WHY
LIBERALS AND
CONSERVATIVES
CLASH

WHY
LIBERALS AND
CONSERVATIVES
CLASH

BRUCE FLEMING

Routledge
Taylor & Francis Group

LONDON AND NEW YORK

Published in 2006 by Routledge
2 Park Square, Milton Park, Abingdon, Oxon OX14 4RN
52 Vanderbilt Avenue, New York, NY 10017

Routledge is an imprint of the Taylor & Francis Group, an informa business

© 2006 by Taylor & Francis

Library of Congress Card Number 2005031273

ISBN-13: 978-0-415-95353-5 (pbk)

Library of Congress Cataloging-in-Publication Data

Fleming, Bruce E. (Bruce Edward), 1954-
   Why liberals and conservatives clash / Bruce Fleming.
       p. cm.
   Includes bibliographical references.
   ISBN-13: 978-0-415-95352-8 (hardback)
   ISBN-13: 978-0-415-95353-5 (pbk.)
   1. United States--Politics and government. 2. Conservatism--United States. 3. Liberalism--United
States. 4. Right and left (Political science) 5. Ideology--United States. 6. Political culture--United
States. I. Title.

JK2265.F54 2006
306.20973--dc22   2005031273

Contents

INTRODUCTION:
CULTURE WARS

Why don't those cowards support the troops? Why are loving couples denied the right to marry because of sexual orientation? Why do deadbeats think they're going to get money from the government for doing nothing? Why do old men force young women to have babies they don't want? How can liberals get conservatives to see how repressive they're being? How can conservatives get liberals to see how spineless they are?

Questions like these are the sparks that set off our current culture wars, the clash between liberals and conservatives. My purpose here is to make both liberals and conservatives realize that the clash gains nothing, and loses much. Accepting the invitation to this battle may feel like something we're impelled to do, like scratching a mosquito bite. However it only makes the itch worse, and if done with enough vehemence, can lead to infection and worse.

Because nowadays liberals and conservatives seem set on polarizing, someone needs to call a time-out. I'm that self-appointed referee trying to get liberals and conservatives to cool off.

My attempt is to explain liberals and conservatives to each other. The reason I think I can do this is that I teach in a generally liberal English department that's part of a conservative institution, the U.S. Naval Academy (USNA). The Naval Academy itself is part of the larger American body, a body now—according to most commentators—split into two parts along the lines of our "red–blue" divide, conservatives vs liberals.

There's a good reason not to let our energies be soaked up by useless confrontation. Both the liberal and conservative worldviews have their strengths—and their weaknesses. Acknowledging that both have their place in American democracy strengthens the larger structure. But in order for this to happen, each side has to be willing to see the other in a new way.

***

People today are drunk on conflict: the military, in one form or another, pervades our lives. We might, in a classical vein, say that Mars, the god of war, has become our presiding deity. He smiled as candidates in the 2004 presidential election touted their military experience as qualification for civil office—experience gained, ironically, during the Vietnam War, until recently synonymous with American political blundering. He smiles as the civilian president dons military gear for photo opportunities—most egregiously, landing on the deck of an aircraft carrier to proclaim "Mission accomplished." Mars has smiled for a number of years at what one author has called "the new American militarism," the post–Desert Storm worship of American soldiers in faraway places, visualized as if figures in a video game that the whole country can follow.[1] He laughed outright, sad to say, when the airplanes hit the World Trade Center; he smiled again when the United States invaded Iraq. And he smiles, too, if somewhat more gently, to see the scuffles, fights, and brawls that take place with increasing frequency between liberals and conservatives—the two groups that, for the sake of simplicity, I take to be the two main branches of American social belief. These are the battles in our culture wars, and the subject of this book.

No one should be surprised by the fact of these culture wars, fought with such intensity by liberals and conservatives. Liberal and conservative are two different worldviews with little in common. The culture wars are simply the weary working out of the fact that the potential for clash between liberals and conservatives is always great. Nor should we be surprised by the intensity of these conflicts. They can get just as bloody as we are willing to let them—in some cases literally so, as when those defending the unborn (as they express it) shoot doctors at abortion clinics, or perhaps even when the doctors themselves perform the abortions.

Do we allow or disallow such things as gay marriage, inscriptions of the Ten Commandments in public places, tax breaks for SUVs and drilling for oil in wilderness areas? Each side, liberal and conservative, attacks the other. The Alabama Supreme Court Chief Justice who smuggled the rock bearing the Ten Commandments into the courthouse in the middle of the night to "acknowledge God" is removed from his position, yet cheered wildly by supporters. Fundamentalist Christians kneel on the sidewalk in front of the Supreme Court in Washington praying for God to intercede as the justices inside strike down the Texas antisodomy law. The "partial-birth" abortion ban is passed in Congress and immediately blocked by the courts. The City of San Francisco marries gay and lesbian couples while opponents of gay marriage ready proposals for a constitutional amendment to block it. People kneel once again before the Supreme Court to keep the phrase "under God" in the Pledge of Allegiance. There seem to be no limits to what one side can accuse the other of being: One side is sinful; the other is fascist. One side is rapacious; the other is unpatriotic. And so it goes.

These issues produce such violent clashes because the conflicts over them are so unresolved, and so unresolvable. Each side has to make up in vehemence what its position lacks in provability—and perhaps surprisingly, intrinsic importance. Paradoxically, it's on the borders of a worldview that the hardest-fought battles occur, not in the more well-defended center of the worldview. Nobody thinks we should be able to kill (as opposed to execute) adults in peacetime, and most people think even newborn infants have the same status for life-termination purposes as an adult. (Goethe didn't, horrified that his Gretchen, in *Faust I*, was condemned to death for infanticide.) The question is merely how far back in time to push the line that defines "person." Those who are sure that "life starts with conception" have to assert this so categorically precisely because the area is uncharted: They have to become more heated about their views because they are talking about something at the edge of their territory. Probably those people eager to have the Ten Commandments displayed in courtrooms would not accept using the Old Testament, with its laws about slaves and its many death sentences as the basis of civil law, as Islamic *sharia* that mandates cutting off the hand of a thief is applied in some

Islamic countries. All they want is this little thing on the edge, and it infuriates them that liberals won't even give them this.

Some people are willing to die for the symbols, the peripheral issues, because in them, the principle comes through most strongly—nothing else is at stake. And the more we let issues like these soak up our attention and energy, the more they will do so. Indeed, they are capable of taking us over utterly, as it seems sometimes they have already done.

Agreeing to Disagree

Each worldview, taken alone, seems self-sufficient. That means that each acts as if it can rule the world independently of the other. In the view of a conservative, we all need only follow the same rules of action, and there will be no strife. In the view of a liberal, each of us needs to define him- or herself and have the room to do it in—there will be no strife here either. The presupposition of most democratic theory is that the goal and, indeed, possible end of democracy is the achievement of consensus. But though this may be the aim of each worldview taken alone, it's not the effect of taking them both together. When we consider the fact that the democratic world contains at least these two worldviews, we come to the conclusion, central to my undertaking here, that the default situation is strife, not consensus.

Nobody need try and understand the other side with a goal to avoiding conflict. It's perfectly possible for both liberals and conservatives to waste their time and resources going down the same self-destructive path they have already well marked. History contains many examples of societies that pursued self-destructive policies to the point of their own dissolution or extinction.[2] Some people think that calling for a truce is akin to giving up, something they have vowed never to do. Sure, we can fight on. Only we should be aware of the price to us all of doing so. Acknowledging that both sides can of course continue full-bore in the direction they are going may cause them to reconsider the advisability of doing so.

Other political commentators have shared with me this view that the default position of democracy is conflict, not consensus. One of the more winning is Boris Dewiel.

> Political beliefs are not just abstract values; they are our beliefs, the highest defining good that we share. Our club is right, the others are wrong. . . . Even among the generally like-minded, dissensus is never far away. The art of maintaining consensus . . . rests on limiting the depth and breadth of discussion.[3]

It's possible to reduce conflict between liberals and conservatives in fact. In brief, we have to agree to stop antagonizing each other. The decision to do this produces a tolerance of the other side, even if it's tolerance born out of necessity rather than love. This toleration of the other structure is sometimes confused with another structure entirely, something between liberal and conservative. It's not a new structure, however. It's just a decision not to push one of the other two structures to its logical conclusion. The "center" is based on what we might call politeness, what I call agreeing to disagree; it isn't defined by its tenets. The center in this sense can be reduced at any moment, in theory, to zero. It has been reduced in recent years in the United States, if not to zero then to a size considerably smaller than it has been.

There is nothing in the structure of either liberalism or conservatism that implies this center. The logic of each worldview, in fact, seems to call out for the tenets of the worldview to be carried to an extreme. As structures, liberal and conservative thought diverge absolutely. If we decide to get along in the world, this will not be as the result of theory, but as the result of pragmatics: merely deciding to get along for the sake of doing so.

The precondition of going beyond the current daggers-drawn stalemate of the two extremes is the establishment of goodwill on each side. Currently, we lack this goodwill.

Each side has its strengths and its weaknesses. Conservatives are better at achieving goals than liberals, better at staying focused, better at being optimistic, and better at looking beyond the individual to something bigger. All these are very good reasons to love conservatives. By the same token, liberals are better than conservatives at looking at long-term effects. They're better at acknowledging difficulties in the world that must be structurally removed, rather than by the individual. They're better at being sensitive to individual variations of people and situations. And they believe that human happiness is a good in itself, not to be lightly sacrificed to yet another "principle."

Constellations

The positions taken by both sides in the liberal–conservative debates are mind-numbingly predictable. They're predictable in the sense that a position held today will most likely be held later. They're predictable in the sense as well that, when we list even one key position of either side held by any given individual, the chances are good that we can sketch the remainder of his or her beliefs.

Let's say we meet a man at a cocktail party and somehow find out that he is opposed to gay marriage. We can probably fill in the rest of the constellation with fair accuracy. We're justified in betting money that he's also going to be against abortion (or, as he would probably say, "murdering the unborn"), for whatever war the United States is currently fighting (unless the casualties are too high), and probably drives an SUV. His equally conservative counterpart who drives a pickup truck with gun racks in the back, if stereotypes hold, won't be at the cocktail party at all, where the poison of choice is wine, but instead will be downing six-packs of beer in the roadhouse down the way with his buddies. Our friend at the party probably also thinks the Pledge of Allegiance ought to say "one nation under God" and isn't too interested to hear that it's only included this phrase since 1954. "Acknowledging God," in any case, is high on his list of priorities. If you learn that he's against gay marriage because he tells you out of a clear blue sky, in the first moments of your acquaintance, the chances of all these things being true shoot up exponentially.

We can fill in the liberal constellation from a single view with equal ease. If we turn to the woman nursing a drink near the shrimp and somehow learn that she is "pro-choice," we can be pretty sure that she doesn't approve of drilling on public lands in Alaska and isn't in favor of giving the rich tax breaks—what the man you've just turned away from would probably describe as "tax relief." Nor, in all likelihood, does she think the Ten Commandments belong in courtrooms.

There's a gender edge to this, too: It's relevant that the person with the first set of ideas, in the example, is a man, and the second a woman. And a sartorial one as well: The person in the dress-for-success suit is more likely to be conservative than the one in the bell-bottoms.

Not everyone is quite so perfect a poster child for pure liberalism or pure conservatism as our imaginary conversationalists. Libertarians, whom Ayn Rand famously and accurately called "hippies of the right," overlap in many instances with John Stuart Mill–influenced liberals.[4] Sometimes you'll find somebody who, usually because of personal experience (an abortion? a gay uncle?), approves of "choice" or gay marriage while otherwise holding fast to the current conservative project of feeding the military and starving all the rest of the government. But such people are the exceptions. So, too, on the clothing front. We'd shake our head for weeks if the woman in the Birkenstocks, multicolored skirt, and clunky necklace just about to get a glass of chardonnay turned out to be a fan of a fulminating right-wing radio talk-show host.

This suggests immediately that liberalism and conservatism aren't merely lists of disparate beliefs, but configurations of beliefs radiating outward from a center. Conservatives predictably invoke the "Right to Life" and the "Need to Acknowledge God"; liberals just as predictably insist on "Choice" and the "Separation of Church and State." The responses of each side to the taunts of the other are just as predictable: One side claims that abortion is murder, the other that anti-choice legislation is medieval.

Listening to arguments between liberals and conservatives, as a result, is like overseeing two touchy children in a sandbox: "My shovel! No, MY shovel!" In the sandbox, there are adults to mediate. But in the equally predictable arguments between liberals and conservatives, there are no adults, no larger figures outside the conflict that can put an end to the strife. Each side vilifies the other; tempers heat up; rhetoric becomes more and more grandiose.

The *Washington Post* commentator Charles Krauthammer summarized the mutual dislike of these two sides in a piece entitled "No-Respect Politics": "Conservatives think liberals are stupid. Liberals think conservatives are evil."[5] Krauthammer is a self-identified conservative. His sugarcoated dismissal of liberals is that "liberals tend to be nice, and they believe—here is where they go stupid—that most everybody else is nice too." Liberals, he believes, misperceive conservatives: "Liberals, who have no head . . . , believe that conservatives have no heart." For the conservative Krauthammer, conservatives are the realists, liberals the dreamers.

The converse is inevitably heard from other commentators. To liberals, it is conservatives who are less realistic than liberals, puzzlingly and hence infuriatingly unconcerned with the long-term effects of their actions. Despite the fact that their actions might well have deleterious effects not too far down the road, they rigorously support drilling for oil on public land, are in favor of forcing women to have babies they don't want, encourage gas-guzzler vehicles for everybody despite their long-term effects on traffic and the environment, and are gung ho to take over shaky countries that have never experienced self-government and then are surprised at the ensuing problems.

Both liberalism and conservatism have what we may call a poster-boy (or -girl) version and a nightmare version. The liberal we have to love is the thoughtful graduate of a "good" college with a commitment to looking at both sides of the picture and helping the unfortunate, who keeps in shape, dresses neatly, knows what that funny thing on his or her plate is when abroad, and listens to National Public Radio. The nightmare liberal extreme is a Hamlet, perpetually mulling over the "what ifs" rather than taking action, or a Woody Allen caricature of himself, all twisting legs and whininess, with his hair flying wild. "DO SOMETHING!" we want to shout at Hamlet. "GET A HAIRCUT AND STAND UP STRAIGHT!" we want to shout at Woody's Woody character. (The problem with Allen's later movies, as many critics have pointed out, is that suddenly we were asked to revere this character rather than despise him.) One popular T-shirt at the Academy shows the international symbol for "no" (the circle-with-crossout) over the word "whining." Enough said.

The conservatism we have to love is that of the USNA midshipman, square-jawed, open-faced, idealistic, eager to serve, running at 5 A.M. with a pack on his back because it presents more of a challenge, tutoring in the local schools. The nightmare vision of conservatism is of racist, gay-baiting thugs, Arno Brecker's muscle-bound nudes for Albert Speer's stadiums (though they might look just like the military's body ideal), and Stalinist or Nazi medals for women who produce sons to serve the Fatherland. When conservatives and liberals go on the warpath, each tends to think the nightmare version of the other typifies all those who hold this worldview.

Who Started It?

A liberal commentator like Paul Krugman, writing for the *New York Times*, sees the sudden upswing in the level of acrimony and vituperation between liberals and conservatives as the fault of the conservatives.[6] In Krugman's view, conservatives—from the time of the disputed American presidential election of 2000 onward—were attempting to effect a revolution, to upset an established equilibrium that has gone unquestioned for decades. Having seen their chance to take the lead after a long time out of power, Krugman suggests, they plunged forward with the singleness of will of the Jacobins of the French Revolution. Liberals, somewhat muffled in their response to these unexpectedly aggressive tactics after the attacks on the World Trade Center on September 11, 2001, in their turn became more vocal. Liberals such as Thomas Frank, in *What's the Matter with Kansas? How Conservatives Won the Heart of America*, or George Lakoff, in *Don't Think of an Elephant: Know Your Values and Frame the Debaate—The Essential Guide for Progressives*, have sketched the outline of a concerted liberal response, one that promises to give as good as it gets.[7]

Yet it's one of my points here that liberalism may not be in a position to fight fire with fire. Liberals tolerate conflict, conservatives court it. So the liberal response may seem, and in fact is, a bit lame: it's too nuanced, it seems, too "yes but" to really knock anybody over. This doesn't mean the conservatives win by default, however, except from their own point of view. Liberalism and conservatism don't frame their ethics the same way, as I consider below; they don't use the same counters to calculate in and don't fight their battles the same way. In any case, you don't convince people by lashing out. Right-wing radio, for example, preaches to the converted, as for that matter do the liberal media outlets. Neither side will ever convince the other.[8]

But that's okay. Democracy is a framework for getting along, where the highest good is the avoidance of internecine doctrinal slug-fests. Politics in a democracy is not based on convincing people; instead, it is based on letting everybody get along.

What I am proposing for the American arena is a sort of domestic *realpolitik,* in the way that international *realpolitik* is based not on hav-ing people do things the same way, but on avoiding wars. I need to admit immediately that this is not ideologically neutral: it will sit bet-ter with liberals than with conservatives, who at their most extreme see value in fighting battles to the last (wo)man.

This fact already helps us understand how it is that liberals and conservatives see the world in fundamentally different ways. They can't even agree on the proper answer to the following question: Is it more important to get along, or to win agreement with their asser-tions? Liberals will probably say the former, conservatives the latter.

To this extent, this book has a liberal cast. Even saying that some things aren't worth dying for has a liberal cast, if seen from the per-spective of the extreme edges of the conservative worldview. But this is so because I'm presupposing that both sides, liberal and conserva-tive, are united in a commitment to preserving American democracy. The fact is that the conclusion that getting along is the highest good has a liberal cast because democracy itself has a liberal cast. Democ-racy is a structure set up with the presupposition that there will be many views. This fact is going to cause extreme conservatives to squirm. Liberals will squirm at other things.

When democracy is destroyed by conservative forces, it falls because its constituent parts are fused into fascism. It implodes.

When democracy is destroyed by liberal forces, it explodes, unable to stick its constituent parts together strongly enough to cohere. Either worldview, if pushed to its extreme, results in the death of democracy.

Without further taking sides in the debate, we must acknowledge off the bat that Krugman is right in one of his assertions: Almost all of the incursions into the minutiae of daily life that form the basis of the culture wars come from conservatives. For conservatives, daily life is not only an acceptable place for battle; it's precisely where the most important battles take place. For liberals, daily life, usually understood as private life, is off-limits to incursion by politics.

Democracy teeters perennially on the edge of destruction and must be continuously set upright again, at least to the extent that either liberal or conservative thought alone is allowed to glut itself on the givens of its own worldview. Living together under one roof implies that each side limits itself. And so, as Hobbes might have pointed out, if either messianic liberals or messianic conservatives think they have a chance of definitively winning over the other side, they may well give it a try, rather than maintaining resentful self-containment in the democratic overstructure.

The democratic overstructure only stays upright if both sides accept self-containment. One reason they can do so may be that they accept that they are getting a good deal, if not the best one imaginable. In return for accepting that they aren't allowed to take over completely, what they get in return is that neither is the other side allowed to do so. Or they may agree to get along because they realize, as I suggest here, that liberals and conservatives each have strengths as well as weaknesses, so the combination of the two is better than either alone. But in order for this to serve as a motivation, both sides have to be aware of it. That's what I'm trying to accomplish here.

Argument

The starting point of my consideration is the fact of clash between liberals and conservatives. Clash is always a possibility for liberals and conservatives, but it is not a necessity. The possibility, however, shows us something about their nature.

The definition I offer here of the liberal and conservative worldviews is produced by the context in which I am offering it, the reason I set about making the distinction. Since this context is clash, my delineation emphasizes the absoluteness of the difference; it also, of necessity, tends to the schematic.

What I am doing here is thus different from the considerations of numerous commentators who have offered definitions of liberalism and conservatism independently of the other, as if liberalism and conservatism were two dogs sedately separated into adjacent cages, not the howling tangle of snarl and fur we currently see at the center of the American scene.

The problem with trying to define liberalism and conservatism without focusing on their clash is that each is what it is only within the context of what it isn't, which here means the other. Thus, if we try to define either of these terms in isolation from the other, we find ourselves fighting a Hydra, a bewildering, twisting mass with many heads, many forms. This is true especially if we try to define one from the other by putting it in its historical context. Every time we consider a new set of historical facts the entity itself changes shape. In this context it's X, but in another context it's Y or Z.

Some of the problems of defining either term in isolation from the other have been noted by earlier commentators. As George H. Nash, an important writer on American conservatism, notes: "Attempts to define conservatism abstractly and universally or in terms of one peculiar set of historical circumstances have led many writers into a terminological thicket."[9]

One of the more useful discussions of liberalism in America, that of Louis Hartz, exemplifies these difficulties in defining American liberalism. For Hartz, American liberalism is liberal "in the classic Lockean sense," namely a reaction to feudalism.[9] But then he admits that it's Lockean in a strange way. America has never known feudalism, and so does not, he explains, produce socialism. We're Lockean, but in a void. Liberalism, in Hartz's understanding is what it is because of being silhouetted against something that isn't there any longer. We're only liberal, it seems, by contrast with something we're unaware of. How are we to understand that?

If we don't work outward from such silhouetting clashes, the web of definition becomes too tangled, and the shifting perspectives that allow us to see someone as, in one moment, conservative, and in the next, liberal, become simply too vertiginous. How, for example, should we classify Adorno's elitist but at the same individualist scorn for what this thinker called the culture industry, the manipulative creation of mass-market entertainment designed only to make money and whose effect was the collective narcosis of society?[11] Is this liberal or conservative? It depends. And in explaining what it depends *on*, we are on our way to writing, or reading, yet another academic consideration of political theory that leaves us more confused than before.

We may have come to dread opening yet another book to read that X is Y, except when it is Z. When compared with A, thinker B is C, but when we compare him to Peirce or Rorty, Derrida or Foucault, he clearly becomes D. And then there is E and F, to whom B's thought is also related, but only when seen in the light of G. The head swims, the book falls from nerveless fingers. It's all so sophisticated, we sense, but finally all these caveats and changes of perspective take their toll. It's enough to make us reach for something we bought in the grocery store checkout line as an antidote.

We need definitions that don't change depending on their context, and that don't presuppose silhouetting against things that aren't there. We get these definitions by silhouetting each worldview against the other, in the moment of clash. My analysis is based on precise circumstances rooted in history, but isn't itself historical. Liberal and conservative are only clearly delineated when they're on opposite sides of something specific. The definitions of both "liberal" and "conservative" that I offer are the result of abstraction from such specific circumstances. Such an abstracted definition is what I'm calling a worldview.

The contrast between liberals and conservatives offered here is a clear one. It can be clear because it's an abstraction. It doesn't tell us what will happen in particular cases; all it does is explain whatever does. Even if, as I claim, the liberal and conservative worldviews are incompatible, this doesn't mean that two men sitting on adjacent stools at a bar, one of whom is a self-professed liberal and the other a self-professed conservative, will be unable to buy each other drinks. The way the encounter works out will in fact cause us to go back and fine-tune or even change the labels. A liberal and a conservative can in fact get along quite well: it's the presupposition that they can do so that underlies both democracy, and this book. It's never individuals that are contraries; it's abstractions. The point of moving on the level of abstractions is precisely that only abstractions give us this degree of clarity.

For the reader interested in things other than politics, I should point out that this recourse to abstractions as a way of both mediating and explaining practical disagreements informs the way, in other works of mine, I've analyzed art.[12] (Thinkers usually think in the same patterns, whatever subject they're thinking about.) We can't arrive at the general from the specific, we just have to jump to the level of the general. But that doesn't mean it's illegitimate to do so. Twentieth-century literary and aesthetic theory has been bedeviled by the attempt to infer the general from the specific, to justify this jump. Typically, such theory asks the question, Is *this* work art? rather than the more general one that the Romantics tended to ask, namely, What is art? I think it makes more sense to ask the abstract question, What is art? And to this the most appropriate follow-up question is, *To what extent* is this work art? There are many works in many gray areas. The only clarity we achieve is clarity in theory.

Thus this work, which claims that the liberal and conservative worldviews are radically dissimilar, isn't (as it may seem at first glance) reductionist. It would only be so if it claimed that in reality, or all the time, anyone who self-identified as liberal or as conservative had to clash with his or her opposite number. Its clarity is precisely the clarity of abstraction, which is the only level where we can achieve such abstraction. The clarity we achieve is the clarity of worldviews, not of individuals, who follow these worldviews to a degree that remains to be determined.

Crying "Uncle"

In an earlier work, *Art and Argument: What Words Can't Do and What They Can*, I considered the fact so central to my analysis here that people rarely convince each other when they argue, whatever it is they're arguing about (not just politics). That doesn't mean arguments never, as we say, change someone's mind. But it's rare for arguments to result in the other person saying, "You're right!" and meaning it. It's more usual for the parties merely to weary, or walk away. The most amiable way this weariness is expressed is one side crying "uncle," which means, "I give up! Let's stop!"

What does make people change their views the relatively few times when they do? We can't say. Sometimes we try for general explanations. A "lightbulb" joke asks, "How many psychiatrists does it take to change a lightbulb?" The answer is: "One, but the lightbulb really has to want to change." When people change their minds, by extension, this isn't necessarily because of what the other person in the argument said. They have to have wanted to change from the beginning.

"Wanted to change" here means "ultimately did change." We can't determine before the fact whether or not someone wants to change; even saying he or she wants to change doesn't show us if that person *really* wants to. Instead, saying the person wanted to change is something we throw in as an extra after the person has actually changed. The circular premise is that the person wouldn't have changed if he or she hadn't wanted to, so this at least has to be present, whatever other factors we can list.

But these factors are many. In order to be convinced of something, we must (to list a few such factors) not be distracted, must not hate the person trying to change our mind, must have the energy to devote to this issue (domestic partners are well advised not to take on a major beef when the other is tired), and perhaps most fundamentally, must have to have sensed problems with the way we currently see things, even if we haven't thought them through. It's rare when all these things line up. Most of the time, arguments go nowhere.

Besides, what's so fabulous about having other people say "You're right"? They can say it without meaning it. They can mean it in the moment they say it and doubt it seconds later, or the next day. Even if they decide we're right for weeks, months, or years, who's to say they won't ultimately change their minds again? If they never change their minds, how are we richer?

Resolvability

Those who believe in the power of trying to change others' minds should meditate, too, on the fact that things we argue about at length are by definition not amenable to being resolved: If they could be resolved, they would be. The longer we argue about them, the clearer it becomes that, for this reason, they are not things for which we already have a resolution mechanism.

Situations delineate an entire spectrum of resolvability, as I've considered in my book *Disappointment or the Light of Common Day*. At one end of the spectrum are things we can disagree about but don't argue about: We say they are "verifiable," such as whether or not the keys are on the table. Only someone (for example) in the next room would disagree with what we said, and then only if he or she didn't realize we were standing right there looking at the table—or if, perhaps, the keys hidden. In any case the disagreement would be easily resolved. At the other end of the spectrum are questions where verifiability is out of reach, such as whether God exists. But even things like this are never totally unverifiable: We have only to die to find out. Or be another sort of creature. Or possess different faculties than we do. So all this means is that we can't verify it, not that it's unverifiable. But I may not be able to verify whether the keys are on the table either: We're locked out of the house and never get in, for example, and then the house is destroyed by a tornado. I'll never know whether or not the keys were on the table. This fact that nothing is ever totally verifiable or unverifiable is what makes all these cases part of the same spectrum.

All we can say is, some things are more unverifiable than others. The more unverifiable things form a realm where the doctrines of religion, among other things, are found. Still, this realm has a

boundary with what's next to it on the scale, and we have to constantly re-negotiate what belongs to realm-lacking mechanisms for
verification and what doesn't.

In the middle of the scale are questions like, What's on the other
side of a high mountain range? We can't find out right now, but we
can imagine what steps we'd have to take to find out. Things change
position all the time, moving from the unverifiable, and hence something about which we disagree, to something we no longer disagree
about. What the moon is made of used to be unverifiable, but it isn't
any more.

We always choose to argue rather than not argue, and we choose to
take as our goal getting someone else to say, "I agree." Getting someone to say this is, after all, a separable thing to our holding the view
ourselves. We can hold a position without arguing for it or against the
other alternatives. Political discourse of the argumentative sort, which
characterizes our world today, only produces more argument: It's the
result of a specific choice. This choice is not the best one.

This is so because of the self-perpetuating nature of argument, as
opposed to things with established methods of verification. If it leads
nowhere, it can go on forever. The things we get heated up about are
precisely the things about which we don't have a mechanism for
resolving disputes. Insisting that another person hold our view that
the keys are on the table does not produce such an endless argument,
nor is there much to get heated about. We're asked to prove our assertion. If we do, the other person accepts. If we don't, he or she doesn't,
and walks away in disgust.

This would seem to be approaching the logical positivist position,
derived from Wittgenstein, that assertions about religion or meta-
physics are "meaningless." But it isn't. They aren't meaningless, they
merely lack a mechanism for resolving difficulties. That's what makes
them the kind of assertions they are. So it's much more likely we'll go
to war over religion than over whether the keys are on the table.

Am I saying there's no point in discussing things? Not at all. Give it
a try, if getting the person to say "You're right" is something you set
store by. It may work, as it may turn out that the person "wanted to

change." Or you may find that you are actually not disagreeing, but instead dealing with things regarding which there are mechanisms for resolving differences. One person says Sarah looks fabulous, another that she looks horrible. Perhaps the first is under the mistaken apprehension that Sarah is going to the beach when in fact she's going to a job interview. Resolving that issue of fact may well make the disagreement disappear. Many disagreements leading to arguments are defused because it turns out we're actually well into resolvable territory.

However the fallacy I'm warning against is the belief that more is necessarily more: Once we've resolved all of these resolvable things, what we're left with is pure argument. And pure argument by definition cannot be resolved.

Immutables

If the world for my purposes divides into liberals and conservatives, then of necessity, it seems, I have to be one or the other. And if my point is that neither side is going to convince the other, what purpose is served by anything I could say? Unless, of course, it's going to turn out, as it all too frequently does, that the person lining the world up in neat rows somehow escapes being one of the things being lined up. I answer the question below, but consider this escape clause here.

Such convenient exceptionalism for the person doing the categorizing is the sign of thinkers I call "immutables."[13] I'm not one of these. Kant's structures explaining change are themselves the only things that, according to him, can't change. Everything else does. Even objections to the structure are only possible because of the structure; whatever Descartes thinks, be it true or false, is still an expression of the self thinking, so the one certain thing is the existence of this thinking self. Locke accepted even more clearly a distinction between primary and secondary qualities. The primary qualities are the more fundamental ones: they don't change. But to later thinkers the distinction has seemed frail.

Indeed, every fencing off of things that "can't change" is ultimately futile. This is so because everything is finite, is merely what it is. And that means, others can disagree with it, or—rejecting it even more absolutely—simply walk away. How do you make something so off limits to the future that you can be sure it "can't change"? I don't see how to do it. Attempts to do it only make it a clearer target. The self, the structure of apperception, the Marxist clash of classes, the Freudian clash of elements of the psyche: these structures fenced off from change in one generation are the mutables of the next.

So, too, my separation of liberal and conservative. It's a specific thing done, which means it can be undone, or simply ignored. It involves a specific separation of immutable form from mutable content. And that means it can be opposed, or merely walked away from.

It's a specific separation because, first of all, the separation is being made in a book. Those reading this book have alternatives to doing so, including mowing the lawn (for those with lawns, time on their hands, long grass, and a functional mower), eating (for those feeling hunger pangs and with the means to assuage them), or staring into space (for practically everybody), among many others. My argument is specific in terms of content too. Even if readers do read with interest, and even end up agreeing with much or all of what I say, that doesn't mean the person next door will do so, or the next generation. The clearer and more absolute I make my points, the easier it will be for the next intellectual generation to see what I took to be structure as only more content and reject it.

So yes, my fundamental distinction between liberal and conservative is itself amenable to being challenged. But at least, I suggest, it's valid for right here, right now: in the moment of clash. This is our liberalism, our conservatism. Perhaps the future will have different things by these names, or lose a sense of the meaning for the names altogether. It's precisely because I accept that I don't control the future that this isn't a troublesome notion. I won't be around to make sure things go my way in a generation or two: all of us have to come to terms with this one.

So the answer to the apparent contradiction raised above—if the world is divided into two types, then I must be one or the other, and if this is so how can I convince the other side?—is this: All works have a polemical edge. Mine is precisely that we have to adapt to each other in order to survive collectively. That is, if we want to survive collectively, which I'm assuming we do.

This polemic involves a more friendly tone of voice than ram-it-down-their-throats proselytizing. The tone of voice isn't merely window dressing. It's part of the point, and a way around the fact that people rarely convince others when they set out to do so. People have to decide they want to adopt your point of view. It's more likely they'll do so if it's attractively spread out somewhere where they can look at it with no pressure than if you're trying to talk your way in and have a foot in the door. It's not just that you can catch more flies with honey than with vinegar, it's that people take things they need, not necessarily what we want them to take. If we're pushing one aspect of our product, we may well have them turn away in disgust if they are interested in another aspect entirely.

Sometimes the shortest distance between two points is not a line. Sometimes it's not even a curve, but a meandering pattern. Sometimes we can't even sketch out what is supposed to happen. Here, I set up a situation where I hope people see my point, showing my wares, smiling, and hoping they'll buy. But if I start trying to force them, it's a sure bet they'll walk away. I can't guarantee that any given person will buy, but those who do, do so because they want to: to them, it seems like their idea. I haven't convinced anyone, only made it possible for them to convince themselves. But I may have sold some of my wares.

Storytelling

The situation I'm setting up both as the genesis and the illustration of my point is my life as a liberal English professor in the conservative military world of the U.S. Naval Academy. Thus this book is partly storytelling, especially in the early chapters, and partly theory. The theory isn't independent of the storytelling. The theory arises from the situation; the situation makes the theory plausible. The theory, however, isn't merely theory for this particular situation. If it were, no one outside the Naval Academy need pay attention. The Naval Academy, where liberals and conservatives reveal that they are in fact doing two different things, offers a microcosm of our deeply divided, contentious American society at large. The Naval Academy mirrors and encapsulates the larger cultural and political conflicts of our time. That's why it's useful to use this situation as a mine of examples.

For, in fact, two different hearts beat within the body of the Naval Academy, one liberal, one conservative. On graduation day, when members of the graduating class throw their snow-white covers in the air at Navy-Marine Corps Memorial Stadium, two separate acts have conferred on them two different things: one, their Bachelor of Science degree (which all graduating midshipmen receive, even if their major was something like English), and then, five minutes later, their military commission. And the paths leading to these separate acts have been separate as well, even contradictory.

The "Comte de Lautréamont" (pseudonym for Isidore Ducasse), author of the *Contes de Maldoror*, created the image later taken as the definition for surrealism as the "the chance meeting on a dissecting-table of a sewing machine and an umbrella." The combination, sometimes clash, of the overriding conservatism of the Naval Academy and the liberalism that emanates not only from individual professors, but from our very means of proceeding and our curriculum in the English department, is in this sense surreal. It's living this contradiction, the surreal quality of teaching people to think for themselves in a military institution, that has produced this book.

***

People frequently say, "The Naval Academy is its own little world, isn't it? Isn't that like studying people in Papua New Guinea?" For the next few pages I consider the possibility that what I'm doing here is a form of domestic anthropology, or sociology. It's one of those considerations of methodology—how what I'm doing relates to what others have done—that will be more interesting to a specialist than to someone interested in my primary subject, the liberal–conservative split as exemplified by the Naval Academy. These readers are well advised to move to Chapter One. Those impatient with stories drawn from the Naval Academy will find they have skipped most of these if they move directly to Chapter Two. I have in any case given a more developed treatment of the Naval Academy in my book Annapolis Autumn: Life, Death, and Literature at the U.S. Naval Academy.

Ethnography at the End of Its Tether

This sort of both-subjective-and-objective work does bear at least initial resemblance to the revisionist anthropological and ethnographic works of late-twentieth-century anthropologists such as James Clifford, Clifford Geertz, and, in the next generation, Renato Rosaldo—all of whom take as their common ancestor Claude Lévi-Strauss in works such as *Tristes Tropiques*. Such writers have given practical illustrations of Nietzsche's point that all objectivity is to a degree subjective as well. In fact, what I'm doing here is the logical endpoint of the changes they have wrought on ethnography. It's ethnography-plus-one-step, and hence no longer ethnography.

Virtually all contemporary ethnographers reject what they perceive as overly magisterial Victorian anthropology (Boas, Malinowski, Benedict, Radcliffe-Brown). They even seek to go beyond the second thoughts of Lévi-Strauss, even, in the next generation, beyond the yet more self-conscious subjectivizing of observatorial position of someone like Geertz.[14] Geertz notes that it's easier to say what contemporary ethnography doesn't want to do than what it does: "The illusion that ethnography is a matter of sorting strange and irregular facts into familiar and orderly categories . . . has long since been exploded. What it is instead, however, is less clear."[15]

Such writers favor a more participatory "dialogic" ethnography, where the subject "Others" frequently speak directly to the record rather than being described by the ethnographer, and where the onlooker makes as clear as possible the specificity of his or her position and the limitations of point of view, not to mention the personal reasons that may have impelled him or her to go among the Others to begin with. A concomitant development of this trend toward acknowledgement of subjectivity is the demand that the ethnographer stay for a longer time with his or her hosts than was normal in the early years of ethnography, and acquire a more profound acquaintance with their language and life—finally be, if possible, one of them. The work of Margaret Mead, to name only one star of the founding generation of American ethnography, has been attacked in recent years for being deficient on these counts.

Clifford and Geertz, in interviews with the now-defunct academic journal *Lingua Franca*, named Rosaldo's *Culture and Truth* the most provocative contemporary book in their field. Rosaldo's book contains a succinct summary of this shift in ethnographic paradigms:

> In contrast with the classic view, which posits culture as a self-contained whole made up of coherent patterns, culture can arguably be conceived as a more porous array of intersections . . .

> This book argues that a sea change in cultural studies has eroded once-dominant conceptions of truth and objectivity. The truth of objectivism—absolute, universal, and timeless—has lost its monopoly status. It now competes, on more nearly equal terms, with the truths of case studies that are embedded in local contexts, shaped by local interests, and colored by local perceptions.[16]

Given the absolute split between "cultures" (the very meaning of the word itself is of course the bone of contention) postulated by the Victorians (we are Us, they are Them), ethnography has had several generations worth of capital to spend down. It started with a very large split that could be progressively narrowed. It seems clear, however, that the capital, dwindling individually with each generation like the fortune of the Rockefellers, is now gone. For if there is no longer a Them and an Us, what justifies Our reporting on Them at all? What justifies talking with Them? Letting Them talk? Some vestige of Otherness must append to the notion of "culture" to justify even going There (in Gertrude Stein's terms, there must be a "there there"), rather than just staying at home.

A certain amount of residual giddiness about our boldness in spending Gramps's fortune, narrowing the gap between Inside and Outside, has taken us into the twenty-first century. But when it narrows to zero, the ethnographic paradigm is dead. If we live indefinitely with the Others, speak their language and eat their food, they aren't Other, they're just the people we live with. At this point it's not impossible to identify Others, but we have to make the case that they're Other, we can't presuppose it. Perhaps at this point ethnography becomes sociology. What else do classic sociological texts like David Riesman's *The Lonely Crowd* do but make the case that those all around us constitute a domestic Other?

Reflections on Rwanda

Drawing on my experiences at the National University of Rwanda, where I taught before Annapolis, I consider how this book is like, and how it is unlike, contemporary ethnography. Ultimately, it's more unlike.

When we act as ethnographers, even the self-reflexive sort we are these days, we start from the presupposition that we are on one side of a fence and our subjects the other. We know we're Outside and are reporting back to the Inside. Otherness is our point of departure. That's not my point of view. Instead, though I may arrive at the conclusion that the Naval Academy is a different world (insert preferred term here, in place of "world"), that's a conclusion, not a presupposition. We have to defend the conclusion of Otherness if we offer it; we can't presuppose it.

One example of second-generation revisionist anthropology is a diverting essay by Laura Bohannan called "Prince Hamlet in Africa." It's a reflection on the author's experiences retelling Shakespeare's plot to a group of West Africans. Bohannan left for Africa, she tells us, with the presupposition that "human nature is pretty much the same the whole world over," and that "at least the general plot and motivation of the greater tragedies [of Shakespeare] would always be clear—everywhere."[17] When, however, she tried to entertain her African hosts during a rainy afternoon by telling them the story of Hamlet, she encountered problems. Her audience of village elders thought that Claudius had done just the right thing in marrying Gertrude (brothers of dead men should always marry the widow), and they were firmly convinced that Laertes had secretly drowned Ophelia to sell her body to the witches. Hamlet, moreover, had done wrong in killing his father's brother; he richly deserved his fate of being bewitched, as clearly he was. Why else does one go mad?

Bohannan's initial presupposition is the assumption that "canonical" Western literature is universal. Yet when she rejects this viewpoint, she goes to the other, related, extreme, suggesting that literature is not universal, but particular to a culture. Her conclusion, with respect to literature, is one of cultural relativism; this ends up essentializing Otherness by creating an Otherness of place. That the culture is Other is never in doubt: Bohannan translates haltingly into the language of her audience, and is constantly at a loss as to how to render certain ideas or relationships to them.

Self-reflexive and self-questioning though she is, she still has to presuppose that there's a There there. Or else why would we be interested in the self-reflection and self-questioning with respect to it? What would a situation like Bohannan's look like where we didn't presuppose Otherness?

It might look like my experiences with reader incomprehension of texts teaching at the National University of Rwanda, before the Rwandan civil war. Unlike Bohannan, I could communicate, in two languages, with my students, so that when they read something differently than I expected, I could formulate both for myself and for them what I took to be the source of the problem. And then we could discuss it. Further, what I was doing was "real" for my students, part of their university training, rather than amusement on a rainy afternoon. It was real for me, too: Teaching in Rwanda was a job for me, it wasn't doing what ethnography, divertingly enough, calls "fieldwork." (The fields in Rwanda are all cultivated and the only people who go in them are those with hoes.) I didn't live in a field, I lived in a house.

Not all differences were differences of the general scheme of things. This was a viable conclusion, but it wasn't one I could presuppose; I had to justify it. Similarly, my students here at Annapolis might be different than I in some fundamental way, but this is a conclusion I have to justify; I can't presuppose it. This is the sense in which my book here is the logical endpoint of late-twentieth-century anthropology.

Some of the problems I encountered with my students were like those Bohannan noted: The students thought a character in John Updike's little fable *Of the Farm* (which I taught because the U.S. Embassy gave me a box containing ten copies of it) was unmanly because he allowed his wife to call him a "bastard" (I explained this was close to the French *salaud* and did not actually question his legitimacy). Unlike Bohannan, however, I explained how things were different in the West. I didn't have to presuppose a different culture, because I assumed we could keep the divergence at a lower level. It seemed the same as a city slicker explaining an unfamiliar street noise to his visiting country cousin. Not all differences equal the absolute presupposition of Otherness.

Some of my students' reactions in Rwanda were determined, I thought, by geography—which is perhaps an influence on culture, but is not synonymous with it. Rwanda is only a few degrees from the equator, with wet and dry seasons rather than fall and spring. The greatest temperature variation is the diurnal one, that between day and night. It lacks seasons, in the Western sense. A great deal of Western poetry is based on the equation of spring with rebirth, winter with death, and so on (as Northrop Frye pointed out).[18] Rwanda at that point was quite isolated, with no television and little outside influence, so its people didn't even have images to fill in the blank regarding the influence of seasons on people's sensibilities that someone born and bred in equally semitropical Miami would have. As a result, most of this aspect of Western literature passed the students by.

Some of their reactions did seem ascribable to more complex things that I could not so easily isolate from the very warp and woof of their lives. The most striking of these was that a whole class of students came to the discussion of Ibsen's *Ghosts* convinced that the young man going mad from syphilis wants his mother to sleep with him, not euthanize him. I had to concede that nothing in the text made this reading impossible; their strongest justification for their reading, which of course I questioned, was Mrs. Alving's horrified reaction to her son's halting and unclear request. "I who gave you birth!" The sense of this is, I take it: You ask *this* of *me*?

My theory was that it was the air of hushed scandal around the unspecified action that made the students conclude it had to involve sex, not death. I thought I understood why. Sex and death in Rwandan society, I had gradually come to think, have a relationship with each other that is the inverse of that in the West. For Westerners, sex is on every billboard, but death takes place alone and is shrouded in a cloud of euphemisms. In Rwanda, by contrast, death even before the civil war and accompanying slaughters was omnipresent. Children died of dehydration, people rendered invisible by dark animal skins walked in the middle of the highways at night to court unfortunate accidents with the few passing cars, and adults died in fair numbers of malaria. If so much hush-hush was in *Ghosts,* my students may well have thought, it had to be sex that was the issue, not something as quotidian as death. So at least was my theory. This was one I never asked them about, perhaps out of politeness or the sense that I would never make them understand. At the most serious level of divergence, we don't talk to the people involved, we just say how it appears to us.

This last example is the kind of absolute divergence that makes ethnographers feel justified that they are dealing with two "cultures." Yet I don't think even something like this justifies the postulation of the absolute Otherness implied in speaking of "culture"—except perhaps in the offhand way we note as we go from Savannah to New York that the whole world seems to change, including people. There are many reasons why we would fail to see a point in saying this to the people involved, including social constraints. The absoluteness of saying, this is Other, is something we postulate, not something we can justify: it involves a quantum jump.

When Bohannan's essay last appeared in the *Norton Reader,* it was paired with another example of dealing with differences, an account of teaching the Romantic poets in the English department at the U.S. Naval Academy, where I sit to write this. The essay is called "Madeline Among the Midshipmen." The Madeline in question is Keats's heroine from "The Eve of St. Agnes," and the midshipmen are earlier avatars of my own students.

This sort of situation is my point of departure here. It's related to the ethnographic one, but different. It's the situation we deal with when, instead of jetting off to Other places, the Otherness of the world now definitively having worn off (why drink your coffee in Borneo if you can do it better on your own back porch? Why go to Borneo to drink what they drink rather than coffee? Why get upset when you get to Borneo and discover the same chain stores that you have around the corner?), people just stay at home and have a life. Along the way they may meet some pretty interesting groups of people, even people that you decide are different than you are. Anthropology, when it narrows to eliminate the previously presupposed distinction between Inside and Outside, becomes something like this work.

Here, as I did in Rwanda, I work up to the distinction between one group and another; I can't presuppose it, as all ethnography, even the most self-reflexive, does. I didn't come to Annapolis seeking the Other; I went for a job and found the Other. And it's Other only in the context of a particular situation.

Fiction too, I've argued in my book *Caging the Lion*, defines an Inside and an Outside, but it has to earn this distinction, it can't presuppose it. The work itself has to define and justify the distinction. Sometimes, to be sure, we express this division in literature in terms that seem taken from Victorian ethnography, as for example when we say the popularity of Indian novels in the United States in the last decade, typified by Arundhati Roy's *The God of Small Things*, may well have been based largely on the exotic sights and sounds the works offered, and on themes that played better in the West than in India. Chinua Achebe's now-classic *Things Fall Apart* offers the even-by-that-point-destroyed Igbo society for the consideration of Anglophones—just as, Achebe himself has pointed out, Joseph Conrad viewed the Congolese of *Heart of Darkness* from the European perspective.[19]

But we need not go outside our own country to taste Other worlds; indeed, arguably what novelists do is precisely to create Other worlds within their own. Faulkner and Flannery O'Connor create an Other world from the raw material of the American South. Proust's great work was set in a world defined by time and social strata, a world that had disappeared even by the time he was writing. It was an Other to everyone, a kind of reporting back to the Inside on an Outside world accessible initially only to its creator. The distinction between Inside and Outside is made by the work itself; it exists only there.

Still, every literary work, not just those that succeed because they offer the sights and sounds of a real place presented as exotic, offers something the reader is assumed not to know. The author strikes out from the known world into the unknown, and reports back on what he or she has found. This unknown-to-the-reader world need not be situated in geographical space at all. Sometimes it's a body of knowledge that's being summarized. *The Curious Incident of the Dog in the Nighttime*, Mark Haddon's popular world-from-the-point-of-view-of-an-autistic-genius work, could be entitled *Autism 101*. It's most interesting to people who know nothing about autism. On top of this, the author has slapped the usual value-added factors that typify Hollywood movies. The people are presented as average, but in fact aren't. Here, the narrator is autistic but also a mathematical genius—one in a million among autistic children—yet will for most readers be emblematic of all of them. More typical would have been a non-genius. But who wants typical? Brad Pitt isn't a typical anything; he brings added value to any role merely because he is, as *People* magazine found him in 2005, the most "beautiful" man alive.

Ethnography at the end of its tether, the capital exhausted of a postulated Other, joins hands with other forms that have been there all along: sociology, seeing our own world as if from the outside, and literature. To the Russian formalists such as Shklovsky, all art was precisely seeing our world with new eyes and presenting it to the reader that way, what Shklovsky called "defamiliarization."[20] Shklovsky is associated with the avant-garde, but he gives many examples from Tolstoy of the more traditional author seeing the world through distanced eyes. Suddenly we, through the author, see things anew.

The title I gave the essay that served as the impetus for this book was "Why I Love Conservatives." This book is meant for conservatives too, but it's written "toward" liberals. Conservatives are its Outside, liberals its Inside.

Reporting Back

In my book *Art and Argument* I proposed that literature, which offers precise situations in the world as content, consists to a large degree of elements that are not meant to convince. It merely says, Here these things are—aren't they interesting? Art—which is a general concept, as opposed to the artwork by definition containing both artistic and nonartistic elements—isn't even communication, though many theoreticians have held it to be so, usually claiming that it's communication between the author and the reader. But how can it be? We're only prepared to say that communication has been effected (lots of attempts to communicate don't result in communication, such as yelling into the darkness, or putting a message in a bottle that's never picked up) when an initial expression, the first part of the communication dyad, produces a response, that is the second part, which is located within the relatively narrow band of permissible responses.[21] If I asked someone I met how they were doing and they told me the time, I would say communication had not been established. If they merely look blankly at me, I don't know whether or not there has been communication. With literature there need be no definable response at all, hence no second part, hence no communication. This fact is the source of the Kantian insistence that art existed merely to be perceived.

The "decadents" who coined the notion of *l'art pour l'art* were right that this is true of the artistic elements of any given work. There may be a reaction, but we can't say beforehand what it should be; there may be no reaction at all. They were wrong to think that works should for this reason contain a very high percentage of artistic elements; it may be technically true that a work with a greater percentage of artistic elements is more artistic, but this is merely a statement of fact, not a value judgment. There exists a spectrum of works between polemics on one hand and, on the other, bits apparently cut from the world. But even the most polemical of polemics has an artistic element—it's one person's view of the world. And the most "objective" of artworks is still offered by an individual for the consideration of the perceiver.

Thus nothing says that art, or at least good art, limits itself to "Here it is" elements. To the extent that the work *is* art, however, it consists of "Here it is" elements. These function differently with respect to the reader or perceiver than "I am trying to convince you" elements. By opening the novel (it might be) and continuing to read, the perceiver leans over to pick up the things lying on the ground. "I am trying to convince you" elements are, by contrast, thrust into his or her hands, probably when he or she is trying to do something else. "Here it is" elements presuppose the cooperation of the reader.

Now we can go back to the question raised above: can I hope to convince either side of anything it hadn't accepted already? Though I am a liberal, and hence one of the two types I delineate, I can offer "Here it is" elements not meant to convince without involving myself in logical vicious circles. Both liberal and conservative can accept the "Here it is" elements; both can understand where my conclusions come from. I suggest that my conclusions are valid for more than the specific situation that produced them, but I merely suggest.

I arrived at Annapolis knowing that it would be military. What I found was that it was also peopled at all levels by people I would call socially conservative, religiously conservative, sexually conservative (the public prudery of the military whose natural Janus face is off-the-record licentiousness is well known), and conservative on gender issues. At first I was surprised: I wasn't expecting to see such a pile-up of conservatives. Then I banged myself on the forehead: How could I not have expected this? It suddenly all seemed logical. Though these groups were conservative in different ways, there was what Wittgenstein would call a "family resemblance" among them. This book is the attempt to articulate that family resemblance.

I
VEGGIE BURGER IN PARADISE

I THINK OF THE NAVAL ACADEMY AS A SORT of conservative paradise. By eating (so to speak) my liberal veggie burger in such a conservative paradise, I've come to understand the givens of the conservative worldview, and to see clearly its strengths and its limitations.

On one hand, it's pleasant to be part of such a place. On the other, such an idyll comes at a price: Not everyone is welcomed into such a world, and outside voices are rejected as Outside. When, for example, I beg to differ, my voice—though I have been a professor here for almost two decades, far longer than any military staff member or, of course, student—is identified as Outside. What do civilians understand about the military? By definition nothing, not being One of Us. In a letter critical of the fact that I had published an article whose content our superintendent (an admiral, but the equivalent of the college president) didn't like, the admiral was forced to come to the unsettling conclusion that I might not be a "team player." This, in a conservative world like Annapolis, is the unkindest cut of all.

In a conservative world, one is either with the program or against it. Other conservative paradises exclude naysayers in much the same way. In a conservative world, everyone aims to achieve the same goal; because everyone else is trying to achieve it, too, they are the "right kind" of people. Those on the outside are not the right kind of people. But this is circular: anyone who disagrees is immediately identified as Outside. Dissent within the conservative structure is unwelcome; dissent within a liberal structure is the name of the game.

Veggie Burger Digested

If we chew for a moment on the somewhat weak Jimmy Buffett–derived joke I'm making here, we can get a taste of many of the themes of this book. Why is it that a veggie burger is so clearly a liberal meal?

Conservatives in the West like eating large animals because doing so valorizes their rather existentialist sense that each of us is alone, and must kill or be killed. Cows are in fact quite passive, so killing them is not a feat of strength such as conservatives imagine shooting large game to be; if people object even to the death of such passive creatures, they must be very effeminate indeed (a bad thing for conservatives). Conservatives like the sense that killing and eating an animal gives humans of being the only entity on Earth that matters. This is sometimes expressed in biblical terms, by saying that God gave mankind dominion over the birds and the beasts. This certainty that human beings are the only game in town—which means humans may use other creatures and things for their own purposes—comes from the fact, developed more fully below, that conservative ethics is expressed in terms of actions, not actors. And that means human actions. For liberals, by contrast, an animal can be an entity whose wants and needs we should consider, since liberal ethics considers precisely the web of relationships between entities rather than the postulation of what I call an Absolute (human) Action.

Eating hamburgers is the societal default in the West: it's something we do without thinking about it. Only liberals, therefore, would insist that we think about it—which is to say, possibly change our behavior. Thinking about something isn't a value-neutral action. In a world where the hamburger is the norm, it will only be a liberal who engages in the two-step action of questioning the norm and looking at alternatives.

Someone who goes out of his or her way to avoid what for conservatives in the West is the unremarkable action of eating a hamburger draws conservative scorn; such a person is a "wimp." This word is surely a portmanteau word combining "woman" with "limp" to suggest impotence: Being strong or firm, as we say, is all about maleness, which (as I argue below) is structurally congruent to the conservative worldview.

Part of the nature of a conservative action is that we just do it. This does not mean, as I consider below, that the conservative position resists changes to the status quo: It can attempt to roll back something that it disapproves of that has become the status quo. It's conservatives who are trying to overturn *Roe v. Wade*, the Supreme Court finding that Americans have the constitutional right to an abortion; it's conservatives who are trying to roll back the American separation of church and state as having gone too far; it's conservatives who support the end of filibusters in the Senate that they fear will be used to block conservative judges.

These are conservative positions not because of any intrinsic qualities of the positions themselves, rather because of the way they interlock with liberal positions. In a world where raising cattle had become uneconomic or impossible, or was controlled by The Enemy, conservatives might well accept eating soyburgers as hardheaded realism. In Hindu India, it's the hamburger eater who's questioning tradition, and so who'll be the liberal, and the "veg" (vegetarian) eater who'll be the conservative.

In the West as it is, however, ordering a veggie burger is an alternative to a hamburger. The liberal has identified this as unacceptable for reasons that seem prissy to conservatives: an animal is killed, blood is eaten, arteries are hardened. As for the last, the long-term health effects, conservatives don't plan, liberals would say, for the long haul: Too-great care with one's self seems to them a bad thing. Conservatives are more focused on the here-and-nowness of the action they take.

Conservatives are proud of the hits they give; this is the reason their imagery is invariably related to the physicality of maleness. This is so because conflict with a brutal world outside is one of the two possible "settings" of conservative thought, the setting of the conservative node facing out toward what for its purposes becomes Outside. Conflict for conservatives is something that is located intrinsically outside the structure. That's the reason it's potentially endless, and potentially so destructive. When you oppose, you oppose with all your force—you don't pull your punch. For liberals, by contrast, conflict is understood as being built into the system, and so is intrinsically held within limits. Conflict isn't threatening to the liberal structure, it's what the liberal structure is all about. And for this reason it has to be toned down to a tolerable level.

The other setting is within the conservative world, what produces the warmth inside a conservative paradise. The wall surrounding the conservative polis bristles toward the outside; within the city, people bask in the mutual approbation of doing what conservatives do among themselves.

No liberal structure produces the same sense of mutual approval for those a part of it that a conservative one does.

Hermeneutics

The Princeton Review (not, as one might think, a literary magazine based at the prestigious New Jersey university but a test preparation service that ranks colleges and universities under many different rubrics based on apparently random student interviews) in its 2005 listings proclaimed the Naval Academy the fourth most conservative institution in the country, just after the Mormon-affiliated Brigham Young University.[1]

Saying that the Naval Academy is conservative is a good example of what is sometimes called the hermeneutic circle. The circle looks like this: How can I say it's conservative and use the Academy as an example of what I take to be conservatism in general without having decided what, in fact, constitutes conservatism? Usually the image of the hermeneutic circle is corrected to that of a spiral: I start with an intuition, test it against what I see, form a thesis, test it again, and so on. That's what I'm doing here.

The midshipmen at the Academy are conservative. I know this because I correct their papers, talk with them in class, and interact with them in their off hours. All but a few of the junior officers who function as company officers in Bancroft Hall, the "world's largest dormitory," are conservative too. Those that aren't don't let it be publicly known: To do otherwise would not be a good career move.

The military administrators of the institution itself are the most conservative of all. They are conservative personally, insofar as I can tell, but are also structurally conservative as a result of their function in the social unit. Their mandate is to keep traditions going, foster respect for authority, and generally keep the lid on things. All these are considered to be virtues by conservatives and are considered suspect by liberals.

Many people would say that the military is what conservatives are all about, so a training college for future naval officers would for that reason alone be conservative. Voting money for military needs is the badge of honor of conservative senators. A yellow ribbon to "support the troops" is right up there nowadays with an American flag in the lapel to show your patriotism, which is equated with militarism. Being at war is a good thing, especially if you win quickly and cheaply, and with no loss of American life. Given that it's rarely possible to do all these things, support for prolonged and increasingly expensive and deadly American wars wanes after a time even with conservatives.

Paradoxes in the Pentagon

Interestingly, as Andrew Bacevich points out in *The New American Militarism*, the conservative military has in recent decades become the means by which liberals are furthering social reforms, notably in the equal treatment of women and people of color—some would argue, the preferential treatment of people of color.[2]

Because the enlisted military ranks are so heavily African-American and Hispanic, the military has moved to aggressively recruit and promote officers of color. The superintendents of all the U.S. military academies filed an *amicus* brief with the U.S. Supreme Court before its deliberations regarding the suit brought against the University of Michigan for what were called "two-track" admissions policies. The Supreme Court found that race could be a factor in a larger whole but not the basis for establishing a second track of admission: In my view, as a former member of our admissions board, this, as of 2005, is exactly what the Naval Academy is engaged in. I've written on the Naval Academy's affirmative action admissions policy.[3]

Race isn't the only issue on which the military follows a policy whose content is liberal. All faculty members at the Naval Academy attend mandatory training in "SAVI" (Sexual Assault Victim Intervention), where it's made clear that even topics treated academically regarding human reproduction can, if they produce in a single person's (student's) mind an "uncomfortable atmosphere," be the basis for a complaint against the faculty member, or the person treating these subjects. To be sure, it's always possible for a committee to determine subseqeuently that a "reasonable person" would not find this offensive. Yet nothing in the directives explains how a single objection can be proof of the existence of an "atmosphere."

This apparently liberal course of action was undertaken, however, as a result of complaints against the military for allowing sexual coercion to flourish, and in particular to a study that found that such things were rampant at our sister academy, the U.S. Air Force Academy. Thus paradoxically the conservative military, which tried to bar the introduction of women into the academies (women were introduced as the result of action on the part of the U.S. Congress, beginning in 1976) and still bars and "separates" (throws out) gays, has become the champion of women's rights.

These moves please liberals, but they are instituted from the top down, as any good conservative structure demands: They have become the new list of what to do and what not to do. Such a list is the sine qua non of a conservative structure. Thus they're liberal in content but conservative in form.

Plebe Politics

Midshipmen, and especially plebes—first-year students—almost all vote Republican, and, unsurprisingly, fully support the use of military force in whatever direction the Commander-in-Chief, whoever he or she is, chooses to send them. Perhaps this is unsurprising: That's what they're trained to do—they want to use their skills. Congressionally mandated neutrality of the military overlaps with the widespread conviction on their part that there's no such thing as a bad war. Most of them think that violence is manly, and that war builds character. Many believe conservatives have a monopoly on "character" (liberals are flip-floppers, lacking principles). Loyalty is important, as is "supporting the troops." As newly arrived plebes during their first summer, they all bid goodnight to Jane Fonda, remembered for having gone to North Vietnam while U.S. troops were fighting in that unhappy country and so for betraying the men in uniform. "Goodnight, Jane," they chorus in exhausted unison before lights-out, "Goodnight, bitch."

Plebes are more doctrinaire than graduating seniors about these things: They're younger, to begin with, and still starry-eyed about the possibility of an unadulterated version of the conservative paradise they have entered. They haven't had the edges rubbed off them by the realization that even a place like the Naval Academy will contain some less than honorable people, or by the sheer complexity of life itself.

I remember their palpable exhilaration after the election victory of President Bush in 2004. Before class began on the day after the election, one of my students, an upperclassman, turned to those around him and asked the rhetorical question, "Why don't the Democrats just *die?*" In the weight room later that same day, two members of the swim team working out behind me traded news that Senator Kerry had conceded defeat. "*Yes!*" said the one to whom the news was new, pumping his fist in the air. He said it in a tone expressing intense satisfaction, but the subtext was, "*Damn him!*"—anger and exasperation that it had been necessary to go to the work of defeating him in the first place.

Way of Life

Yet the conservatism of the Naval Academy comes more fundamentally from the organization itself than from the individuals that compose it. The clockwork, spit-and-polish nature of the surface here at Annapolis is not mere window dressing; it's an expression of the conservative way of life.

Conservatism is expressed in how we lead our lives, what we do: what most conservatives call a "lifestyle." What people do is the point of the exercise, and the way the point of life is expressed. Thus liberals without a structure of actions as ends-in-themselves seem vague to conservatives, unfocused. Conservatives don't see that liberals aren't trying to achieve a structure of actions at all. But it's assumed they're trying to: hence the conservative insistence that, for example, being gay is a "lifestyle"—it's something you can do or not do.

The institutional givens of the Naval Academy are expressions of a conservative worldview, not a liberal one. Liberals tend to find that uniforms get in the way of "expressing their individuality," so the fact that everyone at Annapolis wears a uniform is already a sign of the conservative worldview at work. Midshipmen and officers say "sir" and "ma'am" to superiors, which may stick in liberal throats. Midshipmen salute officers and stand up when professors, including civilians like me, enter the room for class. Most midshipmen attend some form of church service on Sunday, oppose abortion, and are comfortable with (or actively yearn for) a world in which women stay at home and take care of the children while the men deploy on ships for months at a time.

Almost half of the midshipmen self-identify as Roman Catholic. Though Catholicism has its left-wing variant in "liberation theology" (rejected by the Vatican) and American Catholics are much more liberal than Rome wishes they were, Catholicism is most essentially, of all the brands of Christianity, the one most clearly based on authority, as well as being organized in a rigid hierarchy. By closing down doubt and discussion on doctrinal issues, it clears the deck for everyone to try and achieve the same goal, a situation I take as paradigmatic of the conservative worldview.

Our students don't typically know much about the variants of Catholicism, or indeed its dogma. They tend to be comfortable with what they were taught, whatever this was, in church or at home: Religion for them is not something that's open to question. But that is a quality of Catholicism, too, that makes it a strange, and at the same time logical, bedfellow, with evangelical Protestantism and with orthodox Judaism—all groups that support the policies of the conservative George W. Bush. It's not a commonality of content or dogma, but rather of authority: You believe what you're told to believe. Questioning authority shows immediately that you're not a conservative, and hence not worthy of living in the conservative paradise. You're a liberal.

Most of our students were comfortable in other hierarchies in addition to the religious one, and with other group structures—all of which are more compatible with a conservative worldview than a liberal one. Many of them were Eagle Scouts. Many were members of sports teams more focused on group than on individual actions. They show their awareness of the collective: They pick up trash along highways on Saturday mornings, and tutor in the local schools. But all this is as volunteers: They would furiously oppose any government-initiated attempt to force them to do this, as conservatives typically do. Like most conservatives, they can feel compassion for the less fortunate, but they like to retain control over whether it's to be shown or not. Individual compassion is a series of unitary decisions; what they oppose is any program cutting people slack they themselves don't get. Life is tough; everyone should have to compete. Typically, they are comfortable with the vision of a God who damns everyone save those, on a case-by-case basis, He decides for reasons of His own, to pardon. Once in the Academy, however, they themselves are cosseted and tutored to get through; despite the rigors in a certain way of life afterwards in the military, they are taken care of by a system.

Midshipmen believe in the power of individuals to succeed or fail on their own. They are extremely uncomfortable with seeing themselves as the products of their environment, or as predictable by dint of being members of a specific group. They reject with derision government policies designed to buffer any disadvantaged groups from the effects of rampant capitalism: Competition is good, and the fit survive. When I point out that they are the "pampered pets of Uncle Sam"—to quote a line from one of their Navy songs, living on taxpayer largesse—they grow glum, as they do when I suggest that they are the product of many systems other than their individual initiative.

Typically, they defend the way we do things on the grounds that "it's tradition." Tradition, in the conservative worldview, is an absolute good. The more traditions we have at the Academy, the better people around here seem to like it. Traditions let us know how things are going to proceed. They give us a sense of control of the future. Conservatives think this control of the future a good thing; liberals usually find it stifling.

Interestingly, recent traditions, even new ones, aren't of lesser value to conservatives than older ones. A tradition is a tradition, whenever it started; it still predicts the future. The fact that the now-problematic annual greasing and climbing of Herndon obelisk dates only from the 1950s does not deter those who defend it. It's problematic because of the scores of so-far low-level injuries it creates, and the fact that women have to join the puppy pile with the men, and sometimes have been known to be pulled off if they get too close to the prize, a cap on top. To liberals, however, the concept of a "new tradition" seems like a contradiction in terms.

"Outstanding, Sir"

When you ask a midshipman how he or she's doing, the lowest the scale of responses goes is "Outstanding, sir/ma'am," even if the midshipman is failing courses and has just been found guilty of a serious conduct offense for which he or she will be restricted to the Academy for the next six months. Part of the conservative lifestyle consists of putting on a good face to the outside, however outside is defined, and not thinking you're a hypocrite by doing so. The Naval Academy may have problems, people might admit privately, but these are to be kept invisible to visitors. The public affairs officer is there to keep them invisible, and to paper them over if they become visible. In a similar way, individual students may have problems, but these are never supposed to reach the outside viewer. It's an optimistic view, or at least the appearance of one. Yet for conservatives, these two merge into one thing.

Conservatives, even if they are what by outsiders' standards would be considered poor, are likely to be optimistic, to see their relative poverty as a transitory or alterable state rather than as a fixed one. A study of the Pew Research Center for the People and the Press considered the lower-income portion of both Republican and Democratic supporters and came to the following conclusion, according to the *Washington Post*:[4]

> The most striking differences between lower-income Republicans [here: conservatives] and lower-income Democrats [liberals] come in their perceptions of the power of the individual. . . . Where they part company is in their overall sense of optimism, with the Republican group expressing much greater faith in personal empowerment. Three-fourths of the Pro-Government Conservatives agreed that people can get ahead by working hard, and four-fifths agreed that everyone has the power to succeed. Just 14 percent of Disadvantaged Democrats agreed with the first statement, and only 44 percent agreed with the second.

To Europeans, typically more liberal than the average American, American smiley-facedness in general—what the outsider notices about the midshipmen at Annapolis—seems hypocritical. American customer-is-always-right commercial pleasantness, the shining façade of "Hi"s between strangers, and "Have a nice day" to people we know nothing about seem merely lies. (The bumper sticker that growls "Don't tell *me* what kind of a day to have" is a self-deprecating caricature of a liberal position.) It does seem true that Americans are more invested in the surface than Europeans. Many people would agree that the South and the Midwest, the American conservative heartland and the "red" states in the currently fashionable "red–blue" dichotomy, are apparently more concerned with preserving this friendly surface than the Northeast and the West Coast, the more liberal Democratic-voting "blue" states. In the South, they're nice to you.

Saying that things are "outstanding" at Annapolis doesn't mean they really are so any more than saying "Things are bound to get better" means they will: It's a decision, a point of view. Being optimistic means that the conservative worldview is being acted out: You don't emphasize or even acknowledge problems. Perhaps too, in the military, all this sunny optimism is the sign that people want to confuse the enemy into thinking that everything is going very well indeed.

A preponderance of formulaic interactions of any sort, here verbal, is a sign of the conservative worldview. All social structures depend to a degree on formulaic interactions, such as when we ask, "How are you?" socially and expect only to hear, "Fine, thank you. And you?" The military is characterized by having rendered formulaic many more interactions than are typically so in the world outside. This is true of the military etiquette on how to address people of various ranks, what body postures are appropriate at specific times, and what people are allowed to say to superiors.

A midshipman saying that things are "outstanding" is to some degree like one of the five permissible responses to questions during plebe summer, when plebes arrive six weeks before classes start for their "indoctrination," as it is unapologetically called. These five acceptable responses, all placed in a "sandwich" preceded and followed by either "Sir" or "Ma'am," are "Yes" ("Sir yes sir"), "No," "Aye aye," "I'll find out," and "No excuse." This is an extreme and limited situation, even in the military, in that people simply aren't allowed to say anything but this, as they are not allowed to look anywhere but straight ahead ("keeping your eyes in the boat"). But it's an extreme example of the system itself; at USNA it's comprehensible, but elsewhere it would simply be unimaginable. Conservatives don't typically bemoan the impoverishment of expression when responses are limited: you can still act, which is the point of it all. Indeed, you can act more effectively, since your options for actions are limited to only a few. It's liberals who will point out all those things that somehow don't get said as a result, emphasizing the complexity of the individual that is simplified by such limitations.

At least partly because things are always by definition "outstanding" at Annapolis, the smile-production factor for visitors is very high. The very gung ho-ness of the students is lovable—their sense of purpose, the fact that they're always, as I once heard a tourist say, "hot footing it somewhere." Not to mention the fact that they look so "sharp," a much-heard midshipman word. Each midshipman, typically male (about 16 percent are women), has "taped off" offending specks of dust from his natty, close-fitting uniform, stands up tall, calls any tourist "sir" or "ma'am," looks you in the eye, and, if called upon to do so, shakes your hand with a firm grasp. When visitors see masses of these students at parades or football games, their chests out and their spines rigid, how can viewers not burst with pride? Midshipmen really seem America's finest.

What's nicest of all is that they seem so predictable. We know, or think we know, they're not getting into trouble. Adults like to think of adolescents and young adults as predictable: It suggests the world will continue in ways the adults understand, that their lives have not been in vain.

I'd submit that there's no liberal institution in this country where the students come near to putting the same kind of smile on your face as they do at a conservative institution like the Naval Academy. Students at what midshipmen call "real schools" slouch, binge drink, chain smoke, wear caps inside, and never, ever, say "sir" or "ma'am" to a professor. Not to mention that our students aren't—for lack of a better word—sullen. They're not trying to figure themselves out: All they have to do is what people want them to do. What is there to figure out? Plenty, I could tell them, and frequently do; I remember being sullen at their age, lost in the caves of the self back at Haverford College. To conservatives the self points outward like the prow of a boat, it does not look inward into dark and unknown recesses.

Ship, Shipmate, Self

One of the most lovable facts about the Naval Academy, at least when seen from a specific angle, is that it demands transcendence of the individual. The self comes last. The scale of values taught to midshipmen, in order of most to least, is this: "ship, shipmate, self." Self-sacrifice: it's a beautiful thing, and one that, it seems, has all but disappeared in our sharp-elbowed "me first" world. It's a virtue central to the conservative worldview. The very basis of liberalism, by contrast, is a focus on the development of the individual. To the worship of selflessness such as is taught at Annapolis (the reality may be a different thing, of course, than the theory), liberals would say, it's relatively easy for conservatives to sacrifice the self because the individual plays only an ancillary role in the conservative worldview.

The single most striking thing about life at the Naval Academy may well be how predictable it is, which is to say, how controlled: Only things that are controlled are predictable. And control, as I will be considering in greater detail below, is a major goal in the conservative worldview. One of the things that can be controlled is who we live with. That is why the Naval Academy, and more generally the military, offer examples of the conservative love of clustering like to like. Much of conservatism is a way of life, a set of things done in public. If you live with people doing other things, you might begin to wonder if you were doing the right thing. If everyone around you is doing the same thing, you don't have to question it. You can merely act. This is what produces the warmth of conservative paradises.

There's not much room for other-thinking or -acting people at Annapolis to develop their otherness—or in any other conservative structure, which instead of negotiating differences is devoted to following absolute rules. That becomes clear from reading Joseph Steffan's *Honor Bound: A Gay Naval Midshipman Fights to Serve His Country*, the autobiography of a midshipman who realized he was gay about halfway through his "four years by the Bay" (as the school's alma mater has it)—the Chesapeake Bay, that is, our local body of water.[5] Ultimately he was "separated," expelled; he sued unsuccessfully to be allowed to serve in the military. It's the slowly dawning realization on Steffan's part, which he is unable to share with anyone, that he doesn't find the sex jokes of his company mates funny and that perhaps, just perhaps, this might mean something, that is the book's most touching aspect.

Lack of Control

There are many things we don't control in life: aging, for one, or what Freud called the subconscious, or sexuality, the sheer unpredictability of life. I'd say men don't like thinking about these things. We lose all sense of control if we have to deal with the desires of another person, especially if she is female and so intrinsically (it seems) unpredictable.

For that matter, we lose control if we think too much, worry too much, or question too much. We lose control if we consider people too unlike us: What are we to make of this? Does this imply we ourselves should be different?

The aspects of life on Earth that are clearly not amenable to human control are so numerous and all-pervading it almost seems comical to a liberal that we would focus on the few things we can control, though it's hardly surprising. We might go crazy if we thought about all the things we don't; perhaps telling ourselves we do control things is a basic human need.

This need is the genesis of conservative thought. Death, to take the most obvious example, is beyond our control: It happens to everyone. Loss of physical vigor in old age is another. Another is the fact that some humans have to sacrifice themselves to others, such as mothers to children, or women to men. In order to close out such thoughts, the military, and conservative structures in general, emphasize strength, youth, and maleness, a combination which gives people the sense that they are in control of things, at least physically. After all, strong young males are the most able of the people in our world to tell themselves they are in charge of their own destiny.

Youth is the sine qua non of admission to the Naval Academy: No one twenty-three or over can start as a plebe. Despite the presence of women, the Academy revels in masculinity. All military virtues are masculine virtues, or drawn from aspects of the male body at its most aggressive and potent: people in the military are "hard," "lean and mean," and try to be "pumped." (The brigade sponsors a student-body-wide "Gun Show," or contest of biceps.) The inhabitants of the Naval Academy's conservative paradise don't like thinking of themselves as victims, so only "hard-charging" "type A" students are admitted.

Nor is there much talk at the Academy of death and maiming in battle, the reason this institution exists. I've had students say, after we read in class Wilfred Owen's mordant consideration of a triple amputee war casualty, "Disabled," that they had never realized this might be a possibility for them. One former student told me a number of years ago that reading this poem in my class was the reason he transferred to a civilian university.

Hence, too, is the strangely puritanical nature of the military, the fact that so many human beings are physically intimate with each other and are told so repeatedly they are being perverse and "unprofessional" if they notice each other as sexual objects. The reason they have to be told so repeatedly is of course that the danger of their doing so is so great. As Freud might point out, the strength of the repression is correlated to the power of the thing that's being repressed. This problem has grown more acute with the introduction of women into the brigade; sex in "the Hall," as Bancroft Hall is called, dormitory to all 4,000 students, is forbidden. Sex creates sub-units that function like self-enclosed nodes in the social fabric.[6] Intensely social structures like the military, or any conservative paradise, resist the fractionalization of relationships into the nodes required by sexual pairings. The military can't tolerate this. It requires that all its constituent parts be facing forward, at attention and ready for action, unengaged in any personal activity, awaiting orders.

The first female midshipmen at the Academy were admitted in 1976 after vociferous protest from the institution. The same things are required of them as are required of men, with minor variations (upper-body exercises among them); I'd say many of the things taken for granted at the Academy are quintessentially male, from the rigid body postures to the very structure of "Yes sir" hierarchy. Women have been allowed in, but they have to play the same game the men do, and it's a male game. As a result, women frequently act like honorary men in order to get by. Certainly they are dressed like men; the women talk about their "birth-control shoes." Yet for the women it's frequently a no-win situation; my male students tell me they cannot respect a woman who is too feminine, and find repellent a woman who is too masculine.

Conservatives deal with things they don't control by refusing to focus on them. The Naval Academy is structured to make it possible for its inhabitants to focus only on that very small part of life that jibes with the conservative structure—that of young, healthy, largely male people without dependents and freed of other obligations, whose actions are regulated by a structure. To an outsider, the constraints of the Naval Academy are quite clear, and sometimes to the students, too. But to the extent that they simply build them into their lives as something they have accepted, they can forget them. This act of forgetting the very constraints and limitations that are so clear to an outsider allows them to see themselves as free agents. Being a conservative is about how you see yourself, not how others see you.

At the Naval Academy, in sum, men have created a world that banishes the old, the unpredictable, the sexual, and substituted for it the neat hierarchical ranks that parade on Wednesday afternoons on Worden Field as the sun slants across the emerald-green grass and a sea of white-gloved hands slap in unison on the rifles, and at noon meal prayers where 4,000 heads bow in submission to the Almighty. As I write, noontime prayers are being challenged by the American Civil Liberties Union; the administration defends the practice vociferously.

In such a world things are clear: Each person knows who is above and beneath him or her, knows what is good and what is bad. At the Naval Academy, each student has sworn an oath to support the Constitution, though he or she may not be able to tell you what it says, and knows he or she must follow lawful orders by his superiors. In such a world, the predictability of life is intense. This predictability of action is the point, as it's the point of conservative structures elsewhere. Variation is relegated to the level of the individual; it's not part of the structure as a whole. People bear the brunt of succeeding or failing: It's never the structure that's at fault, and individual choices are limited to two—achieving the goal or not achieving it.

Many things still escape control, but in a conservative structure, we choose not to focus on them. We don't know what the people in the apparently identical uniforms on the parade field are thinking, nor do we ask; or what they are muttering under their breaths, or how they dress when not in uniform. Nor do we know what is written on the T-shirts under their uniforms, which no one inspects (I've had students tell me they went out of their way to decorate their T-shirts just so they could feel they were getting away with something), or whether their shoes, similarly uninspected, have holes in them (a surprising number of them do: "It takes so long to get them back from the cobbler, sir!"). Or what they do afterward. If you don't track it, then, for the conservative structure, it doesn't exist.

The illusion of control is produced as a result of a perceptual fact rather than one about the objective world, like seeing the grass as a solid even carpet: An ant would see the fraying ends of the grass, the dirt, the difference in length of one stalk and the next. Furthermore, achieving this illusion requires constant practice, and it is achieved as the result of moral exhortations (your parents are watching) and threats of *force majeure* (your company officer is watching). The uncontrolled can be held at bay, but its force is shown by the elaborate lengths to which we go to keep it there.

Venn Diagrams

The conservatism of the Naval Academy is intense. It is so intense because there is so much overlap between the groups whose thinking is congruent to or inflected by conservatism. These include men, religious conservatives, political conservatives, and adherents of the competitive market economic conservatism (sometimes, confusingly, called free-market liberalism) that most of our students subscribe to—despite the fact that the Academy is a government—and hence taxpayer-funded institution.

The Academy is comparable to the area of overlap in a Venn diagram, which draws circles to indicate the relationships between individual groups; one circle overlaps with another to show the degree of convergence, and the lozenge-shaped area of overlap is colored darker. This darker area can overlap with yet a third circle, a fourth, and so on, and the areas of multiple overlap grow increasingly dark as the color piles up in a single place.

There are numerous circles in the Venn diagram with the Naval Academy at the center. This means that there are many different ways to be conservative in the world outside, related though they may be. There are males, there is the military, there is the Catholic Church, there are the libertarians, and there are the rich with their SUVs and their gated communities, just to name a few groups of people that overlap at the Naval Academy.

My point of departure here is the reality of the Academy. I'm not trying to chart how the groups interact and fold into each other over time. I list these groups of conservatives because they are similar at an abstract level, what I call the level of deep structure. When they overlap at Annapolis, the pile-up of conservatisms is intense, like focusing the sun's rays with a lens to start a fire.

Being one kind of conservative doesn't mean you see eye to eye with all other kinds of conservatives. In the world outside, in fact, some of these groups disapprove intensely of others groups. The military, in what may come as a surprise to some people, typically disdains the (largely conservative) gated-community set as being insufficiently "hard" and self-denying, though the gated-community set largely supports the military. In fact, the more general fact that will surprise many outsiders is that the military, generally speaking, looks down on almost all the civilians it has pledged to defend. Plebes are continually enjoined during their indoctrination period of plebe summer not to think like "civilians" (the word is pronounced with scorn). They're told continually that the military is more moral than the civilian world outside. Moral lapses on the part of the military are excused by the assertion that the military is "held to a higher standard."

There are other divergences between different forms of conservativism. Conservative religion doesn't always approve of the military. Pope John Paul II, as conservative on some issues as one could have imagined, preached for many years against using organized death to resolve national differences—the presupposition of military thinking—and against the illusion that material goods, the goal of all those SUV-driving gated-community types, are the goal of life.

It's possible, too, to be conservative in one aspect and liberal in another. Students at St. John's College, the country's only Great Books college, whose campus adjoins that of the Naval Academy, were famously critical of the Naval Academy and of midshipmen during the 1960s and '70s, seeming to exemplify political liberalism as much as the midshipmen exemplified conservatism. Back then, you never would have mistaken a midshipman walking along Annapolis's neat brick-lined streets for a "Johnnie," or the reverse. Even now, when hair length is not so absolutely correlated to politics, you'd still probably get the school right. The midshipman looks straight ahead, carries him- or herself completely erect, and strides purposefully ahead. You don't get the impression that midshipmen are distracted by their own thoughts.

Yet in its own way, St. John's is as conservative as they come, its curriculum built on an unvarying canon of masterworks studied in rigid chronological succession, its students standing at the entrance of their dean and tutors as midshipmen stand at the entrance of officers and faculty. To explain this, we would probably make the distinction between political liberalism and curricular conservatism.

Some people are politically conservative, supporting U.S. intervention abroad and a strong military, and socially liberal, not caring whether gays marry and supporting abortion on demand. All variations are possible, though this one is the exception rather than the rule. I know it exists because the military officers who come back to the Naval Academy's English department to teach sometimes fit this profile. Sometimes they're even U.S. Marines. I'd say they're atypical Marines, conservative by English department standards, liberal by Marine ones.

***

How My Consideration of Liberals and Conservatives Compares to Two Others

Some readers may want to skip to the next chapter where the thread of the Naval Academy is picked up again. From here to the end of the chapter, I explain how my consideration relates to what may be the best-known attempt to delineate liberals and conservatives, that of Isaiah Berlin, and to the works of the thinker who's developed this contrast most intensively today, George Lakoff.

I'm not offering a historical consideration of the development of liberal and conservative political ideologies, by tracing, e.g., the theoretical roots of modern political thought, usually exemplified in the clash of Kant (liberal) vs. Burke (conservative). Yet because I presuppose that they are two divergent ways of going about things, my consideration bears at least a family resemblance to Isaiah Berlin's seminal essay "Two Concepts of Liberty."[7] According to Berlin, the liberal will typically celebrate "positive" liberty, the freedom to define one's self and achieve one's own goals, while the conservative will typically celebrate "negative" liberty, the freedom from others telling you what to do.

My consideration is more abstract than Berlin's, and the relation of the individual to the structure is different than it is in Berlin's consideration. Though the members of the two groups of liberals and conservatives may indeed hold, respectively, these two visions of liberty, this is merely one of the things on which they disagree, not the terms in which the disagreement is expressed, nor any sort of underlying reason for the disagreement. Both sides agree that "liberty" is a good thing; Berlin's point is that they understand this notion differently. The distinction between "two notions of X" will thus always explain the actions of the individual, never the reverse. This is so because the individual has no possibility of rebutting the theory. Berlin is, in the sense I used it above, an "immutable," suggesting that he alone is able to pull himself out of the conflict to the point of delineating the antagonistic positions.

Here's why I'm not an immutable, or at least am trying hard not to be one. Like most political thinkers, to be sure, I propose something larger than the individual, insisting that at times the reality of a worldview is different than what those who hold it say it is. Yet this is something we can talk about to the individual who holds it. There is room for interaction between the individual and the worldview; typically people will agree that this is, in fact, their worldview. Or they can reject it in favor of another.

In practical terms, this means that individuals can decide they were wrong about the nature of their own worldview, or that of others. Sometimes people are, in this way, wrong about the nature of their worldview, or—more usually—that of the other side.

It usually seems to liberals, for example, that conservatives are actively trying to get everybody to do the same thing. Liberals typically sees, conservatives as intrinsically fascist, bent on imposing uniformity on the world. I argue instead that conservative thought is not focused on forcing uniformity, getting everyone to do the *same* thing. Instead, its real purpose is to get each individual to do the *right* thing.

Because there is only one right thing to do in each situation, this of course means that everyone, at least ideally, will be doing the same thing. To conservatives this isn't central to their worldview; it's a trivial truism, and they don't understand why liberals make so much of it.

Yet confusingly, some conservatives, unclear about the nature of their own worldview, do in the heat of battle with liberals frequently say that they are trying to get people to do the *same* thing. With what I call a worldview rather than a more standard political theory, that's not the end of the discussion. We can suggest to the conservative that the position he or she has taken is not, in fact, central to conservatism, but only a reaction to a liberal attack. A conservative would probably agree that getting everyone to march in step is not, in fact, the primary goal he or she is reaching for but a secondary one that, through argument with liberals, has come to take center stage. Worldviews can be perverted from their natural natures through conflicts with things they are not.

Thus it matters to my enterprise what relation individuals think they hold with respect to the worldview. Whether they agree or disagree with my assertions is itself part of the deciding—for all of us—which worldview underlies their own actions. I don't assign individuals to categories; I propose the categories and invite individuals to help figure out which one they belong to. Most people already know.

Worldview vs. Metaphor

The thinker who shares the greatest number of my presuppositions, whose most important is that liberals and conservatives will never agree, is George Lakoff, whose views on the workings of politics are based on his understanding of how metaphor works. I share with Lakoff as well the fundamental conviction that liberal and conservative thought constitute worldviews, constellations of thought. In order to make clear what I'm doing differently than Lakoff, however, and hence why this "view from Annapolis" needs to be considered, we should consider some of his points. His most relevant book for my purposes is *Moral Politics: How Liberals and Conservatives Think.*

It's important to consider that Lakoff is a linguistics professor, the author of a book on metaphor, *Metaphors We Live By.* Lakoff's central intuition when he turned to considering politics was that politics can be explained as the development of a central metaphor.

Lakoff's master key to open the lock of politics is the family. According to Lakoff, both conservative and liberal politics are the result of applying metaphors for one sort of family or the other, what he calls the Strict-Father paradigm on one hand (conservative), and the Nurturing paradigm on the other (liberal). Yet there's a hitch in applying the metaphor of family to politics: According to Lakoff, we do it but shouldn't. Lakoff's analysis is twofold: First he establishes the metaphor, then he claims it's being applied to something it doesn't really fit.

Lakoff's greatest drawback as a thinker is that, like Marx and Freud, he believes one key can turn many more locks than it actually can. One such key is the notion of metaphor itself. Usually we speak of metaphors when we see both the likeness and the divergence of the terms we use to the situation we're using it in. We say our spouse is "the old shoe" or "the ball and chain" or "the light of my life," but understand that he or she isn't literally a shoe, a chain, or a light. We're focusing on a single quality. To make the metaphor work we have to know which qualities not to focus on.

Metaphors "work" only to the extent that we focus on limited qualities, not on all qualities. We can use the terminology of a ship with the U.S. Naval Academy, but the fact is that we're on dry land, and not moving, among many other reasons why it's literal nonsense. The Naval Academy isn't really a ship, though we daily work the extended metaphor of calling it one. Hallways are "passageways," students come to an "attention on deck" when I enter the room, and everyone goes to the "head" rather than the toilets or bathroom.

Metaphoric language causes problems for people with disabilities on the autism spectrum because such people don't know which qualities out of so many to focus on. Even mildly autistic people typically require literal use of language, or need to have each instance of figurative language explained. Instead of a general concept, they tend to visualize a specific instance. When someone says "shoe," they imagine scuffed, brown Oxfords. In a similar way, the metaphoric comparison is visualized with all its qualities. They don't foreground one quality and consign all others to the background. These secondary or irrelevant qualities so to speak come along for the ride, not just the ones that "fit." This reaction of people with disabilities helps us see that these qualities are there all along: it's just that people without this disability have learned simply to ignore them.

The weakness of Lakoff's insisting that metaphors are so central is that deciding something is a metaphor is as much a fact of perception as of any objective quality. It's not true that there's a category of some words that's intrinsically and clearly, for all circumstances, metaphoric. If you can't make your explanatory category stand still, you can't use it to explain anything.

If we say, to indicate we're adopting a new course of action, that we've "changed horses in the middle of the stream," that's pretty clearly a metaphor. But to say we've "changed course" isn't so clearly so. Do we literally "adopt" a new course of action? No, if this is literally what we do with a baby. Yes, if "adopt" is correctly used not only with babies but also with courses of action. Do we adopt a "course" of action literally or metaphorically? If we say we "change our mind," is this literal or metaphoric? The mind itself isn't changed.

If we use the metaphor without knowing it's a metaphor—so that someone has to point out to us it is—I'd say we're using the language literally. For the poet Shelley, this was the process of metaphors "dying."[8] I think what Shelley saw as the death of metaphors is just the way language develops new denotations. Legions of people in the United States today say that something "sucks" to indicate it is a bad thing, or distasteful, or painful. To me, and others, this is clearly a vulgar word, part of male recess slang in junior high school, and its use in public places inexplicable. Yet when I explain to my students what clearly is the genesis of using this in a negative way (it's a homophobic, and possibly misogynistic, slur—just what do they think is being sucked, and why should it be negative?), they are taken aback. "Sir," they say, "nobody thinks of that."

Some people do. I do. But if we stop doing so, or are simply out-voted, or die out, to say that something "sucks" will be as literal as saying it is "distasteful" or "painful"—I don't suppose it's literally painful, in a medical sense, to do things we don't like, or that they have anything to do with our tongues. Yet we use these words without blinking. They're not dead metaphors, or if they are, virtually all literal language is. Is it metaphoric or merely technical to speak of a "dead" metaphor? There's no way to answer this question.

So Lakoff is wrong to think that he can easily or definitively separate off "metaphor" from things it isn't. Whether or not something is a metaphor largely depends on our point of view, what we're aware of and what not. For that reason metaphor can't be used as the key to explain all the other ways we use language, which is constantly changing.

In my book *Disappointment*, I make the point that we have to use language in new ways all the time to produce explanations. Every new explanation describes the layer beyond the layer we have an explanation for, and so uses language to describe new, because hitherto unseen, things. Proust's *Remembrance of Things Past* had to be so long because there was not available vocabulary to describe the workings of the filmy process of memory he wanted to articulate. Now we sum up this whole thing by referring to Proust, speaking of a "Proustian" experience, or a "madeleine moment." Similarly, we speak of a "Kafkaesque" world: Without all the words of Kafka we wouldn't understand that this meant a vaguely threatening world of endless passageways leading nowhere and punishments we are unaware we merit but somehow vaguely accept, a Byzantine bureaucracy that will draw us into its deserted labyrinth, which we will wander until we die.

Lakoff is interested in the way, e.g., spatial concepts pervade the way we talk about the mind: put something higher on our list, before others, lower than other things. But who says this is metaphoric? We can say just as easily that this is just the way we talk about the mind, words used in a technical sense. We'd say of the language we use to talk about politics that's the same as what we use for the family that it's just the way we talk about politics. "Attention on deck" is just what the students *say* when an adult comes into the room, even if there's no deck, and even if "attention" is somehow a synecdoche for standing up straight, apparently paying attention. That's what "attention" means here.

But let's say we're focusing on the historical genesis of the terms here. It's clear why we'd think of the Naval Academy as a ship. It's not so clear why we would be impelled to use language initially used to describe the family to describe the social unit. Both are groups. But why use one to describe the other, rather than, for starters, the reverse? Do we assume we privilege the paradigm for the family we ourselves were raised in (rather than, e.g., those of the kids next store we'd wished we had been)? And why should we be impelled to apply its language to something quite different, namely the state? We may be the head (is this metaphoric?) of our family, but we can hardly argue we control the state. Why should we see state and family as similar enough to transfer the vocabulary? Why is it even remotely feasible that the family explains the state?

The family provides Lakoff with an explanation for politics because, it turns out, the family is what really interests him. At the end of *Moral Politics*, he makes clear that he thinks people raised in dysfunctional (for him, Strict-Father families) go on to perpetuate the same mistakes in their own families. Apparently there's no escape possible if you've been raised in such a family: It leaves its imprint on everything.

Even if you're a woman? If you're a man on whom the Strict-Father paradigm grated horribly? Lakoff thinks people raised in Strict-Father families shouldn't project (his word) this paradigm onto anything, as the Strict-Father paradigm doesn't work even for children. But if it doesn't work, wouldn't the children raised in such a paradigm be acutely aware of this fact? Wouldn't that mean they wouldn't perpetuate it? Or are they condemned to do so? If so, by what forces? Even showing that the Strict-Father paradigm doesn't work in a family doesn't necessarily mean it won't work for something else, such as the state. Lakoff's point is after all that the state is not the same as the family.

Why should we say that an adult supports strip-mining (typically beloved of conservatives) because of the way he or she was raised (which seems to be the implication of Lakoff's metaphor of the family)—or even because the adult accepts a certain view of child-rearing? Why not say the adult adheres to a view of childrearing because of his or her views of the proper role of the state? Who says a view of the family isn't already itself a metaphor for something?

Lakoff has to explain why it is that conservatives, who by rights should be supporting the Strict-Father in their application of this paradigm to the government, in fact attack government at every turn. This, he explains, is the result of a tweak in the Strict-Father paradigm: that adult children are no longer under the power of the father. So they don't have to perpetuate it? Suddenly it seems as if the metaphor isn't that of a family with a strong father, imagining the children as minors, but of the family with independent major actors who have to decide what nursing home to put Pops in. Is that really the family at all in the sense Lakoff was using it to construct his paradigms? Certainly it has nothing to do with raising children.

Lakoff encounters similar difficulties in explaining why the military should be so attractive an institution to conservatives, from my perspective a glaring flaw. First off, it's unclear who the "father" is in the military: the whole institution? One's immediate superior? The whole chain of "fathers" up to the very brassiest brass? But if conservatives don't want a "father" in the form of the government, why should they want one (or many) in the military? Certainly the military, as Lakoff notes, doesn't allow much latitude for personal expression. So why would it appeal to the same people who demand that the market allow us to be free to make money?

Nor does Lakoff's explanation of the liberal and conservative worldviews as the (illegitimate?) transfer to politics of the language of childrearing explain phenomena like the conservative love of rich people. In Lakoff's explanation, the conservative assumption is that riches are earned, so that wealth, to conservatives, implies the individual has worked harder. But the fact is that conservatives typically like rich people who have inherited their wealth too. Maybe more than the ones who acquired it. Nor do they really require that this acquisition be the result of work rather than luck, e.g., on the stock market. Conservatives simply like "winners," whatever the source of their victory, and abhor "losers." Liberals go around trying to identify the "losers" so they can help them; conservatives typically snort and look the other way.[9]

For Lakoff, the differences between conservatives and liberals are differences of words. Of course, things would seem this way to a linguist, especially one who initially expressed disagreement in terms of metaphors. Thus Lakoff, most troublingly for me, misses the fundamental point about conservatism: It's not about argument in words at all, but action. The conservative's words are only produced, when necessary, to justify actions. Liberals, by contrast, are essentially about words, because they are trying to change something. They're the ones trying to convince the conservatives.

Conservatives only use words defensively; they're perfectly happy doing what they do. They have what I call in *Art and Argument* the "home-field advantage" in any subsequent argument: They're where they are; it's someone else who's questioning what they take for granted. That's the nature of their worldview: It's the one that's not in need of change. That's why conservatives like "winners," however they got their position (and/or money): That's a stable situation that no one is looking to change.

We need a more abstract notion of the nature of liberal and conservative thought than is provided by metaphor, argument, or words. Lakoff gets close to this view in a later chapter of *Moral Politics*, when he lists the assumptions of Strict-Father morality. The first is quite close to my formulation: "There is a universal, absolute, strict set of rules specifying what is right and what is wrong. . . ."[10] In my view, this is what underlies the conservative worldview—including family, ethics, state—rather than one of these being primary over all the others.

As Lakoff points out, this is an assumption, something the person him- or herself would certainly be in a position to agree or disagree with the analyst about. The individual could say, "Yes, I hold this assumption," or "No, I don't." And we would be inclined to take that person's word for it. The childrearing metaphor as explanation, by contrast, is a liberal "gotcha." Like Freud and Marx's explanations, it's valid whether or not the person agrees—in fact, it's probably held to be more clearly valid if he or she disagrees. But conservatives aren't going to be listening to any liberal "gotcha." They're going to be off acting, living the conservative lifestyle. It's part of the conservative worldview to think everything part of a "lifestyle," a choice: It is for them, why not for everyone?

Lakoff's theories lose air quickly when we ask, "How well do they explain the reality of the Naval Academy?" Here, childrearing seems far away, save insofar as it is kept artificially alive by the Freudian assertion that it continues to determine us even when we're doing something else entirely. To be sure, I'd say, in Lakoff's vein, that most midshipmen came from strict, conservative families. It's true too that many of them seek to be told what to do, as their own biological fathers (or their stand-ins) did. But why argue that the superior officer is a stand-in for the strict father? Perhaps it's the reverse, that the father was the caretaker until the military could take over. Certainly that's the way the powers that be hereabouts see things, regularly thanking the parents when newly arrived plebes are sworn in for "giving" them their children.

2
DEEP STRUCTURE

The primary difference at the deepest level between liberalism and conservatism is that liberal ethical pronouncements are expressed in terms of actors, conservative in terms of actions. The currency of liberalism is words; the currency of conservatism is actions. Conservatism tells us what to do; liberalism doesn't.

This sums up the current chapter. If you read it and say, "That's why liberals are such wimps," you're making the assumptions of the conservative worldview. If you read it and say, "Yes, and that's why conservatives are proto-fascists," you're making the assumptions of the liberal one.

* * *

Why We Need Deep Structure

I propose a way out of the bellicose stalemate between liberals and conservatives that defines our current scene through what I call, with apologies to Noam Chomsky, a consideration of the deep structure of liberal and conservative thought. We need to think in terms of this level precisely because it's impossible to make sense of the conflict in terms of particular positions: We can list what positions conflict with what, but that's all we can do.

Liberal and conservative are relative concepts, not absolute ones. They're made to describe complementary but opposing viewpoints. That means opposing or complementing in a specific context. This is the reason why it's possible for someone to be conservative on one issue and liberal on another; to hold conservative views that in another time or place would have been considered liberal (or the reverse); or to go from being liberal to being conservative (or the reverse) with age. We can still say what it is that makes a position liberal or conservative in the particular circumstances in which it is so.

You're a conservative on a specific issue in a specific place because you're not a liberal, and the reverse. Liberal and conservative aren't groups of people here, but ways of seeing things, world-views—though certain groups of people tend to adopt these one way or the other. The groups that converge at the Naval Academy tend to adopt the conservative worldview. The fact of binary conflict on the American scene allows us to speak of two groups of people, as if this were the level at which the distinction occurs. It isn't. If we try to say what the divergent natures of liberalism and conservatism are merely by looking at what the two groups say about themselves, we will soon give up in frustration, since both make claims to the same things.

Conservatives claim that they are better defenders of life because they oppose abortion ("killing the unborn") and refuse to pull the plug on patients who are deemed beyond saving by medical professionals ("miracles are always possible"). Liberals claim that *they* are better defenders of life because they typically oppose the death penalty and because they ask more often than conservatives do such questions as what the cost in human lives of war will be, and what will be its effect on the country being invaded. Conservatives claim that they are better defenders of freedom because they oppose government interference in people's lives, whereas liberals claim that *they* are better defenders of freedom because conservatives would have all women barefoot and pregnant and everyone forced to go to the same churches on Sunday morning. It seems an impasse.

Other Explanations

We need some notion like deep structure, among other reasons, because previous explanations of the nature of liberalism and con-servatism haven't proved adequate. Feminist theory has offered a broad-based explanation of conservatism—namely, that it's about protecting the patriarchy. According to feminist theory, this produces the conservative abhorrence of abortion (killing off off-spring, the ultimate proof of masculinity); the support of war (men are naturally aggressive, plus look how phallic all those guns and rockets are); and the belief that everybody ought to be driving an SUV, if not a motorcycle or a tank (men like big throbbing machines between their legs).

Feminist thought correctly perceives a link, considered further below, between conservative thought and male thought. But it makes too much of this. Maleness is one of the overlapping circles in the Venn diagram of the Naval Academy—or the conservative side of things in the political arena. But it's not the underlying explanation for their pattern. We see this from the existence of female conservatives (feminists can explain this only by calling female conservatives brainwashed, co-opted by the patriarchy, or pawns), and plenty of male liberals, not all of whom are 98-pound weaklings who can't change a flat tire. Masculinity can overlap to a large degree with conservatism, but it can't be identical with it. Many high-profile gays and lesbians are liberal, but others are fervent Republicans and devoted Roman Catholics.

Another common definition of conservatism holds that conservatives are the ones trying to keep life the way it was, whereas the liberals are the ones trying to change things, trying to move forward to the future. This is the sense in which liberal thought is "progressive." This comes closer than feminist theory to being useful as an underlying principle but still comes up short of being a full explanation.

There's nothing intrinsic in a position that will let us say, outside of the context in which it was advanced, whether it belongs to the future or the past, we just have to see how things turn out. Nor can we say with any degree of confidence that conservatives always support the status quo. The George W. Bush administration's neoconservative strategists advanced a theory of global change to justify the invasion of Iraq, after giving up on talking about the weapons of mass destruction that were initially held to be the reason for the American invasion. The Middle East was to be made democratic out of the barrel of a gun. This policy surely has nothing to do with the status quo.

Conservatives can go on what President Bush unwisely called "crusades," too: In their own eyes they're removing an aberration, but from the outside it looks like trying to change the way things are.

It's not a good idea to accept without question what each side says about itself and its opponent. In arguments you always emphasize differences with your opponents. Yet in reality you're likely to be quite similar to any opponent you'd be interested in distinguishing yourself from. The differences between liberals and conservatives create their clashes; what allows them to clash is that each has adopted a worldview—which, since it's a worldview like every worldview, is a view of the same world. A tomcat doesn't fight with a lemon; it only fights with another tomcat that wants what it wants, probably a female cat. The commonality of goal and desire is what they have in common, though what they say, in tomcat-talk, is that the other one is the enemy, and has nothing in common with it.

This is why we need to sketch the deep structure of each worldview, the pattern beneath all of the particular tiffs and tussles that makes the conflicts foreordained. These deep structures tell us what things in the world each side privileges and what it ignores, what kinds of evidence it holds relevant and what irrelevant, and what issues it finds worth talking about and what it simply will not touch. Both worldviews are views of the same world, though quite different views.

The two views are as divergent as the paintings by two art students assigned to paint a bowl of fruit in the front of the room. Both paintings may be recognizable representations of the bowl with three pears, a banana, and an orange, but what they choose to include and what they leave out will determine their individuality. One of the views of the bowl of fruit may be cubist, the other naturalistic; one in black and white, the other in color; one upside down and the other sideways. One may have the fruit float over the bowl while the other anchors the curves and shining surfaces of apples and oranges in the bowl's embrace. Different versions of the fruit, like the divergent worldviews of liberal and conservative, are merely different versions. Unless, of course, we are one of the artists, who presumably thinks his or her version alone captures the "reality" of the fruit.

Both artists would agree that they are offering versions of the same fruit. (However everything being a "representation" doesn't mean there's no such thing as the objective world.) It's precisely the fact of clash that shows us that liberals and conservatives agree at least to this extent. If conservatives and liberals weren't fighting over the same turf, they wouldn't be fighting. That still doesn't mean we can articulate the turf by merely accepting the language of either side.

My presupposition is that the people involved can react to and negotiate their distance to the deep structure. An individual can decide the extent to which he or she approaches the theoretically "pure" version. Again, when I say that liberal thought exhibits a certain deep structure, this doesn't determine whether any individual is a liberal or not. But it may help us determine the extent to which that person is so. Deep structures as I propose them don't have any determinative power. They are primarily aimed at the members of the group they purport to describe, not at describing them willy-nilly. They can be either embraced or rejected.

* * *

Consider the snort. Conservatives snort much more often than liberals do. Usually the snort means: There they go again, those liberals! What wimps! It's the fury of conservative talk radio, and the fury of my student that Senator Kerry even had to be defeated. Conservatives conceive of themselves as striding toward their goal, killing dragons as they go, and dogged at their heels by a pack of yipping liberal curs that do nothing but cause trouble. For the dogs, they have nothing but contempt. Hence the snort.

If you snort derisively, you're a conservative; if you shake your head in disgust, you're a liberal. To liberals, conservatives are lumbering bears, not yipping dogs, hardly nuisances that can be snorted away. So liberals snort less. Conservatives seem instead, to liberals, to be major threats to personal liberty. A typical liberal knows he or she can't afford to snort when confronted with yet another fulminating conservative demagogue.

Asymmetrical Views

Liberal and conservative worldviews are structures, not just lists of contents. Their content is produced by their structures. The distinction between structure and content is all the more necessary because the two worldviews are asymmetrical.

We get a sense of this structural asymmetry in the liberal bumper sticker addressed to conservatives: "Against Abortion? Don't Do It!" It's meant as a taunt showing (liberal) consciousness of the asymmetry I am emphasizing here. This asymmetry is found in the fact that the *kind* of thing conservatives want to see happen is fundamentally different than the *kind* of thing liberals want to see happen. Liberals know that what conservatives want is not merely that they themselves be allowed to forgo aborting, but that the action itself be forbidden, to everyone.

For the same reason, conservatives mount a "defense of marriage" by ensuring not merely that they continue to be able to marry people of the opposite sex, but that everyone who marries will marry someone of the opposite sex. Liberals, by contrast, envision a world where those who want to abort do so, and those who don't, don't. It's also a world where those who want to marry someone of the opposite sex do so, leaving those who want to marry someone of the same sex free to do so. "Each to his or her own" runs the liberal creed.

This difference in kind between liberal and conservative thought is the source of the otherwise inexplicable surface divergences. Consciousness of this structural divergence helps us answer questions like these: Why is it that conservatives are apparently unconcerned with the lives of soldiers or of civilians caught in wars? Why is it that liberals seem to be unconcerned with the lives of defenseless "unborn children"? Why are conservatives spending so much capital on keeping two words, "under God," in the Pledge of Allegiance? Why don't liberals seem to care who gets married, or if anyone does at all?

This asymmetry is captured neatly in an editorial by the liberal commentator Ellen Goodman.[1] It concerns one of the manifestations of the culture wars, the attempt to discredit the teaching of evolution in schools and to place alongside it—and ultimately, perhaps, supplant it—an explanation that involves God. It's called ID, or intelligent design, the insistence that so much complexity (design) in the world implies a Designer, not merely the working out of Darwin's principles of natural selection. It was an argument against Darwin in the Victorian age as well. Goodman quotes a member of the Kansas committee responsible for deciding whether to require that Darwin's evolutionary theories be challenged in the classroom, William Harris. Harris, who thinks they should, announced: "Our overall goal is to remove the bias against religion that is in our schools. This is a scientific controversy that has powerful religious implications." Goodman comments, acerbically, "Science that doesn't teach his religious beliefs is biased against his religious beliefs."

Yes, this is the case. Goodman means it ironically, but Mr. Harris would probably agree with no irony. This divergence captures neatly the asymmetry of the liberal and conservative worldviews. For the conservative, the contents of his or her belief expand to fill the world: Allowing them but limiting their applicability (you can hold them at church or at home but not at school) is to violate the very nature of the belief. Relative or limited belief is no longer belief. The worldview is just that, a view of the world. From the liberal perspective, that's the problem with conservative belief: Every conservative wants his or her personal worldview to be imposed on all others.

Thou Shalt Not

According to conservative thought, the action itself, regardless of the nature of the actors involved in it, is forbidden or allowed. Liberals, by contrast, express ethical dicta in terms of actors. As a result, the particularities of the person's situation are relevant to the liberal, and irrelevant to the conservative.

For conservatives, the individual is a relatively meaningless unit that is constantly found wanting with respect to the Absolute Action, that great looming thing outside of him or her that nonetheless he or she is constantly attempting to attain. This is what's behind the Naval Academy's ordering of priorities: ship, shipmate, self. The conservative individual is constantly struggling to achieve what he or she perceives as something greater than him- or herself, to fulfill a dictum.

A statement of the form of "Thou shalt X" or "Thou shalt not Y" is an intrinsically conservative dictum. Conservative ethics are expressed in rules of actions, not in a consideration of individual situations.

Negatives are even better than positives, from the conservative perspective, because they're so much clearer: With positives, we still don't know how we're going to accomplish them. A negative, however, both tells us what we want to do and that we're not going to do it. One of the most fundamental facts of life for conservatives, and one of the most puzzling for liberals who look on, is the conservative love of forbidding—for everyone, including, and to some degree primarily, themselves. Yet this is merely another sign of the intrinsic divergence between the liberal and conservative worldviews. Conservatives, puzzlingly for liberals, seem in love with their self-forged fetters. In feeling the comforting strength of the bounds beyond which one may not go, conservatives taste the edge of their world, which therefore seems solid. A negative is a complete little drama, all in itself. It makes certain that particular bit of the future.

Thou shalt not, for example, steal. Only a liberal, to whom the particularities of the actor's situation are relevant, would ask, "Is it all right to steal if you're starving and the bread you're stealing belongs to a millionaire who won't miss it?" It isn't that conservatives always say "no" to such questions. The question itself doesn't figure as legitimate in the conservative worldview. Asking it produces only a snort from die-hard conservatives. They're annoyed that it's even being brought up. Such questions themselves are inappropriate. Liberals, by contrast, tend to think that all questions are appropriate. The liberal worldview consists precisely of such questions, the conservative worldview of answers.

Other People

Relationships between the self and others are also different in conservative and liberal thought. The conservative matrix at its deep-structural level has nothing at all to say about other people; they enter the structure only as a second step. The action does not vary according to who's doing it. Thus, as a logical corollary—rather than something that needs to be asserted—all others should be attempting to achieve the same action.

Conservative thought is absolutist thought. Things are this way and no other. There is no slot in the structure of its thought for internal dissent, so when it encounters the other, it responds either with incomprehension or aggression: This wasn't supposed to be there. Opposition is to things outside the system, and for that reason the more unbridled. This is also circular: if something opposes conservatism, it is by definition Outside, it can't be part of the conservative paradise.

When conservatives seek to express their fury with liberals by calling liberals "relativists," liberals don't understand why this is a term of opprobrium. It is so for conservatives because to be "relativist" is to deny the fundamental nature of their matrix, its absolutism. To a conservative, "relativism" seems to imply chaos, because it lacks the quality that for conservatives is the sine qua non of any ethical system—namely, that it tells you what to do. For the liberal, by contrast, "relativism" is part of the givens of ethics. Of course things are relative, but this for liberals is not the primary quality of liberal thought, merely an uninteresting fact that decides nothing in particular.

Consideration of situational specifics is something only liberals engage in, not conservatives. If you ask two people "what do I do?" and the first one says, "Do X" and the second one says, "Weeeell, it depends on A, B, and C," the first is the conservative and the second the liberal. Liberals always tailor their actions to the particular givens of the situation, because their ethics are written in terms of actors rather than in terms of actions. So we have to know something about the actors. Actions are inhuman things that humans aim at, and the more forcefully the individual does so, the better. For liberals, it's the human doing the aiming that's the point.

Thus, force constitutes a good in itself for conservatives. You're supposed to be decisive, even if you later "reverse yourself" (as we say at Annapolis) and charge just as decisively in the opposite direction. The point for many conservatives is the charge itself. Liberals roll their eyes at the sight of all these charges, which in many cases seem to them like that of the Light Brigade in Tennyson's poem: valiant, but quite the wrong thing to do. Indeed, "The Charge of the Light Brigade" will be read quite differently depending on whether the reader is a liberal or a conservative. The conservative will cheer on the valiant cavaliers who rode "into the valley of death"; the liberal will note that "somebody blundered." In looking at the U.S. engagement in Vietnam, liberals decry the waste and destruction produced by the involvement, whereas conservatives emphasize the individual bravery of soldiers.

Conservative thought can be visualized as composed of individuals, each of whom is connected by a string to the same Absolute Action. As a result, conservatives don't see the perfectibility of the group as something that figures in their structure. We perfect ourselves only individually. That is why each of us, according to the conservative movement we call evangelical Christianity, accepts his or her Personal Savior. Conservatism is interested in each person doing this, but it is not—and here the distinction is subtle, but real—interested in every-one doing so. This may be the end effect if each individual does so, but for conservatives, individuals do not add up to a group. The lines of the conservative structure do not go sideways, nor do they cross.

This makes clear how impossible it is to say without caveats whether it is liberalism or conservatism that is more interested in the individual. Conservatism requires each person to try and achieve the goal, but it does so without taking much account of variations of indi-viduals. Each individual is defined by his or her relation to the abso-lute, external action. Liberalism defines the individual by relation with other individuals, not with absolutes. The lines of the liberal structure form a web that connects individuals to individuals. For a conservative structure, groups have no ontological meaning. They are only 1 + 1 + 1 + 1. For liberals, it is meaningful to see a group as hav-ing ontological weight.

For conservative thought, the individual is (only) the doer of the action, so the individual takes last place in relation to things outside him- or herself. Because conservative ethics looks like many threads going from countless individuals to a single external action, the individual follows his or her thread to the action, not necessarily looking sideways to the other individuals at all. Liberal thought, by contrast, is based on what may be as many actions as individuals, which for that reason are not conceived of as primordially external to the person. For liberals, these actions intersect and sometimes interfere like threads tangling between individuals, a maypole dance gone awry.

Liberal Views of Conservatism

My view of the nature of conservatism departs from articulations of conservatism inspired by classic apologists like Hume, Smith, and Burke. Such defenses of conservatism, as Boris Dewiel puts it, see "the fundamental social good in terms of continuity, structured cohesion, and civil order."[2] Yet this, according to my view, is a deformed view of conservative thought, because it is produced from without. The notion that the individual needs to have his or her goals defined by a society in order to be fill-in-the-blank (free, fulfilled, good) is the liberal version of a conservative view, not an intrinsically conservative one.

Any theoretical justification of conservatism comprehensible to liberals will already be expressed in terms of liberal givens. And to assert that conservatives believe society needs to tell us unstructured individuals what to do is to express the conservative worldview in terms of the liberal. This is so even if it is conservative thinkers themselves doing the expressing: One side can learn the language of the other, and use it under proper circumstances.

While thinking we can express the essence of the conservative worldview by expressing it from the point of view of liberals is a mistake, it is a very common one. Usually it is liberals doing the expressing, and so making the mistake. The short-lived poet and literary theoretician T. E. Hulme provides such an example in his delineation of what he called "classical" (conservative) from "romantic" (liberal).

> [The] root of all romanticism [is] that man, the individual, is an
> infinite reservoir of possibilities; and if you can so rearrange society by

the destruction of oppressive order then these possibilities will have a chance and you will get Progress.

One can define the classical quite clearly as the exact opposite to this. Man is an extraordinarily fixed and limited animal whose nature is absolutely constant. It is only by tradition and organization that anything decent can be got out of him.[3]

. . .

To one party, man's nature is like a well, to the other like a bucket. The view which regards man as a well, a reservoir full of possibilities, I call the romantic; the one which regards him as a very finite and fixed creature, I call the classical.[4]

This definition, like the comparable definition of human nature as requiring fulfillment in society, is intrinsically a liberal definition of both liberal (romantic) and conservative (classical). This is so because it primordially separates the individual from the society. It hurries on to assert that the individual finds his or her fulfillment or good in achieving the goals set by the group. But the more essentially conservative point of view is from the point of view of this fusion, without having to assert it. The conservative individual is already one with the group; he or she doesn't have to achieve oneness with it.

My insistence that conservatism and liberalism are different types of things echoes the distinction Friedrich von Schiller drew between two sorts of poetry in "On Naïve and Sentimental Poetry." Naïve poets, Schiller thought, citing Homer as an example, feel "naturally." Sentimental poets, by contrast—we would say he was describing the then-nascent Romantic poets—seek "the natural." They're always on the outside looking in. Yet the apparent paradox is that it will be those who are outside Eden who will sing the most beautiful hymns to its beauty. Those inside Eden are just going about their business.

Thus, it's liberals who will define conservatives as holding the view that the individual is completed only in society. The conservative, who may in fact act as if he or she holds this view, merely sets about completing him- or herself, not holding the view. If you have to assert the fusion, as many Romantic poets did—and as liberals writing about conservatives do as well—you'll never achieve it. Indeed, if you're too aware of the necessity of the fusion, the chances are good that you'll never achieve it either.

Such justification for the conservative worldview, presupposing as it does that the individual must strive for completion in the society, assumes the split as primary. This justification can't be primary in a correct definition of conservatism. Conservatives don't feel they have to justify what they do: What is primary is not the split, but the fusion. Action becomes primary. Conservatism is about things done, not things said. Liberalism, by contrast, is all about articulating your own position with respect to someone else's. It's about words.

It's only when conservatives have to talk to liberals that they come up with justifications like those of the classical theoreticians regarding the nature of the individual and his or her completion by society. All academic debate is carried out in terms of one of the two worldviews, namely the liberal. This is a fact of the structure of the debate, not of its content. That's why academics almost invariably misdescribe conservatives, who represent the world of action rather than thought. Conservatives would more nearly express conservatism not by coming up with justifications of conservatism in words that are comprehensible to liberals, but by walking away—as many of them in fact do.

Loyal Opposition Is, It Seems, Disloyal

Conservatism pervades the air at Annapolis, but this doesn't mean liberalism is absent, as I can attest from the English department. It just means that liberalism is raucously attacked each time it raises its head: Conservatives correctly see that it presents a threat to the conservative social fabric. Indeed, the conflict of liberal and conservative, which to an extent means academic vs. something else, is a very real one here at the U.S. Naval Academy, where students go to class in such subjects as English and History, and then go and drill on the parade field.

What's most interesting is that liberal dissent is attacked in terms that seem, to liberals, illegitimate. Liberals are berated not for what they say, but for the fact of saying it—for dissenting, something that for liberals is a given. This fact once again indicates the asymmetry of the two positions.

The mere fact of my disagreeing publicly indicates that I'm not a conservative. When, as I periodically do, I write an article suggesting that the Naval Academy could be doing things better, I typically get outraged e-mail from the officers teaching in a department that for a time was called Professional Development, "Pro-dev" for short. How *could* I? To them it seems perfectly natural to blast me for "disloyalty," which is to say, for saying that things aren't as squeaky-clean and happy-faced at Annapolis as they are repeatedly asserted to be.

For many of the military officers, the mere fact of articulating dissent publicly clearly means that I have broken the rules. There is by definition no such thing as "loyal opposition," in the British sense—loyal, that is, to something or someone higher than the people you are disagreeing with. They rarely argue about the content of what I've said. The fact of saying it has already shown that I'm not one of them. A liberal would accept the fact of disagreement and demand that the content of the assertion be responded to: Facts matter. But facts, which presuppose an objective world, are in a fundamental sense irrelevant to the conservative worldview: What matters is the front you put up to defeat enemies. I shouldn't be disagreeing with company policy at all.

The same is true in other forms of conservatism than the military: Once you've got it right, there is no merit in questioning it. Questioning religious faith, for example, can lead to people losing it, so it's better not to do it. "Yes, but," or "have you considered" are not considered acceptable positions in the conservative worldview; instead, they are merely the sign of the unconvinced, the weak, or the contrary-minded. In the conservative worldview, you don't get any credit for being the clever one in the back who raises objections. In the liberal worldview, you do.

This is an example of why most academics, who tend to be liberal, do not grasp, and so misdescribe, the fundamental nature of conservative thought. The very form of liberal thought is out of sync with what the conservative worldview requires. Liberals think of themselves as intrinsically neutral, ready to question everything but with no preconceived ideas. But it's the questioning everything that is part of what makes the liberal view non-neutral. That's why it's content, at least from the conservative point of view.

Literature and Motivation

Part of the conservative worldview is this demand that we emphasize only the positive. All of us, according to conservatives, are striving against things that challenge our attainment of the Absolute Action. We give them too much credit even by naming them, much less acknowledging their power, or worse, concluding that they will defeat us. Asserting our own strength isn't understood by the conservative as being literally true, at least not now: It's meant to discourage enemies by describing what the conservative hopes will be the outcome.

The Naval Academy, as a conservative institution, demands unrelentingly good news. Sharing bad news is "unmotivational." Reactions are keyed to encouraging shipmates (which at Annapolis means fellow students—is this a metaphor or simply the term we use at Annapolis?) to achieve objectives, not talking about situations where the objectives weren't achieved. For our students, and conservatives of all stripes, literature is a handmaid to this project. They don't see the point of literature whose purpose was not, in this sense, motivational.

The problem this creates for our classroom is that great literature only allows within its canon works that are nonmotivational. Works that end in a "how-to" lesson are too simple to stand the test of time: They're made for specific circumstances, and so are disposed of when those circumstances fail to be the case. From the perspective of my students, what we read—all of it taken from the canon of high literature or contemporary candidates to that status—is negative. It wants you to think about all the possible consequences of actions, even (or perhaps, especially) the negative consequences.

Great literature is literature that lasts, meaning literature that lasts when it's taken out of its context. It's almost a tautology to say that great literature isn't very polemical; it's not out to have us take actions in the world. Some proportion, here a larger proportion, is merely what I call "Here it is." The more polemical the literature, the more closely it's bonded to its circumstances, and so the shorter the lifetime of its successful transmission. The tendency in the nineteenth century was to get the causality backward and speak of a realm of art, conceiving of art as existing separate from the world, a type of thing somehow superior to the sweat and dirt of real life. From this comes the notion of people who devoted themselves to this realm as being "high-minded" or "too good for the world," as the heroine of George Eliot's *Middlemarch* initially imagines her dried-up pedant of a husband to be.

Art isn't something we create because we're in a realm. It's what gets sifted out of the world precisely because its connections with the world are so weak, and so ends up in a category by itself. It isn't used to incite wars, or to make people better, or to change the status quo. All it does is make us think. This is a liberal goal, since it is alien to action in the world. Merely thinking means not acting.

Kant isn't wrong that all we can do with art is perceive it; he's only wrong if we take this to be something we can tell about any given object beforehand. We do what we do, and when we find ourselves merely perceiving, this object is assigned to the category of "great art." This is a category liberals acknowledge as valid and conservatives, by and large, don't: It doesn't imply action. That's why conservatives, as Lakoff points out correctly, tend to want art to be good for something, e.g., encouraging public morality.[5] In the stereotype—which like all stereotypes is based in fact—it will be liberals who go to museums and read serious books, and conservatives who go to car races and ride motorcycles.

Because the liberal agenda of serious literature is such a given for those who take the validity of art for granted, they usually fail to see it. They are surprised when conservatives reject the arts (conservatives can rarely marshal the reasons to question the arts), or dismiss the conservatives as "philistines." From the outside, by contrast, this liberal agenda, in conservative terms the lack of clear "motivation," will clearly be seen by conservatives as the content of literature.

The war novels I have my students read for class, such as *All Quiet on the Western Front*, are never stories of heroism to rally the troops; instead, they show the waste and pointlessness of war. The novels about marriage that we read, such as *Madame Bovary*, show us that marriage frequently not only solves nothing, but even makes things much worse. Poetry typically aims for a realization that we can't have it all, what the literature professor thinks of as its "complexity."

The take-home point of Keats's "Ode on a Grecian Urn," which I read every year with plebes, is that we humans are caught between a rock and a hard place with our desires. They're necessary to keep us moving. But we do not, save in an almost trivial, momentary sense, ever achieve them. Once we achieve our goals, they are no longer goals, and we must find new ones. They slip from us like wraiths. This, I am now no longer surprised to hear, is not what our idealistic students want to hear. They want to hear that war is worth it, that marriage is the ideal state, and that we can attain, in every sense, what we set out to own. So, too, for the officers who lead them, who are constantly suspicious of the goings-on in the English department, that font of nonmotivational thinking.

Literature professors would say that telling my students what they want to hear would be to tell lies. But, the conservative would respond, "so what?" Truth is not the currency of conservatives; action is. Thus people are allowed to say anything that achieves the goal. It doesn't have to be true that life is controllable and that goals can be achieved. But it keeps us moving forward better than admitting that it isn't controllable and that goals are rarely achieved. The proof is that the conservative continues to run after the Absolute Action. What we say is, for conservatives, more a part of the larger puzzle and less outside of it, as it sometimes seems to liberals.

Truth Is Liberal

The conservative/liberal divide also, I have been implying, clarifies the nature of the philosophic debate about "truth." Truth is a specific relationship with the world that isn't always appropriate. It's more the distanced "representative" relationship of high literature than it is the rhetorical, "heat of battle" relationship of popular literature, or of action. No one says that Napoleon's victories are "true"; they merely are. They're the result of actions.

One of the greatest goods for the liberal worldview is truth. The comparable good for the conservative worldview is belief. In liberal thought, the relations between individuals have to be worked out. Thus the presupposition of the liberal worldview, before any particular liberal assertion, is that everyone is equal. This at least is the point of departure. Thus everyone must have the same relation to an outside manifold. Assertions made between people must be in a sense extrapersonal. Scientists, perhaps for this reason, are almost invariably liberal. The jewel in the crown of science is the assertion of extrapersonal truth. But you get to this by listening to what others say about it: you put forth your theory for possible disproof. Conservatives never do this; they merely state the truth and defend it. It doesn't matter what others say if you've already said what your Absolute Action is. Belief is to a much greater degree something the individual has access to; truth by contrast must be arrived at by considering other people.

The conservative worldview has on one end the individual, and on the other, the action at which he or she is aiming. Relations between individuals are not part of the conservative worldview, so belief, given importance by the mere fact that it is the individual's, fills the role of truth. An assertion of belief has intrinsic value for conservatives, and none at all for liberals.

Conservatives, being focused on the action, will say and do many things in the pursuit of their action that do not stand the test of truth. Yet this isn't to say that, for the conservative worldview, they're false. These things aren't meant to stand the test of truth; they're meant to change the world in some way, to move forward the cause. If I say I have twenty men behind me and I only have ten, it's not true, but that's not the point: The point is to fool the enemy.

Where in a world of action would truth be able to enter? What you say is determined by whom you're saying it to: To yourself, you say that you will prevail; to your fellows you say that they are fighting the good fight; and to your enemies you don't say anything, as you are using all your energy to raise your sword and swing it.

Not admitting difficulties in a proposed course of action doesn't mean you're denying they're there (as liberals sometimes think conservatives are saying), only that you don't talk about them. Confusingly, to throw enemies off the scent, conservatives sometimes *do* deny that there are any difficulties. However this is merely what you say to others, which need bear no relationship to what you admit explicitly to yourself, or implicitly admit through the fact of trying to counter these difficulties.

If you start with knowing what to do, as conservatives do (rather than, as liberals do, spend your life trying to figure it out), truth isn't really something you need to worry about. It doesn't go away, but it's not very important either. You'll remain optimistic yourself, say encouraging things to the people around you who are fellow believers, and smite your enemies ruthlessly.

This is the reason why the military isn't interested in "truth" about things it's done, or things going on in the military world, when it encounters opposition from civilians. Opposition is opposition, and the military's knee-jerk response with any sort of opposition will be to deny everything for as long as possible and circle the wagons. Only when denial and attack fail may it be forced to admit "truth." This is consistent with the conservative, military worldview.

Liberals tend to be very upset when the military, or conservatives, lie to the world outside. For the military, this is just another attempt to overcome enemies. Similarly, for religious fundamentalists, as liberals call them, the mere fact of belief is its own end. Liberals, by contrast, try to show them they are wrong about their facts, something that merely annoys conservatives without affecting them because for them it's completely beside the point. This is the nature of the conflict between Darwinian explanations for the development of things and the Intelligent Design advocates. Those for whom belief is primary can let others talk until they are blue in the face; if the end result is not the belief, it's wrong. This makes perfect sense to the conservative, and none at all to the liberal.

Conservatives might express their relationship with language (it's a means to an end) by saying that language plays a role in the world; it isn't outside of it. Conceiving of language as being outside of its particular use is a liberal position. The twentieth century's philosophical turn into language philosophy presupposes the adoption of a liberal perspective, because it focuses on the truth of an assertion rather than on the assertion's place in the world. Actions not in words aren't assertions at all. Only someone operating from the distanced perspective of the liberal that sees, first of all, the fact of language and only secondarily what is said would focus so strongly on assertion, or on truth, as twentieth-century philosophy derived from the early Wittgenstein has done.

The question so central in Western philosophy of whether literature is true or false, which I considered in *Art and Argument,* belongs as a result as well to a definable place in the liberal/conservative divide.[6] Being worried about whether something is true or false is already a sign that the person worried is a liberal. Yet the fact of trying to get a clear delineation between these two places the person trying for it on the conservative edge of liberalism. Literature contains things that seem, if excerpted from the fact of being in literature, to be all but identical to mom telling us that there are fresh cookies in the jar. Either there are or there aren't, we say. If we can't judge an assertion in a novel the same way as mom's assertion about the cookies—say, the assertion that "the countess left the house at ten"—we seem to have a paradox on our hands. It's an assertion, written the way we write other assertions. Yet we know we won't find any trace in the real world of the countess, her house, or her carriage.

We'd be disappointed if we didn't find any cookies in the jar; by contrast, we don't even look for the countess. What's the difference? The only thing that makes this assertion different from mom's assertion about the cookies is the fact that the assertion about the countess is in a novel. And this seems to push us to the nineteenth-century view that literature somehow exists in another "world" or "domain," a sort of parallel manifold like the real one, only not.

But this is to accept the premises of the particular position I call "conservative liberal," namely that the question can and should be decided. It's one of these questions that seems interesting because it comes from an area just outside a boundary. Assertions in novels are enough like assertions at home that it occurs to us to ask what the difference is. But things even further away don't even seem enough like the thing we're sure of to pose a problem—any objects, such as our raincoat and umbrella in the umbrella stand.

John Searle's conclusions in this vein that literature deals in "pseudo-assertions" seems downright comical given the vastness of things that are even more "pseudo" than the assertions of literature, being no assertions of any sort at all, but something else entirely.[7] Why doesn't it bother Searle that mowing the lawn isn't any sort of assertion at all, not even a "pseudo" one? It's because he's trying to colonize the area closest to what he's focused on, trying to bring the border area inside the wall. Territories further away are merely beyond his reach. He's expending all this effort for what actually is a very small possible expansion of his territory. But this is always the way arguments work. You attempt the possible, not the impossible.

Assertion is merely assertion. It isn't murder, or mayhem, or standing on one's head. It may be true that only assertions are true or false, but the limited nature of assertions helps us see that truth or falseness isn't a particularly interesting quality for most of the world. If we happen on an area where we're unclear if what's going on is assertion or not, the correct answer is precisely that: We're unsure, which means, it's the gray area. But the gray area isn't, e.g., merely half white, it's also half black, and the all black, the vast area outside, isn't amenable to any sort of connection with assertion at all.

Philosophy, to be even more general for a moment, typically tries to decide all these border cases: Is X an example of A or of B, and why? But the fact that we need to decide indicates that we don't really have to. Instead we can walk away. Similarly, the fact that liberals and conservatives could get up a really good knock-down argument that could last forever shows us the pointlessness of doing so. The better the argument we can get going, the lower, in the larger scheme of things, the stakes.

Misapprehensions

Each view, to itself, is as clear as air or water. From the point of view of the other side, however, each medium seems opaque. Liberals think it's only conservatives whose view has content; conservatives think it's only liberals. This is so because each side assumes of the other that its worldview contains certain sorts of elements: unsurprisingly, those that its own worldview contains. This leads to false assumptions, and to criticism of the other side for not being like one's own.

Thus liberals who think that the point of conservative thought is to get everyone to do the same thing make the mistake—though it is a comprehensible mistake, fueled by conservative thinkers—of believing that what is merely a secondary quality or mere corollary of the conservative structure is central to its nature. They do so because liberal thought contains, at its fundamental structural level, a space to specify relationships between individuals assumed to be different. Indeed, we may say that liberal thought is all about relationships between individuals assumed to be, at least potentially, divergent.

For this reason liberals who consider conservative thought look for the pronouncement of conservatives on how to mediate differences between individuals. Finding it absent, they assume the point of the structure is to make all individuals identical. But the absence of something doesn't mean it's been excluded; it can mean it's just absent, not a fundamental part of the structure.

The influence of Michel Foucault on late-twentieth-century thought, as I consider below, has been to obscure the difference between, on one hand, failing to do something, and on the other, overtly not doing it. And if you're suspicious of someone else, you tend to regard his or her omissions as conscious slaps in the face at yourself: We all assume our own preoccupations are others' as well. Conservatives don't assume they have to mediate between individuals, because their focus is elsewhere. Of course, this is exposed as a weakness of conservative thought when we need to mediate between individuals. Liberal thought has other structurally determined weaknesses, but not this one.

Liberals, whose ethics is articulated in units of actors rather than actions, see other people—who, as a result, can in theory be talked with rationally—where conservatives see The Enemy. Conservatives make the mistake of assuming that liberals must be just like them, and then go from perplexity to anger when liberals act differently than conservatives do.

As conservatives see it, liberals believe everyone can be convinced by reasoning: They can talk their way out of anything, they need never act. This is Krauthammer's point, above. According to him, liberals think everyone else is as nice as they are. Presumably, instead of blowing them away, liberals want to talk with enemies, or invite them to tea. This, to conservatives, means that liberals are indecisive and weak, as well as stupid.

Much was made at the Republican National Convention in 2004 of John Kerry's statement that the United States should be waging a more "sensitive" war on terrorism. This was presented to the Republican faithful as synonymous with "kinder, gentler," when the context suggested "not so ham-handed, more effective." "Somehow I don't think Al Qaeda would be impressed," Vice President Cheney chortled to the pro-Bush delegates. Hit 'em hard, hit 'em repeatedly; that's the conservative way of dealing with problems. Indeed, according to them, it's the only way. Those who don't agree are "girlie men," as California Governor Arnold Schwarzenegger called those he held in contempt.

The disadvantage of the liberal worldview is certainly that you always have to gather information about circumstances before you act, since what you should do is determined by the specifics of the situation. Information gathering is laborious, and usually slow, not to mention frustrating. The advantage of the conservative worldview is that it allows people to know exactly where they're going before they start: They have access to the Absolute Action in which conservative ethics is expressed, and can act immediately if threatened. When liberals do not initially see an Enemy, conservatives conclude that liberals are "soft."

This reaction by conservatives is based on a misunderstanding of liberals by the conservatives—albeit a comprehensible misunderstanding. For a liberal, the fact that he or she can articulate the other person's point of view doesn't mean it has to be accepted. What if that point of view is utter rejection of all the person articulating holds dear? In that case a liberal is perfectly comfortable resorting to the conservative's default of violent opposition. But because the liberal doesn't make that decision until determining what the other person is thinking, the liberal seems indecisive and weak to conservatives. The action remains to be determined; liberals can't say a priori what their reactions are going to be. The nature of conservative ethics is, however, precisely such *a priori* actions, achieving a list of actions independent of the individual.

Disagreement vs. Conflict

Liberals integrate friction into their system as disagreement, conservatives banish it to the outside as conflict. Thus liberals want to disagree with conservatives; conservatives want to attack liberals.

Again: conservatives like conflict with the outside—it reminds them of who they are by giving them a clear sense of who they aren't. The greater the opposition, the more they are defined. Conservatives insist that the world is made of scary people: This is "realism." The only language possible with them is the language of force. This is the basis of the neoconservative Robert Kaplan's insistence on the necessity of armed intervention by the United States in foreign places. His book *The Ends of the Earth* is permeated with bitterness bred from disappointed surprise: These guys just aren't very nice![8] And his other books develop his love of soldiers, whom he calls, indicatively, "warriors."

Thus the attraction of conservatives to the military is based on structural congruence; it is not the result of chance. Typically, liberals like to assume that conflict can be kept in the family, and defused. Disagreement, the liberal form of conflict, is like the formerly wild animals that they, as the ringmaster, keep in line. Liberals see themselves as the grid that allows the contents of the particular units within it. Any unit that threatens the grid is failing to act according to what liberalism thought everyone understood the game to be. The proper response is to explain to the recalcitrant one that it is out of line.

Conservatives like to focus on their force, but this is only applied to the Outside. This means that many more people are Outside for conservatives than for liberals. Inside, they are astonishingly warm and fuzzy, approving of all their fellow conservatives doing the right thing. Conservatives are tigers with those without and pussycats with their own. When they self-present to outsiders, however, what they emphasize is the tiger. That's the square jaw and unflinching gaze of the Marine Corps: Beware. Thus liberals may be unaware of just how pleasant conservative paradises can be, though of course they are so only to like-minded people.

Liberals take these two extreme attitudes applied to inside and outside, what we may conceive of as black and white, and mix them to gray, for everybody. Conservatives criticize liberals for not being forceful enough to the world outside. It's true; they're less forceful. Liberals aren't initially as aggressive as conservatives, because as a result of their structure, outside isn't populated by absolute Others. But by the same token this means that liberals aren't as warm and fuzzy to those on the inside. Liberals don't approve of other liberals to the extent conservatives approve of like-minded fellow conservatives. Liberal structures are actually quite chilly.

Peace Is Patriotic

A liberal bumper sticker insists: "Peace is patriotic." It's a response to the conservative equating of patriotism with the military. And it reveals once again, as bumper stickers do—given that they rely on pithy sum-it-all-up phrases—the asymmetry between liberals and conservatives. Conservatives would say, "How can a lack of action, doing nothing (peace) be equated with patriotism?" Patriotism is something you show, which means, something that requires action. For liberals, patriotism isn't something active; it underlies other things that have yet to be determined.

Because action is to a degree its own end for conservatives—they're aiming at an external action, not something expressed about the actor, conservatives tend to think patriotism is most properly expressed in the most forceful action.

Military action is specific, well-defined action against an outside foe. Thus it fits neatly into the conservative worldview. For this reason, conservatives tend to think patriotism is expressed most essentially, or only, in military action: perhaps by being in the military, or at the very least supporting the military and voting for a president who seems to like using the military.

A liberal, by contrast, might more typically think patriotism is best expressed in inaction rather than action, e.g., in allowing people with different viewpoints to express themselves. But this is a non-thing to conservatives, a lack of action rather than the definable action their worldview demands. (This is Berlin's "negative" liberty.)

Military action provides the structure for action against the outside, but it doesn't say what actions we should do inside. For this reason the military has always had organized religion as its Janus face. I consider this intrinsic link below.

Historical Context

It is part of liberal thought and not conservative to historicize and contextualize rules and absolutes, and to point out that they can't be so absolute if they were made by individuals. This is not something conservatives deny the possibility of, but they do resist doing it. Rules are rules; the specific contexts related to their creation are irrelevant. Liberals will assume that because conservatives resist defending their structure, they have no valid structure to defend.

The biblical hermeneutics of the nineteenth century was intrinsically a liberal undertaking, as is any movement that seeks to apply reason to revelation. Modern biblical scholarship, such as that of Geza Vermes, that tries to explain what, in the context of the Aramaic original, the terms we translate as "Lord" or "Messiah" would have meant, is also an intrinsically liberal enterprise.[9] Conservatives always resist this sort of research, not because they hold it to be untrue, but because it is held to be irrelevant. Usually this comes out as, "It is irreverent and destructive. We shouldn't be doing it at all." It's illegitimate the way it's illegitimate for a civilian professor at the Naval Academy to "bad-mouth" (which is to say, question) the decisions of the military administration in public.

Liberals and conservatives have indicatively divergent reactions to such historicizing. When liberals look at the genesis and history of terms and concepts, they tend to feel proud of themselves, as if they have succeeded in piercing the veil, looking behind the curtain at Oz. For conservatives, the issue is not whether what the liberals come up with is true or not, but rather that these things muddy the waters. Conservatives typically feel that liberals are poking around where they should not. For conservatives, whatever way we currently use terms like "Lord" and "Messiah" is what it is, which usually means what some charismatic preacher, right here, right now, who knows no other language than English, says it is. What it was once plays no relevant role.

Conservatives sense correctly that invoking history is not innocent, though liberals typically act aggrieved if it is suggested that they are acting with an agenda. Liberals defend their actions by appealing to the "objectivity" of their findings: These things are, after all, true. Yet the action of finding these things is not objective. History is almost always used to relativize and so debunk the present. Understanding historical context always means making the present seem merely contingent, and hence robbing it of its force to compel us. Burrowing around in history is itself a liberal undertaking.

Conservative resistance to it is not fear of truth, merely showing an understanding of the fact that they are threatened. The world is full of truths. Why emphasize these? This is a question conservatives might ask of liberals if conservatives naturally reached for the same weapons as liberals. But they don't, so liberals never have to answer this question. To liberals, saying something is "true" is equivalent to the conservative Christian saying "The Bible says it." Both may be the case, but in each situation we can legitimately ask, "Why focus on *this* thing that's true or in the Bible?"

The emphasis on an apersonal or interpersonal structure is intrinsically the sign of a liberal worldview. It says, "What you believe is irrelevant." The vocabulary of objectivity or interpersonal structures always aims to paint as limited what it's opposing. It does this by adopting the vocabulary of a larger overstructure, usually an impersonal one. Science is such an impersonal structure, as is the system of liberal democracy. Both are examples of the two-step liberal thought structure, which claims to have transcended the conservative as one-step.

Confusingly, the liberal two-step structure can even take on the coloring of the one-step thought when this is used at a meta-level. The insistence of thinkers like Nietzsche, or those late-twentieth-century literary theoreticians demanding representations from authors other than "dead white males," that everything is subjective is an example of this. It's the liberals who are insisting this, yet the content of what they are saying is conservative.

Such thinkers look at the pretense to objectivity of the scientific system, or the claim that literature like that of Homer and Dante is more "universal" or "classic" than that by, e.g., black lesbians, and reject the pretense of the overstructure. The literature of Homer and Dante isn't classic or universal, such thinkers say; it's the literature of white males. Thus it can take a number, or, indeed, be eliminated. In any case, it's not the universal donor; it's just another blood type. Similarly, ultraliberal theoreticians of science like Paul Feyerabend have emphasized the subjectivity of the scientific enterprise, and Thomas Kuhn's wildly influential book *The Structure of Scientific Revolutions* has been used to justify seeing a scientific structure as merely another "paradigm," not true or untrue.

This argument is in turn echoed by conservatives seeking to resist the liberal claim to a structure larger than their one-step structures. This is why we in the United States currently see the Christian right insisting that evolution is "just a theory" and should be offered as one option, with "creation science"—the nineteenth-century "argument by design" (the presence of such intricacy in the world implies a designer)—being another option.

But the difference between liberal thinkers like Feyerabend—or those demanding greater representation for black lesbians in "the canon" (an issue that in the twenty-first century, after the attack on the World Trade Center, seems close to dead)—and the proponents of "creation science" who reject the claims to hegemony of evolution, or indeed of any scientific viewpoint, is that the first group wants everyone to hold to whatever subjective views they themselves hold. This group talks the vocabulary of plurality, but in fact this is merely because plurality including them is the best they can get right now. Once the pretense of objectivity transcending belief is dead, they are home free. Belief reigns supreme.

Yet liberals remain liberals, even when they seem to be turning into conservatives. The assertion that all is subjective allows a plurality of subjective points of view. Conservatives don't want a plurality of subjective points of view. Indeed, they don't even see their own views as subjective: This is a label applied by liberals who want to put conservative views in a lineup with other views. To conservatives, their point of view trumps all others.

No liberal will ever convince a believing conservative by reason. Reason is irrelevant to the conservative who keeps his or her eyes firmly fixed on the belief. Whatever impinges on that must be rejected, and usually is. Changes of point of view can take place, but in that case we'd have to say that the person who changed, like the light bulb, "wanted to change." It wasn't the argument that accomplished the alteration.

It's not a sign of stupidity that a conservative measures all arguments by the ruler of whether they will end up eliminating the belief, the Absolute Action that is the conservative's North Star, the thing that guides action. That's just the way the conservative worldview is set up.

Socrates and Respect

The military is intrinsically conservative because it is devoted to action, not justification of action, to unanimity of purpose, not to discussing the purpose. Thus from the conservative, or the military, point of view, liberals are afraid to act—they must be, because they don't seem to privilege action. In fact liberals aren't afraid to act; the currency of their ethics is simply that of talk about specifics, considering the particular situation. Action comes, if at all, much later.

Conservatives' natural medium of expression is things done, not things articulated—action rather than thought. Places devoted to talk are thus intrinsically liberal bastions. Places devoted to action are conservative. Sports teams are conservative; the philosophy club is liberal. The Naval Academy, which prepares midshipmen to become officers in the Navy and Marine Corps, is conservative—but what I do there, in the academic buildings, is liberal, because talk is both its medium and its end.

Civilian universities, our academic buildings writ large and stripped of what for us is the military context, are intrinsically liberal bastions because they thrive on words and proof, not on actions in the external world. This is so because debate is more compatible with the liberal worldview than it is to the conservative. Universities are institutions that exist with the premise that debate will never die out, just as some cynics have suggested that international aid organizations to the so-called Third World exist with the premise that they will always be necessary. For the conservative, debate can at best be a means to the end of action, something that should, to adopt a Marxist image, wither away. For the liberal, the act of questioning, the fact of disagreement that's mediated, is the presupposition of the structure.

For this reason, in the larger American structure, the conservative's archenemy is the ever-active American Civil Liberties Union (ACLU), constantly finding something, in conservatives' eyes, to question. Conservatives object as much to the fact that the ACLU is meant to go on forever, sees its mission as perennially stirring up trouble, as they do to what it is that's being challenged. For liberals, the fact that challenges are possible is a sign of the health of the system. To conservatives they're cankers on the otherwise perfect rose. "Can't they just *die?*" conservatives seem to say of the ACLU, snorting each time they hear the organization has once again kicked into action, echoing what my student said about Democrats.

The academic world is proud of adopting the "Socratic method," constantly questioning presuppositions. This itself is a liberal action, anathema to conservatives. For the same reason that the elders of Athens found Socrates, influence contributing to moral decline—they'd rather the youth of Athens simply accept what they were told, not question it—conservatives will never accept that questioning assumptions is a good in itself. Some things, according to conservatives, merely are, and should not be questioned. For liberals, everything is grist for the demand for justification.

To conservatives, this means liberals respect nothing. And respecting nothing is tantamount to a rejection of all ethics. In our building, at USNA housing the English and History departments, things aren't true merely because someone in authority tells you they are. You have to think about them yourself. What we do is summed up in the '60s bumper sticker that enjoins tersely, "Question Authority." You can respect rules or you can question them. You can't do both.

Showing you respect rules is a form of action. It's something people do, though speaking can be a form of doing if it's something people say in public. Public acknowledgement, for conservatives, is the point of a show of respect. Many of the actions that are part of the conservative lifestyle are therefore public actions. Their very publicness is the point, from "acknowledging God" in the Pledge of Allegiance and the public exhibition of moral codes such as the Ten Commandments, to saying "Sir" and "Ma'am" to acknowledge earthly superiors. Because they are public actions, they are necessarily formulaic. The point is carrying out the formulae, not understanding them.

Respect at the Naval Academy is shown in time-honored military ways, including saluting and standing at attention. A group of many midshipmen will all shift their weighty book-bags from their right hands to their left in unison to salute a single officer coming toward them along the walkways, shift the book-bags back in near unison after they are behind him or her, and then shift again as a group twenty paces further along. Here, the liberal would say that all the midshipmen are doing the same thing. In fact, for the conservative each one is doing the proper action; it just happens that they are all doing it at the same time and the same place.

The conservative worldview contains no internal conflict, being governed by absolute rules that everyone is supposed to follow. The conflict only comes when liberals object. Thus to conservatives, liberals create the problems—as the ACLU is perceived as doing.

That's why conservatives frequently have the sense of being "blindsided," as the military puts it. Being blindsided is the quintessential military nightmare. It constitutes an attack from within, when you need all your energy to attack without. Conservatives assuming that inside the walls, everything is flowing smoothly, and point their aggression outwards. Dissent comes as a surprise. It isn't supposed to be there at all. Usually conservatives discover the existence of other points of view only after hearing protesters outside the gates, telling them that they are bad people, or are doing something immoral. "Huh?" they probably said the first time. "What's immoral about my SUV?" The protesters outside have already come up with the reasons for their stance; if and when conservatives do so it's only retroactively, and probably defensively.

For conservatives, the way you build the intrinsically unknowable into your system is to create a force to destroy whatever it is that you encounter. It doesn't mean you've dealt with these things, or even know what they are. But at least it means you've checked off the box relating to them: You've acknowledged their presence, and taken steps to deal with them if and when you encounter them. By contrast the liberal worldview, as liberals put it, doesn't demonize the outside. In the view of the conservatives, liberals fail to acknowledge that demons—or at least, major threats—exist. Conservatives think liberals believe they're going to talk at everything.

Sometimes the conservative worldview is the more useful, sometimes the liberal. If we really are blindsided by a huge threat from the outside, the situation is more in sync with the conservative worldview, which can tell us how to react. By the same token, liberals would point out that we are more likely to perceive something as a huge threat from the outside to the extent we are adherents of the conservative worldview. Perhaps it isn't outside at all? We've only defined it to be so. And if it's inside, we can talk at it, reason with it. To a degree, according to liberals, conservatives make their own problems.

When do we stop talking and pick up a gun? An extreme conservative would never have talked to begin with; an extreme liberal will be murdered rather than give up his or her conviction that if only he or she could reason with this other being, things would be fine. Neither worldview by itself can sketch the line of intersection between these two worldviews. As a civilian English professor in a military institution, however, I walk this line every day.

Conservative Brilliance

There are as many brilliant conservative thinkers as liberal ones. Indeed, a common misconception of liberal intellectuals is to think that conservative intellectuals are identical with conservatives in general. In fact, conservative intellectuals are quite atypical of conservatives, because they have learned to fight fire with fire, take on liberals using the weapons of words. Other conservatives are off acting. Liberal intellectuals, by contrast, are much more typical of liberals than conservative intellectuals are of conservatives. They're better than the average at what they do, but what they do is the same sort of thing as other liberals, namely talk.

What conservative intellectuals defend with all their individual brainpower is an insistence on the insignificance of the individual in the face of principles: People are binary; either they achieve or do not achieve the Absolute Action. No other quality of the individual matters, save his or her attempts to achieve the Absolute Action. The self exists to serve the principle; this is sometimes misunderstood as saying that the self exists to serve others. But conservative thought is fundamentally unconcerned with others, as others. Everyone is assumed to be engaged in the same enterprise, attempting to achieve the action defined by "Thou shalt" or "Thou shalt not."

Some of the most committed neoconservatives working today, not coincidentally, became conservative as a revolt against their liberal or alcohol-soaked youths. They got tired of asking so many questions, or of not knowing what The Answer was. They realized that finding The Answer was as simple as accepting you'd found it. You stop looking for it, declare you have it, and set about acting according to it. The realization that you can just as well spend your life carrying out a principle you've found as looking for it is the realization of the convert to conservatism.

By definition, what such a convert to conservatism finds is not just his or her answer, but The Answer. And the thing about The Answer is precisely that it's The Answer. What a relief! Things are changed utterly. This is the well-known phenomenon of the rootless cynic becoming the most convinced of absolutist believers. T. S. Eliot is an example of someone who apparently lived this trajectory, and many people before and since have done the same.

That's why the conservative economy that trades in the currency of action—where the idea is that each individual must aim at the same Absolute Action—works best when greased with relentless "can-do" optimism, the smiling hustle-bustle that makes the Academy such an appealing place for visitors. You're breaking the covenant if you admit difficulties with action. The sacred phrase is "Let's do it," not "Let's talk about whether it would be a smart thing to do."

Of course, you can upbraid the people who are getting in your way—that's a different story. In fact, there's a long tradition of conservative complaints against liberals, what Thomas Frank calls the plen-T-plaint. It's the point of view of the biker dude with the ponytail convinced that the government is taking over because it tells him he has to wear a helmet, the backwoodsman who takes potshots at "the Law" when it comes down the lane to see if he's got the still up and running again. It's odd when this mentality is transposed to those running the show rather than the marginalized. Carping at "Beltway mentality" seems odd from the people themselves stalking the corridors of power. Apparently it plays in Peoria.

It's also the furious "*Yes!*" of the midshipman on hearing that Senator Kerry had conceded defeat. Those damn liberals.

Henry James

For the same reasons that the liberal–conservative divide has grown in recent years, the America–Europe dichotomy has been flogged more relentlessly than during the time of Henry James, once again a relevant author. Americans, according to both James and George W. Bush's Secretary of Defense, Donald Rumsfeld, are more active than Europeans, less cynical and morally purer. Americans act and Europeans think—which is to say, Europeans *talk*, instead of taking the bull by the horns, as Americans do.

From the American perspective, this means that Americans are unfettered by the chains of tradition. They dare. For the Europeans, it means the Americans are criminally destructive. James suggested this meant Americans could never understand the Europeans, unable to conceive of the depths of moral turpitude to which this more complex, but at the same time more decadent, people would of necessity sink.

Europeans tend to know from the beginning that attempts to remake the world will fail. Usually this is expressed by saying that bitter experience has taught them so. But of course it's a postulate to say they'll fail, just as it's an American postulate that acting like a bull in a china shop isn't so bad and, indeed, may work. In any case, there's no harm in saying it will—the point is the assertion of motivation, not to say something that is true, in the liberal sense of speaking defensible truth, truth in the cold light of morning.

Considering consequences is not high on the conservative list of priorities; indeed, to the extent that doing so may sap motivation, it is a thing to be avoided. For liberals, not considering consequences is a sign of rank stupidity: Consequences, for liberals, are implied in actions. What liberals fail to see is that, for conservatives, consequences aren't implied in actions. The actions are their own ends, precisely as an alternative to thought. "Nothing ventured, nothing gained"—this is an American point of view, not a European.

Another aphorism still heard occasionally is that "Americans live to work; Europeans work to live." In a noteworthy study of the victory of American merchandising techniques in twentieth-century Europe, *Irresistible Empire*, Victoria de Grazia[10] suggests that this distinction between two roles played by work on the two sides of the Atlantic has disappeared, thanks to the victory of American consumerism. De Grazia regards this process at least with equanimity, perhaps even positively. Americans who sit in the shaded arcades of sunstruck Italian piazzas, sipping their cappuccinos and watching the young congregate and socialize, may be fooling themselves that this world is different. Perhaps the young are only here socializing because they can't get a job.

For de Grazia, the old way of doing things is represented by Thomas Mann's crumbling bourgeoisie from *Buddenbrooks*, the Nobel Prize–winner's 1925 masterpiece about the dissolution of a merchant family into artistic creativity and death. A hundred years is a long time by modern standards, and if that's the last time Europe had a sense of difference, it may be true that it's irrevocably gone. But I'd suggest at least that more people in Europe have a notion of what this world was, and bemoan its absence, than do Americans—who know it not from any personal associations, however tenuous, but merely from books.

The stage sets of a different age not only dot the European landscape, but define it. They may be irrelevant to those who live in the changed world of the big-box store and the stock exchange, which feels no nostalgia for the vanished hegemony of aristocracy and the Church. But intellectuals—still widely respected in Europe—are not unaware of this world, and keep it alive at least by contrast with what is the more standard tenor of daily life around them.

Inside/Outside

Liberals and conservatives diverge on the issue of what constitutes Inside and Outside. For liberals, everything is Inside unless proven otherwise. For conservatives, everything is Outside unless proven otherwise.

All of us are ignorant of many things; liberals are no different from conservatives in this. Yet when liberals tax conservatives with ignorance, the liberal is always able to say what it is the conservatives are ignorant of. The conservative, by contrast, is merely ignorant of it. This is the reason why, as Krauthammer puts it, that "liberals think conservatives are stupid."

Gun ownership in the United States in noncriminal circles has become the sign of the conservatives. It's true that liberals are loath to resort to violence, in the same way that a host at the party wouldn't immediately throw out a guest who uses a tone of voice he or she thinks inappropriate. The host will make a joke, or try to get the guest to change things him- or herself. That's the presupposition that people know how to behave and have momentarily forgotten themselves. Of course, there are some actions that require immediate reaction—for example, upsetting the punch bowl while laughing loudly. Here even the most liberal of hosts must assume that the guest needs to be evicted.

Conservatives and liberals overlap in the case of an egregious affront. In such a case, a liberal would react as negatively, and as immediately, as a conservative. The clearest modern example of this is the attack on the World Trade Center. But this agreement on an extreme case should not occlude the fact that in the case of affronts of lesser intensity, liberals and conservatives react quite differently.

There is no theoretical difference for U.S. conservatives between opposition physically located within the United States and opposition outside of it. Outside starts well within the boundaries of the nation-state for conservatives. By contrast, the fact of someone being in France or Bangladesh is uninteresting to a liberal; the presupposition will always be that this person can in theory be subsumed within the liberal grid, unless proven otherwise.

Similarly, conservatives rarely make distinctions between slight and stronger opposition. Everything is opposition, and so equally a sign of following bad actions. If you're not with a conservative, you're against him or her.

The pen is the archetypal liberal weapon, the sword the conservative. And it's only liberals who say, somewhat predictably, that the pen is in fact mightier. Liberals will always be trying to convince conservatives; conservatives will always react to this liberal attempt by circling the wagons with their like-minded already-convinced brethren. This is the nature of the way things are.

It can be argued that because conservatism offers absolute principles for action, it's more congenial with what average people want and need than liberalism and so should be propagated for that reason. This is similar to the argument of Dostoevsky's Grand Inquisitor, who, though not a believing Christian, ran the Inquisition because the common folk need the illusion of something unquestionable. This isn't real conservatism; it's cynical liberalism.

Conservatism and Wealth

To liberals, it frequently looks as if conservatives defend privilege for self-interested reasons. The fact that it doesn't seem that way to conservatives is something that needs to be taken account of, if not necessarily adopted as correct. Here, this helps us understand more fully a topic broached earlier: the relationship of conservatives to wealth. Certainly safeguarding individual wealth may be the motivation of individual conservatives. But it is not an intrinsic feature of conservative thought.

Liberals who make this accusation about conservatism in general rather than about some individual conservatives are once again getting the causality wrong; each side does this with the other because it assumes the other side is a variation of itself.

Privilege is a position that the people in it don't want to change. Hence it's a position that can be expressed with action, not thoughts. Because it is a desirable position, it is seen as a stable situation, and this makes it amenable to expression in conservative terms. Undesirable situations imply change, or at least discussion of the inability to change them. Thus the way you express a situation that has reached a point of stasis is through a conservative worldview, not a liberal one. The liberals are always those who want things to be other than the way they are. For this reason the marginalized almost always gravitate to the liberal worldview.

Max Weber, in *The Protestant Ethic and the Spirit of Capitalism*, is the most famous theoretician to suggest a connection between material wealth and a specific set of moral beliefs. Though the logic of predestination, which for Weber was central to Calvinist Protestantism, means we remain in ignorance of our ultimate moral worth, we can try to convince both ourselves and others that we are predestined for the better alternative though doing well materially. At the same time, Weber noted that people who have done well want to believe that they have done so as a result of divine intervention. Being wealthy is a sign that they are moral people—or in the case of Calvinism, destined to be saved.[11]

It would indeed be surprising if materially successful people failed to believe that their success was a state of affairs that a) was meant to be, b) was morally better than others, or c) was the end point to which all things were tending. It's such a satisfying view of things. The particular form of Protestantism Weber chose as his explanation for this, however, provides an improbable basis for this phenomenon.

The problem is the predestination itself that Weber thought was so central. We should be suspicious from the outset of this being the most relevant explanatory factor, given that it is absent from the belief systems of many other conservatives equally convinced that their material success is somehow God-ordained.

The more fundamental fact, that I noted earlier when considering Lakoff, is that rich people tend to look approvingly on other rich people, whatever the source of their wealth. This has to be the case for reasons unrelated to predestination. In fact, these reasons are found in the very structure of conservative thinking.

People become conservative by reaching a stable state. They express that conservatism in action, not intellectual justification of the state. In order to avoid having to provide justification, or perhaps because they weary of being asked for it, they associate with people like themselves. In this case, these people are well-to-do conservatives. Not everyone need see his or her choices mirrored in others. Conservatives do, because of the absolutist nature of conservative thought that isn't set up to include divergence as part of its structure.

It would be theoretically possible to have a conservatism of the poor, except that virtually no one sees being poor as a state worth preserving. Yet the fact is that there is also a conservatism of classes other than the highest. Indeed, the paradox that Thomas Frank is focusing on is that people at or near the bottom of the economic ladder in America have helped elect a president whose policies apparently make it more difficult for them to move upward.

The apparent paradox Frank is pointing to is that we sometimes call the free market that allows for upward mobility "liberal," whereas in fact people we call in other contexts conservative are its most fervent supporters. This is only an apparent paradox; it's the result of the fact that people can be liberal in one context, or from one point of view, and conservative in another. The reasons they are each never vary, but the situations do.

The pattern of the conservative worldview is of individuals, each of whom is tied by a thread to the same Absolute (external) Action. Conservatism is the structure of a stable state, one where people merely act, and do not discuss the reasons for their acting. The individual, however, determines what for him or her is a stable state. Being poor rarely is, but being, e.g., middle class may be. In terms of Frank's analysis, being a factory worker about to be laid off may—surprisingly for him—be a stable state. The patterns of liberal and conservative thought don't say when we'll be which. Frank is trying to get those blue-collar factory workers who have been laid off by the policies of the Republicans, at least in his argument, to reject that party. If the workers, or ex-workers, got mad enough, presumably they would. But for now, they apparently see their situation as being the way things have to be.

What you see is determined by what your point of view is. Midshipmen at the Naval Academy think of themselves as rugged individualists. They see themselves working, each alone, to achieve certain abstract goals, Absolute Actions. To an outsider, they look like a group. To Frank, blue-collar workers with dwindling incomes look like a social fact. To themselves, however, they seem like individuals.

Frank's mistake with respect to definition by economics is to assume that everyone always wants to be at a higher economic level, and so must be perennially dissatisfied. If true, I'm arguing this would create a country of liberals. In fact, many people in the United States are basically satisfied. This creates the conservatism Frank finds so inexplicable. If someone takes the possibility of mobility for granted and thus doesn't want to change the system, even if he or she is in fact not mobile, then the system seems fine. That person will be a conservative. If, one day, he or she wakes up dissatisfied with lack of mobility, or sees things as Frank does, that person becomes a liberal.

Frank is a liberal, and he assumes that people do want to move up the ladder. The assumption that the ladder makes this possible is what is "liberal" about liberal economics. Yet the fact is that people can lodge at various rungs of the ladder.

A writer like Paul Fussell, the author of the mordant *Class: A Guide Through the American Status System*, would not be surprised by the conservatism of less than wealthy voters. Indeed, for Fussell, people lodge at wherever they are in the economic spectrum and make their lives there—even (again an apparent paradox) those who are trying either to get out of the class they're in, or look as if they are. Fussell is most unforgiving to what he calls "upwardly mobile proles," blue-collar people trying to act as if they are in fact middle class. This is itself a stable state. My analysis doesn't tell us whether or not a particular individual will see his or her state as stable. But if so, that person is operating with the conservative worldview. The state itself is stable; this is what allows the individual to act. That's all there is in the conservative worldview: the individual, acting to achieve something outside.

Fussell's view is intrinsically liberal for seeing the ties that bind all these individuals to each other in a class. Those Americans who deny there is such a thing as class are going to be conservatives; those who insist that there is will be liberals.

It would have been equally logical, reasoning from what should have been rather than what was, for Weber to say that because Calvinists are cut off from any real influence over the hereafter, they would have a tendency to simply throw in the towel and vow to live it up while they can. The fact that reality could, in theory, have gone either way—toward parsimony and the acquisition of riches, on one hand, or toward a spendthrift "devil-may-care" attitude on the other—shows us that the relationship between capitalism and conservatism is two-sided.

To the extent that capitalism is the means by which many people achieve material well-being, it fuels the conservatism of material stasis. At the same time, we call the market system "liberal," by which we mean that it is the agent of continuous change. Capitalism is capable of merchandizing the marginalized, such as hip-hoppers or rappers in our day, or otherwise unsocialized sports figures with specific talents, and making them millionaires. It searches incessantly for something to sell.

This is the reason why some otherwise diverse conservative belief systems have in common their criticism of the capitalist market system. Some of these include the Catholicism of Pope John Paul II, the belief in the primacy of "gentlemen" who by definition do not work for a living expressed by Victorian writers like Trollope, and the views of Marx in his more Romantic idealizations of preindustrial society.

At the same time, some liberal groups disapprove of the market as well. It leads to shallow consumerism rather than the development of the self; it is aggressive and male-dominated; it is heartless and punishes ruthlessly those who lose. Removed from a context, the market of capitalism is neither liberal nor conservative. As a framework allowing action, it is conservative; as something allowing the individual to shine, it is liberal. Its primary activity, which is simply making money, transcends both liberalism and conservatism.

Defending Liberalism

Liberals get conservatives wrong. Sometimes they're not much better with liberalism. Usually, if asked for an expression of liberal thought, we point to John Stuart Mill's "On Liberty." Yet the intellectual center of the book is a technical argument, namely the proposition that the state does not have the right to limit individual freedom of thought and action except to protect other individuals. Doing so would be inefficient in the long run, Mill claims, as it's precisely these people who ultimately give society the greatest benefit. As a result, Mill offers a critique of groupthink and celebrates the uncommon, the individual, even the eccentric. This is to confuse a side effect with the point.

We may well question Mill's optimistic insistence that encouraging individualism is the most efficient way of keeping a society healthy, as well as his eugenic belief in the infinite perfectibility of mankind's notions, if only people are allowed to point out their errors. The conservative, if pressed, would certainly say that eccentricity does not help perfect mankind, because the only thing that will perfect mankind would be to accept a fixed set of rules, or perhaps Jesus Christ as their Personal Savior.

So what reason do we have for defending, as Mill does, the freedom of the individual to make his or her decision about things if the conservative points out this freedom isn't intrinsically good. Perhaps that it causes less frustration if people are allowed some leeway to do things their own way in cases where, as we might say, it doesn't really matter? But surely the conservative would say we would only have to embrace X, Y, or Z (e.g., the rules of Jesus Christ) for all to be well. If we are still stuck back at the level of asking why we should practice Christianity rather than Hinduism, conservatives do not know how to respond. Conservative thought does not provide justification for accepting one set of absolutes rather than another; indeed, the notion of competing absolutes is a liberal one and not a conservative one. So freedom for strangeness as a justification for liberalism doesn't seem to cut it. At least it won't convince many conservatives.

3
RELIGION AND SEX:
TWO BONES OF CONTENTION

In a deep-structural sense, the conservative's world is unitary rather than binary. The conservative is located within this unitary world; the only boundaries he or she sees are from the inside, as if we were in New York looking up toward Canada or in Toronto looking down to the United States, with no knowledge, in either case, of what might lie on the other side of the border. The possibility of other alternatives is simply not part of this worldview. If conservatives could conceive of real alternatives to their point of view, they wouldn't be conservatives, but liberals.

The rancor against the outside world that seems to liberals to be such a constituent part of so many conservatisms only comes subsequently, as the outside world inexplicably, for conservatives, is given the opportunity to become like them, and refuses—or, worse, laughs or merely turns away.

Faith and the Military

The military has reached this stage of feeling rancor. If you don't support military intervention in X, you're a traitor. If you don't "support the troops," you're a traitor. Supporting the troops can be done by simply saying, "I support the troops," or by putting a bumper sticker to that effect on your car. Now we've graduated to magnetic yellow loops that are meant to look like ribbons but in fact plaster flat against the car's body. Slap one on and you support the troops. Lack of such an object can be taken to mean you don't.

Other conservatisms in America have had a long time to develop their rancor, too. The rhetoric of the Hebrew Bible, the "Old Testament," which casts all struggles as the struggle of an oppressed minority and which has long since been taken up by African-American churches to express the situation of outsiders in American culture, is also attractive to political conservatives, who see themselves as persecuted, vilified, attacked. "Everybody's against me" is a comfortable position for conservatives, even when they're in power. Yet it's not intrinsic to conservatism; it's a learned behavior in a world that also includes liberals.

The sense of struggling against great odds that must be vanquished was probably behind the statement in 2004 by the unusually frank Lt. Gen. (Ret.) William Boykin that God had put George W. Bush in the White House.[1] When the Bush administration woke up in 2000 and found itself in power as the result of a decision by the Supreme Court, how the administration must have thought that finally God had heard their prayers after so many years in the wilderness! When things go badly for conservatives, they typically conclude that God is taking His time. And when things go well, they have proof that He does not sleep, and that though the night may be long, the morning always comes.

The military's link with God is through its conservatism, its approval of moral tenets expressed in terms of actions. Many military organizations enter battle invoking God, or their gods. The German army went into both World Wars with belt buckles saying "*Gott mit uns,*" "God with us." (The British replied to this, rather sweetly under the circumstances, by saying: "We've got mittens too.") Islamic militants famously invoke God before setting off on their suicide and murder missions. General Boykin, with his invocation of a God who was "stronger" than the opponent's Islamic one, is an example of the assertion that God is behind military maneuvers. So too, for that matter, is the Roman Emperor Constantine, converting to Christianity because of a dream of the True Cross promising him victory in the next day's battle, which he duly won.

A liberal would try to reason with General Boykin, not realizing that the very act of reasoning means that the conservative will not engage with him or her. Such a liberal might point out to General

Boykin that "Allah" isn't a name, any more than "God" is. "Allah" means God, and according to the Qur'an, this is the God of Abraham and of Jesus of Nazareth. Thus the God of Christianity cannot be "stronger" than the Islamic God, as they are the same. The primary characteristic of monotheism is that God can't be defined any more precisely than with negatives and superlatives with respect to human beings. And that means that any god defined as "the" God is identical with any other that's defined that way.

The conservative response would surely be to say that the history of these terms is irrelevant. In practice, Allah for the conservative is not the same as the God of the Christians; this is clear because Allah is invoked by people attacking people who invoke the God of the Christians. For those who see their actions as the only moral ones, being at war with another group means that the other group worships a false god. The rhetoric of the Hebrew Bible is useful here, too.

Candide, or Optimism

Beyond the things an individual controls, American conservatives typically insist that God takes over. Mid-level sources of control between the individual and his or her Maker are not allowed. God is what takes over seamlessly when the individual reaches his end.

Whatever happens, thus, God has everything under control: If there is a tornado that kills thousands, there has to be a reason for that. If the angelic little girl next door dies of leukemia while a no-good hoodlum dies in his bed at the age of ninety-four after causing death and destruction his whole life, there is a reason for that, too. This is a way of taming the lack of control we feel over the major decisions of life—whether we get a terminal disease isn't really up to us.

This is precisely the attitude that Voltaire skewers in *Candide, or Optimism*. I frequently read this with plebes, and though Voltaire has set the book up so that he makes the character Dr. Pangloss, who enunciates the optimism Voltaire is rejecting, the dupe, I have an easy time showing my students that, in fact, they agree with Pangloss.

Pangloss' philosophy is derived from Leibniz, with his notion of possible worlds. Of all the possible worlds—worlds we can imagine or postulate (and a possible world can be identical to our own save for a single particular—e.g., no AIDS, no lemurs, or no peanut butter)—this actual world has to be the best, since it's the one God in fact made, and God is omnipotent, omnipresent, and omniscient, as well as good. What looks like a bad thing—death of thousands from an earthquake or a tsunami, death of the angelic little girl down the street to a lingering cancer, an apparently senseless drive-by shooting—has in the larger scheme of things to be good, since God allowed it, and God is good.

Voltaire makes fun of Pangloss' ruthless logic that proves not only that what is, is good, but also that what is, is intended. It's the necessary result of imbuing the world with a divine consciousness presupposed to be working for the good. (If you respond that the reason there are bad things is original sin or free will, of course the next question becomes, "Why did God make people knowing they would pluck the apple and hence be miserable? What? He didn't know they'd pick the apple?" etc.) My students properly laugh when Pangloss tries to prove that noses were meant to hold up glasses: The proof Pangloss offers is that they do hold up glasses. Similarly, according to Pangloss, legs were meant for trousers. The proof is, we put trousers on legs.

Yet it's more difficult for them to laugh when Pangloss, similarly, tries to show that the reason something apparently goes wrong is because it was meant to produce the silver lining, as we would call it. It's too close to the way they themselves reason. Why did the athlete break his or her leg the night before the All-State track meet? God was testing his or her fortitude. In a similar way, right-wing religious figures claim that various illnesses or natural disasters—AIDS, the tsunami of 2004—are God's way of punishing the unrighteous. Those for whom the bottom line is "God" are never discouraged.

Similarly, those for whom the bottom line is "science" are never discouraged either. In the first case, believers just haven't found the reason God does something. In the second, scientists just haven't found the natural explanation. Both groups can live forever in a state of not understanding God's purpose, or not having the scientific explanation. The difference between them is that the scientist feels he or she can be actively looking for an answer, where the person with the equally firm belief that the explanatory principle is "God" is frequently left waiting for revelation.

A belief in a controlling God is congruent to the conservative worldview; it isn't identical. It's possible to have conservatism without God, to derive rules for action that are as strong from other sources—fascism, e.g., or atheistic communism. That's not the way it's worked out in America. Still God, so to say, is a means to an end—at least if what we start with is a characterization of conservative thought, rather than religious. Belief in an intentional God who knows where things are going allows us both the action of seeking to learn this divine will, and of seeking to carry it out.

American conservatives tend to be appalled by those who proclaim themselves atheists or agnostics. Failure to believe in a higher power seems to fly in the face of the hierarchy that is so important to the structure of conservatism, and so to contravene the order of things. The nature of conservative thought is to insist that individuals are relatively insignificant, constantly trying to achieve actions external to them. For conservatives, it is the rankest sign of hubris to deny this, as if claiming that human beings can fly just by flapping their arms.

Conservatives set what for liberals is great store by insider references to religion that identify them to each other as members of the same group. Echoes of the well-known King James translation of the Bible into English are usually enough to establish insidership: If you read the Bible you're the right kind of person. Many conservatives apparently believe the Bible was written in this English, so that its phrases are literally "the word of God"—something only Islam claims for the Qur'an, which is the reason why the Qur'an is always memorized in now-inaccessible Arabic, and why translations are called by purists "interpretations."

Insider phrases can come from specific church doctrines. President George W. Bush, for example, frequently uses the phrase "culture of life" in addressing Catholic groups; because this is a code phrase for antiabortion, he was perceived as being one with the Catholics. In the 2004 presidential election, Republicans were sent out to tell Hispanics, in Spanish, "Republican values are Hispanic values." There is no discussion of what values are meant. The point is that the message is delivered in Spanish, since speaking Spanish is the identifying quality of the group. This love of code phrases identifying insider groups is related to the conservatives' perception of the outside world as Outside, and their correlated love of tasting the sameness of Inside.

For the vast majority of my students and the officers who lead them, bowing your head to a higher power, however you understand that Power, is part of living correctly. For conservatives, only belief in a higher power keeps things running on an even keel. If you tell conservatives you're happy they believe in a higher power but don't yourself, they look at you in horror. If you don't believe in a higher power, what's preventing you from raping and murdering?

To liberals, this question seems silly. Yet it is justified in the conservative worldview, in which there is a conceptual vacuum between the individual and the absolute Rule. Liberals would say there are many things that prevent us from raping and murdering that, in a structural sense, come between the individual and the Rule. These might include respect for people, or understanding the implications of our actions. But since these are keyed to the individual case, they cannot be listed beforehand and so earn conservative scorn when presented as justifications for the assertion that the liberal individual can act morally.

All conservative thought links the individual by a straight line to the Absolute Action, and so it can also link them to God without having to answer questions like whether other very different people are similarly linked to God, or what justification the conservatives have in believing that they themselves are so linked. This is the reason that conservatives almost always appeal to their "faith," as if this were a sort of garlic clove holding the liberal vampires at bay. It's a belief, and hence sacrosanct. If I believe it, you can't disagree with it. Liberals, by contrast, take individual belief as being neither here nor there. Belief is what you believe, nothing more: what *you* believe, not necessarily me, or the next person. It doesn't offer the protection conservatives are seeking in it.

There are no intermediate structures in the conservative view; individuals link directly to the Absolute Action that is beyond discussion. Because their worldview has no intermediate structures between the individual and the external rule, conservatives tend to be sure that God, somehow connected to the rules, is personally interested in the things they do. At Annapolis, this means, God is interested, at least according to those who pray to Him, in whether or not the midshipmen's football team wins, in whether or not individual midshipmen graduate from the Academy, and in what they, as future officers, think and do each day.

And why should they not think this way? The most colorful stained-glass window in the turn-of-the-century chapel (cornerstone laid in 1904) is "The Heavenly Commission" from the Tiffany workshops. The hand of God reaches down from a cloud to hand to a newly minted officer, resplendent in his "choker whites," a rolled-up paper: his commission as an ensign in the U.S. Navy. After all, in the "Navy hymn," known elsewhere as "Eternal Father Strong to Save," God is imagined as protecting those at sea. When we pray we say "Thou" to God, as Martin Buber pointed out—we're on intimate terms with our Creator.

Prayers before noon meal formation, those under attack by the American Civil Liberties Union, make eminent sense to our conservative institution, as prayers before football games do for the League of Christian Athletes. For conservatives, the point is to bow the head, in public if possible. The liberal might wonder here again what's intrinsically good for conservatives about faith. The answer is that, for conservatives, it acknowledges the smallness of the individual in the same way that postulating the Absolute Action outside of us postulates the smallness of the individual. George W. Bush's support of "faith-based" initiatives on all fronts gave an example of the fundamental irrelevance for conservatives of the particular nature of religious doctrine. Faith is what trips the wire, not faith in anything in particular.

Still, what conservatives support is not any possible faith whatever, it's faith in a fairly limited range of options that they have approved beforehand. Faith to conservatives in America means belief in some brand of Christianity or Judaism, almost inevitably the most doctrinaire sorts. I doubt conservatives would be so quick to support "faith-based" initiatives if the faith in question is Wiccan teachings (witchcraft), or a belief that, e.g., frogs are the highest life form. Nor, in all probability, would they approve of worshiping a god with the head of an elephant, usually accompanied by a rat—though many Hindus are devotees of Lord Ganesh, one of the most popular gods in the Hindu pantheon. As for Islam, religion of a large percentage of the world's population, General Boykin rejects it. It's only because even stranger options aren't seriously proposed, and so can't be rejected, that many conservatives would probably say, and really mean, that it was faith itself that was valuable.

At Annapolis, we're tolerant up to the limits of current conservative approval. Nobody is trying to get you to follow a particular form of monotheism. But the assumption is that you won't be doing anything else either. There are services for Catholics and Jews, and a nondenominational Protestant service. The embattled noon meal prayers invoke God the Father. Probably the U.S. Naval Academy administration thinks it is being broad-minded by eliminating references to Jesus. The possibility that faith could involve, e.g., God the Mother, or many gods as instantiations of the whole Godhead (Hinduism), is an uncomfortable one.

Liberals like diversity. This is the way they internalize conflict, turning it into the more manageable entity of disagreement. Conservatives always consign disagreement to a position outside their system. Conservative in America at the moment means flag-waving antifeminist, antigay Christian, or some cluster of positions from that list. If too few are chosen, the person is merely a reprobate liberal, not a real conservative. But of course the world offers many other varieties of the same sort of absolutisms, the most remarked upon at the moment being fundamentalist Islam.

American conservatives are living under the comfortable illusion that their most threatening enemies are liberals. They have been given a free pass because their particular brand of conservatism has ruled the roost for so long. American conservatives fail to see that their more worrisome enemies in fact, rather than in theory, are not liberals, but equally absolute conservatives of other stripes entirely.

In all likelihood, they will not attempt to talk to them, as liberals do, but probably attempt to blow them away. The attack on the World Trade Center allowed American conservatives briefly to see radical Islam as something Outside. The more recent bombings in London and the riots across France in 2005 have made clear that radical Islam is no longer Them, but in fact Us. And this is not a situation that the conservative worldview is able to contemplate.

In Islamic fundamentalism, fundamentalist Christianity has finally found a kindred spirit. Of course, fundamentalist Christianity doesn't like what it sees. My truth! No, MY truth! Your revelation's a fraud! No, yours!

Islam holds that the Holy Qur'an is the prophecy necessitated by the perversion of God's message sent through such great earlier prophets as Jesus of Nazareth. God kept trying to get through; people kept getting it wrong, so God sent Gabriel down one last time to get things straight. Most fundamental is the fact that God is One. In the context in which Islam arose, that means He isn't hundreds of specific gods, like those worshipped in Arabia in the seventh century C.E. But it also clearly means He isn't three, as the Christian teaching has it. The Qur'an makes gentle fun of the notion that a virgin is supposed to have given birth and that God has a son. How absurd this is! And from the perspective of strict monotheism, it clearly seems so.

The unitary structure of conservative thought means precisely that the particular tenets of the conservatism can't be defended, save by rejecting through force other options. Someone who believes that God has had a Son, someone we call a Christian, can't defend this against someone who says it violates the tenets of monotheism, who might be a Muslim (of course the Christian can claim it doesn't, not really, for the following reasons, and so on). A conservative structure isn't constructed so as to be able to defend its particular tenets against other conservatisms' particular tenets, just to provide an alternative to a multipart worldview.

Bernard Lewis, the distinguished American scholar of Islam, proposed that the West had developed religious toleration and Islam had not because the West had already, both literally and figuratively, been through the wars—in this case, religious-based wars of Catholics vs.

Protestants.[2] We in the West, he pointed out, had the Protestant Reformation and the St. Bartholomew's Day Massacre behind us, and after a few centuries of bloodshed, realized that we had to get along. Islam, Lewis said, never had this experience, so it has charged into religious conflict with the enthusiasm of the neophyte.

This was an interesting theory portraying the West as the older, jaded, civilization that had already made the mistakes the Islamic world was in the process of making. It was especially interesting because another pillar of Lewis' argument was that the Islamic world remembered its high level of development from a time when the pre-industrial Christian West was, by comparison, quite primitive. This raised the question, "Which ultimately was the older civilization?"

Fundamentalist American Christians are about to make the same mistake with Islam that Lewis claims we long ago decided to avoid with divergent Christian denominations, and more recently with Jews. American Christians seem to be spoiling for a fight, drunk on the possibility of scratching the itch of Difference rather than merely tolerating it. Islam infuriates fundamentalist Christians in the same way that putatively "Christ-killing" Jews once did.

Many Christians are infuriated by Islam as well, I would guess, because Islam makes the same claims to historical irrelevance about Christianity that Christianity makes about Judaism. When evangelical Christians talk about our "Judeo-Christian" society, they don't mean that Judaism is an acceptable alternative to Christianity, only that Judaism was necessary for Christianity to come to be. The "New" Testament reinterprets and fulfills the "Old." New allows Old, but Old without New is incomplete. The revelation of the Holy Qur'an supercedes and complements earlier revelations just as the New Testament does the Old for Christians. And it announces itself as the final one. This time is it. Of course Christians don't like the notion of being superceded any more than Jews liked it when Christians said they'd done it to the Jews.

At any given time, whatever fills the blank left in conservative thought for Holy Writ is defended vociferously by conservatives. This is so because it is impossible to defend the concept of Holy Writ as an undefined blank to be filled and remain a conservative: Doing so makes one a liberal. Still, what conservatives really want is not a specific blueprint for life, but the certainty of having a blueprint, whatever it is. We see this from the fact that conservatives can digest specific alterations, and then go on being conservative incorporating the changes.

The greatest good for conservatives, because it defines their worldview, is lack of questioning, getting on with the actions of life, not the content of whatever specific unquestioned list of beliefs they are defending. Here as elsewhere, the liberal/conservative divide reveals itself as a thought/action contrast. Yet one of the paradoxes of conservatism is that conservatism always expresses its defense of the Law as a defense of the letter of the law, and typically repulses any attempt to change that specific content. In fact, any other letter would work just as well for conservatives, and does work after such time as, for whatever reason, it is accepted. But because what's being defended is the whole worldview, conservatives can't bargain over individual elements of it. Bargaining means discussion, and discussion is for liberal wimps.

This need to have something specific in the blank conservatives leave for Holy Writ fuels contemporary conservative attempts to "acknowledge" God in forms like the "under God" phrase of the Pledge of Allegiance. It also leads to attempts to put into legislation references to the Christian nature of U.S. society. Although the politically correct terms nowadays in speaking of the "Judeo-Christian" nature of U.S. society; soon it may be "Judeo-Christian-Islamic" and with enough immigrants from India and southeast Asia, the "Judeo-Christian-Islamic-Hindu-Buddhist" nature of society. Liberals might ask, "Why does God need to be acknowledged? How are we doing so by including this phrase in a pledge to a flag? Why does this have to be a public action?"

Conservatives become exasperated quickly when questioned in such a manner. It's not that they would be unable to provide answers. It's that asking rather than obeying is itself not a part of the conservative worldview. If we're questioning, we can't be engaging in the public acts of respect that are the end goal of conservatism. Probably their annoyance also comes from the fact that they know they're trying to tidy up the edges of their worldview: Nothing is really accomplished by "acknowledging" God, or by mandating the Pledge of Allegiance to begin with. They have to assert so strongly because they realize they are on such thin ice: The only justification they can offer is the principle itself, expressed in terms of respect.

Questioning public symbols such as the Ten Commandments, similarly, is an intrinsically liberal undertaking. It never fails to incense conservatives. Liberals, for conservatives, are the spoilers rendering impossible the consensus that would otherwise be obtained. But this argument, like all arguments between liberals and conservatives, is asymmetrical. Conservatives are put in what for them is the false position of having to defend this doctrine against other doctrines, an absolutist worldview against other absolutist contenders. Of course, the liberals who oppose one doctrine with another aren't interested in having the second substituted for the first as a new absolutism. They want the absolutists to admit that there are alternatives to all absolutism. This the absolutists can never do.

Liberals would point out that even those conservatives claiming allegiance to the Ten Commandments as the basis of American democracy pick and choose which of the commandments they'll focus on. Why choose the ones we do? It seems we could get many religions out of the Bible simply by applying different filters, each of which chooses some parts to emphasize and others to ignore. What about that commandment that says, in King James English, "Thou shalt not make unto thee any graven image"—presumably of God? No one in the West puts much store in that one nowadays. The liberal might point out that there are plenty of paintings in the Western tradition of God (though none at all in the Islamic world of God, and only a few in the Persian world of Mohammed, usually veiled) and some statues. Apparently Islam is much more in consonance with the Jewish commandment than the Christianity that claims these Jewish laws as its basis.

Nor is it at all clear what these commandments mean. Does "Thou Shalt Not Kill" mean people must be vegetarians? That they may not go to war? Neither would be particularly congenial to conservatives in the military. It tends only to be orthodox Jews, rather than Christians of any stripe, who insist that the commandment about doing no work on the Sabbath (Exodus 1:10) means you can't even turn on a light (but you can set a timer the previous day to make the light turn on during the Sabbath). And no one is out policing us anymore to make sure the poet doesn't write on Sunday, the hobby-woodworker stays away from his lathe, and the gardener doesn't pull a weed. In early Puritan New England, people were policed in this way. This is one of the absolute rules that has altered over time without changing the fact of conservative existence.

Conservatives are what they are by nature of the structure of their belief, defined against the structure of another belief, not (though this is the opposite of what they say) because of the precise nature of that belief. Thus the conservative position alters constantly, as we emphasize different aspects of an Absolute Rule, or accept new ones. Showing conservatives their own alteration flies in the face of the most fundamental given of conservative thought's view of itself: that it is absolute and unchanging. To a liberal, this may seem absurd. However, the conservative position is not absurd. At any given moment in time, conservatives are absolute and if they resist change, they can believe they are unchanging.

The fact that the particular content of conservative viewpoints changes means that we can only identify what is conservative by comparing it to what it is not, its liberal opposite/correlate. A religion we qualify as conservative is a religion that trumpets its faith, and downplays its reason. Catholicism is conservative with respect to established Protestantism, as is evangelical Bible-based Christianity. The source of authority varies (priests, Bibles), but what makes them all conservative is that the individual isn't supposed to ask, "Why is that?"

Conservatives and Sex

Conservative thought almost inevitably evokes the language of "purpose" to describe and explain human actions. By this is meant, purpose beyond the individual. Purpose *is* beyond the individual, and so allows us to justify actions as absolute. It lets us say what we should do.

Logical positivism, disseminated by such thinkers as A. J. Ayer, insisted that it is never justified to derive a "should" from an "is."[3] This is a quintessential liberal position. It separates out as two discrete states things that, because separated, allow of no mediation. No two entities that are once separated conceptually can ever be put back together with the degree of fusion their unseparated selves enjoyed. A similar problem beset Descartes, who had separated body from mind. Putting them back together again proved nearly impossible. Another related problem plagues poets who remember their young selves and compare this with the older person they have become. The more absolute the distinction between these two states—and this is the result of making this distinction—the more difficult it will become to ever mediate between them. The melancholy of Proust, similarly, is a self-created problem, one that solidifies the state of longing by separating the longer from the longed-for.

Ayer and the logical positivists do not speak for conservatives. For the liberal, "is" is separate from "should" and thus can never imply it. For the conservative, by contrast, there is no substantial "is" that requires subsequent linking to "should": The individual is a geometric point at the end of a vector arrow culminating in the Absolute Action, the "should." All assertions of purpose are therefore attempts to articulate vector arrows, things that, if accepted, do not require further linking between "is" and "should" because they are themselves the linking. If we accept the purpose, we also accept the actions that lead to that purpose.

Much philosophic ink has been spilled over whether saying we "should" do something means we are in fact obligated to do that action. The two positions on this topic, as on so many others, are those of liberals and conservatives. The problem is that the language used by both sides is the same: A liberal is perfectly capable of saying that he or she "should" do something and yet will not do so; the conservative, for whom "should" is the vector arrow, is already moving as soon as the word "should" is pronounced. The same is true of promises or intention: They are grist for the conservative mill and suspect to liberals, for whom there are many slips between the cup and the lip.

These slips the conservative calls momentary setbacks, since the point for the conservative is simply to continue to drink.

One of the most well-known conservative assertions of purpose is to hold, with Saints Thomas and Augustine, that the purpose of sex is the production of children.[4] Sex undertaken with this intention, or at least with no known reason why it should not produce this result, is held to be "natural." Sexual acts that, as acts—rather than individual cases, which are never the currency of conservative thought—cannot produce children, are "against nature": masturbation, sodomy (usually defined as nonvaginal intercourse), homosexual sex (which overlaps to a large degree with sodomy), and so on. So, too, are actions that directly contravene having children: abortion, for example, or birth control.[5]

This view of sex as purposeful produces a long list of rules. These rules are expressed in terms of actions, not in terms of the actors, or the particularities of the actors' situations. Liberals are on the wrong track when they offer as "disproofs" of conservative reasoning individual cases that they take to be like things forbidden by the conservative rules, yet which conservatives condone. For example, by saying that sex involving a sterile partner or a postmenopausal woman is as incapable of producing children as sex between men. Why, they ask, aren't conservatives busy denouncing these things as well? But this is not an argument liberals can win, because conservatives express their rules in terms of an Absolute Action. This means, the rules themselves cannot admit variations as mitigating factors. The fact that the man or woman is sterile is such an individual variation on the rule, as is the woman's age.

Conservatives are beating the drum as I write to create a constitutional amendment defining marriage as being between two people of opposite sexes. Marriage implies sex, and sex implies children; it therefore follows inexorably that marriage can only be between a man and a woman. Conservatives find themselves put in the position of forbidding other sorts of unions. But from the conservative point of view, they are merely asserting what is the case—that marriage is between a man and a woman. Forbidding other things is secondary, not the primary purpose.

That forbidding other things is precisely the way they will define themselves against liberals produces some unintentional comedy. Demonstrators against the legalization of gay marriage before the United States Supreme Court carry placards urging the Justices to "Save Marriage Between a Man and a Woman." But, liberals respond, no one is thinking of prohibiting marriage between a man and a woman! To liberals, it seems as if conservatives aren't thinking straight. In fact, the need to prohibit other alternatives, once they are articulated, is a result of the nature of the conservative deep structure. The content of the Absolute Action isn't defensible to conservatives as content, merely as opposed to a lack of any Absolute Action.

In the sense that St. Augustine held that evil was not a substantive alternative to the good but merely the lack of good, alternatives to what conservatives hold to be the Absolute Action are not substantive other options, as liberals make them out to be, but merely the lack of the correct one. For conservatives, this is an area that at the most fundamental level of their point of view does not exist. These things, here same-sex unions, are merely the absence of true marriage, not a substantial alternative. It is a liberal argument to merely accept the existence of other sorts of unions, and ask why these are unacceptable.

Conservatives are unmoved by liberals pointing out that many marriages between a man and a woman are unhappy, that a male/female marriage can be entered into frivolously, as by the post-teen pop singer Britney Spears, and that many same-sex marriages would be anything but frivolous. For conservatives are not arguing that all male/female marriages are ideal, only that they are male/female marriages, which is to say, marriages. For them it's binary: Either the actual case fits the principle, or it doesn't. If it doesn't, it slips off the charts; it ceases to exist.

It's not absolute numbers that matter to conservatives, only that the rule be upheld. Say they were successful in keeping same-sex pairs at the current status of "living together" or perhaps "civil unions." Even if everyone opted for this rather than for marriage, the die-hard conservative would not be discouraged. Conservatives will not be swayed if no one is getting married as long as marriage is defined as being between a man and a woman. It's enough that marriage, regardless of how many people actually do it, be defined in a certain way. Because not all actions can be regulated, the world is full of actions that conservative ethics do not touch: Conservative ethics only regulates the actions it regulates, which are a tiny minority of all those possible.

Arguments between liberals and conservatives sometimes take on the air for liberals of tilting against windmills, arguing not about the substance of issues but about their public forms, such as marriage. Liberals miss the point that by the nature of the conservative worldview, public forms have intrinsic value. It might be true that unmarried gay people are having the same amount of sex they would be having if they were married, if not more. But for conservatives, gay marriage is a contradiction in terms, a public insult to marriage.

Contraception

If the purpose of intercourse is children, then clearly it is acting "against nature" to take any steps to prevent this from fulfilling its purpose. This includes, for virtually all conservatives, abortion, and for many—strict Catholics among them—birth control. Liberals sometimes try to co-opt the conservative term "natural" by saying that if something happens in nature, it can't be unnatural. Research showing that, e.g., penguins engage in homosexual behavior is taken to valorize human homosexuality.

But here "natural" is a circular term, and such research typically leaves conservatives unmoved. We can of course admit that not only animals do it, but people too, and still hold it to be "unnatural," or "against nature." The possibility that people can do other things than the right action is always a real one in conservative thought. Just because people do something (e.g., engage in homosexual sex) doesn't make it, in the conservative view, right. Here "natural" should be taken to mean actions that are deemed acceptable by those doing the deeming. Because conservative thought accepts only one right answer, by definition many vying for acceptance are left out in the cold.

The conflict between liberals and conservatives once again turns on the relationship between "is" and "should." If somebody separates "is" from "should," by definition nothing but an outside agent can unify them again, e.g., threats, or societal pressure. Yet someone who acts has transcended what for liberals is the split between "is" and "should." "Natural" is the over-the-shoulder justification thrown by conservatives as they are in the process of acting; it's not what lets them proceed.

Liberals sometimes try to trip up conservatives by asking why the so-called "rhythm" method of contraception (avoiding intercourse during ovulation) is acceptable, but using a condom is not. For conservatives, this is a false comparison. If the purpose of procreation is the production of children, the principle only becomes applicable when you have intercourse, not before. Rhythm isn't a substantial method, only the lack of the thing you're supposed to do. Similarly, liberals may well point out that Catholics allow chemical intervention to cure illness. They ask why, if this is so, conservatives do not allow chemical intervention to prevent pregnancy. But no one says that illness is the point of life, as most conservatives hold that procreation is the point of sex.

If liberals offered another, equally absolute candidate for "the" purpose of X, here intercourse, conservatives might well be given pause. But typically the challenge from liberals addresses much more than the merits of a particular version of purpose. More typically liberals simply attack the only available candidate for "the" purpose of something, proposing nothing in its place. Conservatives conclude, quite correctly, that what is being attacked is the notion of there being a single purpose at all. This is what disgusts them: Their candidate is being attacked and, worse, no other candidate is being proposed. Liberals seem to conservatives to be nothing but destructive. Indeed, in a typical argument between conservatives and liberals on any subject, the conservative will feel the liberal is questioning what the conservative holds to be the Absolute Action without telling us what to do instead. For liberals, this isn't destructive, it's being liberal. We don't replace one Absolute Action with another, we leave it up to the individual.

Asking what is "the" purpose of a body part, or a bodily function like intercourse, is already to have made a decision: that the question itself makes sense, and can be answered—that a body part does have a single purpose or function. The way we describe the body part or function makes some answers better than others. If we ask what is the purpose of intercourse, we've already begun to "point" the action toward an end by the words we use to describe it. If we called it "having an orgasm," this might push us toward giving another answer entirely if asked what its purpose is.

It is intrinsically conservative to assume that the answer to the question, "What is the function of X?" will be a single one. Liberals might say, "Who says that actions have only one function to begin with? That they have any purpose or function in this sense at all? Perhaps they have as many functions as we can find to put them to." But, of course, this view is unacceptable for conservatives, as it makes it impossible to deduce any "Thou shalt" or "Thou shalt not" from the identification of any function. We have only to wait and see what other functions we can come up with later on; if we find them they are functions.

Some gradations among conservatives are possible, as are gradations among liberals. This is why we can speak of liberal conservatives and conservative liberals. Perhaps liberal conservatives, people who are fundamentally conservative but who can see the point of the liberal objections, could accept actions and body parts as having secondary functions in addition to what for them are primary ones. A conservative conservative, for example, would almost certainly insist that the purpose of eating is to nourish our bodies. A liberal conservative might add: along the way, if possible, please our taste buds.

Certainly there are times when the only function that is being fulfilled is the function the liberal conservative allowed but relegated to secondary status. If "the" function of hair is to keep our heads warm, as a conservative conservative might insist, then coloring or even combing hair might be proscribed. A liberal conservative would allow such things, so long as the primary function was fulfilled. A more liberal conservative yet would allow head shaving on the grounds that we live in heated houses and have hats. A true liberal wouldn't have an opinion about hair treatment one way or the other—or would encourage it as a form of "self-expression."

In a similar way, if "the" or "the primary" function of sex is to have children, a liberal conservative might accept that sex also typically feels good. At the same time, such a liberal conservative might well want to limit the times when we can serve only secondary functions, or even insist that it is only legitimate to serve the secondary function if the primary one is being served as well. Liberal conservatives might well accept that sex feels good, but insist that this feeling cannot be pursued as an end in itself.

Because the ultimate goal of conservative thought is absolute rules for action, such thought is unlikely to accept the liberal rejection of the basic idea of purpose. All actions are possible; conservatives want to eliminate all but a small handful as options. The nature of conservative thought is to produce invariable formulations of action. Catholicism, for example, requires the same template from each individual because it is conservative thought; the precise content it offers to justify this is what makes it Catholicism, not what makes it conservative.

Abortion

Differing views of the notion of purpose are behind many otherwise inexplicable battles in the culture wars. The liberal vs. conservative debate regarding abortion has as its central conflict that one side accepts that intercourse's purpose is procreation, while the other side questions the very premise that an action need be seen as having a single purpose. This is rarely articulated, however. Instead, the nuts and bolts of argument come from the fact that, once an action has been determined to be on the conservative "do not do" list, the inevitable variations introduced by the individuals involved are irrelevant.

Abortion is on the "do not do" list as a result of conservatives having decided that the purpose of intercourse is the production of children. If this is so, then clearly we are going "against nature" if we try to undo this result once it has been gotten underway. (People oppose contraception for the same reason they oppose abortion;

abortion is merely a little further along in the process.) This is the reason why hard-core conservatives do not allow exceptions even in cases where abortion, according to liberals, can certainly be allowed: rape, in what for most liberals is the best reason, tapering down to mere disinclination of the woman to be a mother to this child. This is why opponents of abortion, with a Republican president and two Republican-led houses of Congress, geared up in 2005 to attack the thirty-year old Roe v. Wade decision guaranteeing the mother's right to an abortion in the early months of the pregnancy. Later in the year conservatives seemed to be pinning their hopes on the appointment of conservative judges to the United States Supreme Court.

Here too, the conflict between liberals and conservatives is expressed in terms of second-order doctrine, but it's based on a divergence at the structural level. For conservatives, the notion of purpose for sex will go up in smoke if we allow actions designed to interrupt pregnancy. If we can legitimately prevent or stop the process of producing children, this suggests that the purpose of sex can be something else, or at least something else as well. But the terms of the structural divergence are not the terms in which the argument actually takes place. Instead of focusing on structural differences, arguments are always expressed in terms of what follows from these divergent structures. And these, being once removed from the true source of the disagreement, can never dovetail into one another, only be asserted with increasing vehemence. They're not what the disagreement is really about.

A logjam of this sort always occurs when two groups of people are tussling over the same space. If they want to occupy different spaces, there is no tussle, hence no logjam. If, for example, conservatives were happy with "marriage" for two people of the same sex and liberals were happy with "civil unions" for two people of the same sex, and each side failed to care about the other's victory, there would be no argument. It's only if one side wants the same thing the other side wants that things get difficult. At the deep-structural level, both sides do want to occupy different spaces. It is therefore by considering this level that we may be able to reduce the vehemence of the argument on the surface.

At the deep-structural level, liberals and conservatives looking at the subject of abortion are seeing two different things, much like the blind men feeling different parts of the elephant and disagreeing about the nature of the entire beast. For the one who grasped the leg, the elephant was like a tree, for the one who grasped the trunk, the elephant was a snake. The argument occurs when each of the blind men asserts that he has found the whole elephant. By definition there's no way of reaching agreement so long as we continue to look at different parts of the same thing and assert that each one is the whole. There's some hope for reducing the acrimony if we realize that the mere fact that they can argue means that all these are parts of the same elephant.

The justifications of each side to say that its position alone should be adopted never offer the deep-structural reasons for their positions; if the deep structure were articulated, those who accept it would realize that it is indefensible. This is so because only secondary positions are defensible, not the underlying structure that determines them. But remaining at the level of conflicting secondary positions ensures conflict.

Conservatives would say that for them the argument of primary importance is the assertion that "life begins at conception." This choice of conception as the absolute point of departure may seem arbitrary to liberals, who may well ask, "Why pick conception as your point of departure?" In fact, a large proportion of zygotes fail properly to implant, and so are aborted "naturally." At the very least it seems conservatives should be insisting that life begins at implantation, not conception. Or why not two-thirds of the way through gestation, at which time a fetus might survive outside the womb as a child? Why not birth? Why not, for that matter, some time after birth when danger of infant mortality has dropped below a certain level? Conservatives are welcome to pick any particular time they want, and may do so without giving up their nature as conservatives. But the more possibilities we enumerate, the more arbitrary their particular choice seems.

Their argument with liberals is not, and cannot be, over which particular point is chosen. It is couched in terms of tail-for-whole, or leg-for-whole, namely as being "pro-life," as if the only alternative to their position were death. It isn't the particular time chosen that's central to the conservative position, but the fact of having an absolute beginning, something the liberal does not require for his or her position. When conservatives oppose liberals, it is always because the liberal is denying the necessity for a particular absolute time that divides the world into two realms, not countering the conservative assertion that a particular time is such a dividing point with another candidate for this slot.

In the same way, conservatives always defend Holy Writ in the particular, but the fact is that all that's necessary for the conservative position is that there be some Holy Writ, not particularly this one. This again is the reason why, if liberals would propose another absolute purpose to sex other than the production of children, they might have a shot at making conservatives scratch their heads. They won't, since to do so would only mark them as conservatives, not as liberals. This is why the most deadly disagreement of all is not between liberals and conservatives, but between two conservatives of different stripes, e.g., an evangelical Christian and a fundamentalist Muslim. Only this isn't expressed as a disagreement, a conflict in words, but in action, usually involving weapons and death.

Other candidates exist for the blank that conservatives fill with "conception." In the eighteenth century, the beginning of life for practically everyone was not conception, but birth. (Conservatives will fail to be impressed by such historical relativizing.) An epigram of Voltaire speaks wonderingly of the fact that for human beings, dying is worse than never having been born. Why does Voltaire not say, worse than never having been conceived? Perhaps for the good reason that people in the eighteenth century didn't know the facts about conception and gestation.

Even liberals must acknowledge that the development of technology to see the fetus/unborn child humanizes that fragile creature. What parent-to-be has not felt more protective toward this pulsing blob within after seeing the beating heart? Conservatives seem unaware of the extent to which technology has shaped their insistence that "life begins at conception." But what has produced our current way of seeing things can also change it. Ultrasound and Neonatal

Intensive Care Unit (NICU) nurses that can make a person out of a prematurely born baby change the nature of the world. What we know changes our viewpoint of what is, rather than merely confirming a doctrine.

Why conception? It seems clear that conservatives, in order to shore up their position, have pushed the beginning of life back to what for them is the beginning of the time line, so as to avoid having to argue over differentiation along it. The deep-structural nature of conservative thought means that we do not make individual distinctions based on situations; everything is about action. The action says something like "Don't murder people." If we have to argue about who a person is, the conservative worldview is stymied. So the conservative position is to make such argument impossible.

For conservatives, gestation is what we may call a "hard process," one of the many examples of slides down slopes that, once initiated, are logically followed out to their conclusion. Adopting a passive posture before such hard processes is what I call "process-thought." We all engage in it, seeing the ineluctable hand of Fate in things that must be. We all "count chickens"—assuming that we know how the future will turn out. Of course, the future can always surprise us.

Notions of what counts as a hard process change over time and according to circumstances. Geza Vermes points out that for Christians in the early Common Era, illness was such a hard process, the result of the sufferer being in a state of sin.[6] As a result, intervention by humans was illegitimate; only God could remove the sin, and hence the illness. Nowadays almost everyone thinks intervention in illness is legitimate, since for us health is postulated as the default position. Even Christian Sciences allows prayer to remove the illness. Illness, like evil in St. Augustine's view, is merely the lack of something—health, or the good.

Conservatives see gestation as a hard process; liberals do not. Interestingly, conservatives rarely see childrearing as being as automatic a biological process as they do gestation. It's clear to all conservatives that parents have to be actively involved, or things can go very badly indeed, or even not go at all. This is the reason conservatives are so happy to uphold what they call "family values." Conservatives typically think that sparing the rod spoils the child. Liberals, by contrast, tend to take a more laissez-faire attitude to the growing up process (Rousseau is the classic example): People are basically good and will mature willy-nilly. Families for liberals typically do not take on the almost holy status they have for conservatives.

Conservatives may be made to pause if they are forced to consider that there is nothing self-evident in the assertion that "life begins at conception." Nor is it self-evident that abortion is the same as murder. Murder, after all, kills a person. Whether or not the entity we are looking at is a person is precisely at the center of the debate. For liberals it still trails clouds of nonbeing, as we might say in a Wordsworthean vein. For conservatives it is merely an unformed being.

Conservatives are adamant that "life begins at conception" largely as a result of what they consider and what they don't. Typically they don't consider as part of their worldview any time prior to conception. Of course, life begins at conception if that is the beginning of the time you consider. The liberal point of view typically considers conception as the end point of a prior period of time, a period of possibility that ends with the emergence of this one fetus, implanted in the uterus. These two different periods of time, each one the object of one of two conflicting political philosophies, are as different as the elephant's leg and trunk, two different excerpts from the same time line.

The split between liberals and conservatives is mirrored in the terminology each group uses. To speak, as conservatives do, of an "unborn child" implies that what they consider is a subset of a child, though of the unborn variety. The time line points forward. Liberals are more comfortable speaking of a "fetus," which brackets this thing with entities before it, including a zygote and the constituent parts of the zygote. The time line extends into the past.

Conservatives frequently talk as if their whole goal were to have any one given fetus be born, this unborn child come to term. Yet each fetus in a sense denies life to all the other eggs that are not fertilized. Conservatives defend the rights of unborn babies, but not unconceived ones. This is so for the good reason that conservative thought starts the clock running at conception, and so cannot consider a situation that predates it. A liberal, who does include this time of possibility as part of his or her worldview, might point out that aborting baby X might well allow baby Y to live as a result. This is frequently how liberals see the debate. A liberal couple may well reason as follows: We don't want this child now, but not having this child now will allow us to have one when we wish.

Surely at some point technology will allow us, perhaps by pheromone typing, to determine which people are more likely to pair up and produce babies. Will conservatives claim the first meeting between the prospective parents as the beginning of a new hard process? Or the conception of these parents-to-be, each in his or her mother's womb? Or the first date of *their* parents? If we include the time before conception in our worldview, there seems to be little sense in making this an absolute demarcation line.

Allowing baby X to continue to birth precludes the birth of at least one of the eight or so eggs that would otherwise be released during the gestation period, if the mother were not pregnant. Why do conservatives not sense this child, prevented from coming to being, as a loss? Similarly, conservatives fail to mourn all the other children that might have resulted if women produced as many eggs as there is available sperm, and if there were wombs enough for all of them.

The notion of "unconceived children" is one a liberal can understand, but not a conservative, who typically will reject it out of hand, usually as counterfactual. Conservatives frequently see themselves as pragmatics, and, indeed, are so in the sense that they wait to see what happens before they commit themselves. What didn't happen is no grounds for lamentation. This is so because situations not covered in the Absolute Action that is the basis of conservative thought are ontological negatives in the sense considered above, that evil for St. Augustine was not written with a majuscule, and was merely the absence of good.

Conservatives simply don't conceive of alternatives to the actions they outline: Having these become real alternatives muddies the clarity achieved by expressing things in terms of actions, just the way seeing same-sex unions as other kinds of unions is already to bestow ontological valorization on murky things outside of a definition of marriage as the union of a man and a woman. If this is the definition to exclude other things, as it is quickly becoming, the conservatives have already lost, because implicitly they have acknowledged the existence of alternatives.

For liberals, causing this fetus (unborn child) not to be born is perhaps somewhat worse than, e.g., preventing the myriad of wasted sperm from finding other eggs, or than the fact that during the process of gestation no other child will be born. But not much worse. Aborting a fetus for a liberal takes the process back to the realm from which it came. Liberal thought typically allows a vast realm of nonbeing before the conception of this child. Conservative thought does not. For conservative thought, the only choices are two: Should this baby be brought to term, or should it not be? The only thing that is being compared with this postulated already-born baby is its nonbeing. No wonder, for conservatives, abortion is tantamount to murder.

Let us say we agree that life begins at conception. For liberals, the issue is precisely, the life of what? According to liberals, something not yet a person. Even infants, whom everyone agrees we should not kill, Jonathan Swift notwithstanding, seem in some way incomplete people. They lack so many of the qualities that make people people, being devoted only to eating, sleeping, and pooping. And if newborns are even to this degree not yet whole people, how much more so is an undifferentiated blob that may, if all systems remain go and many conditions are fulfilled, some day grows into a person.

It's difficult to talk about an entity that, in its early stages, lacks almost all of the qualities we associate with a person—lacks visible sexual characteristics, lacks organs, lacks limbs, and lacks tastes in the things people have tastes for (pepperoni pizza, the Red Sox, baked brie and red wine). The unborn (fetuses), in short, lack many of the qualities we think of as human: They don't reason, they don't love, they don't have tastes, they don't even (at least up to a certain stage) have a specific sex or even organs. At the same time, they are clearly on the track to becoming human. Whether it is legitimate or illegitimate to derail them on this track is precisely the thing that is under discussion; it cannot be concluded from this strange half-and-half situation itself.

In the same way it's difficult to talk about almost people at the other end of the spectrum—namely, after death. Once people argued about angels, or looked to divines to tell them what was the case. Did angels have sexes? Church teaching ultimately ruled they did not. Did angels have extension (take up room)? The way this question was expressed by later skeptics was, "How many angels can dance on the head of a pin?" If angels weigh, e.g., 150 pounds, then no angels can dance on the head of a pin. If they weigh nothing and take up no room, then an infinite number can do so. But if they take up space, can Heaven get full? Do they weigh down the clouds? Do their bottoms get sore from sitting on the clouds, their fingers calloused from playing the harps?

The questions do not stop here. Do angels remember their taste for pepperoni pizza here on Earth? Are they aware of their earthly mate in the form of another angel over in the corner? How old are angels? Some distinction was made between infant deaths, the cherubim, and everyone else—but does the person who dies at the age of ten end up the same as the person who lived to ninety? The Church finally gave the answer that angels were thirty-three, like Jesus. But what if they weren't thirty-three on Earth but two? Ninety-two? Do they in any case have exactly thirty-three years of implanted memories, like the creatures in *Blade Runner*? Or no memories at all? What does it mean for an eternal creature to "be" thirty-three anyway? Are his/her/its teeth (do angels have teeth? what for?) the teeth of a thirty-three-year-old? Do spouses recognize such other?

Nowadays we get around arguments about angels by not having them. Instead, we spend our time arguing about an equally unclear realm, that of the beings on the other end of life, creatures in the transition from nonexistence to existence. The development of a human being, like a halfway state after death, is a conception that strips the gears of our language: We talk of people, and the unborn are in some ways like and in some ways unlike what we mean when we do. But then again, the most vociferous debates are about limiting cases at the edges of a worldview.

The liberal/conservative debate regarding abortion centers around the conservative need for ontological clarity to justify absolute rules for action: We can't debate the nature of the actors if we are to concentrate on the actions. Debate regarding actors is in any case a liberal enterprise, not a conservative one. Conservatives "solve" the problem of what for liberals is the "neither fish nor fowl" state of fetuses/unborn children by stating loudly and clearly something that cannot be justified, namely that black is absolutely separated from white at point X, and that the status of these beings is absolutely Y.

Choose Life

The conservative bumper sticker points out, correctly, that "Abortion Stops a Beating Heart." "Choose Life," says another conservative sticker. Yet we have no compunction about stilling other beating hearts, such as those of enemy soldiers in battle, or—a conservative favorite—criminals condemned to death. A liberal will say, all right, let's reason about this. What do we get in return for stilling this beating heart? Such a question is intrinsically a liberal one, because it deals in horizontal questions linking individuals, rather than being couched in terms of an Absolute Action. Vegetarians and Jain try to avoid taking animal life, but all of us have to eat at least plants, which clearly are alive, and many conservatives are ardent hunters. Most, as I have noted, are enthusiastic eaters of large animals with the capability of becoming attached to people, like cows, not to mention the ones they themselves kill. Does this mean they're not "pro-life"? To liberals, this oft-asserted conservative reverence for life, even human life, rings hollow. They don't hold the position they do regarding the unborn because they reverence life; they hold the position they hold, and this they call "choosing life."

Because liberals are willing to consider the circumstances of particular pregnancies, they are more closely identified with "rights of the mother." The mother's situation, after all, varies according to each situation. Conservatives, as a result of couching rules as Absolute Actions, do not consider such particular circumstances. From a liberal point of view, the conservative exclusion of particularity seems tantamount to a denial that the rights of the mother matter at all. Liberals feel that conservatives regard mothers as mere vessels. Liberals sometimes respond in kind by seeming to imply that the unborn child/fetus has no independence whatsoever, is as much a part of the mother's body as her limbs.

For liberals, the baby literally cannot come to be without the active participation of the mother. Abortion for liberals is simply the mother refusing this active participation. For conservatives, by contrast, development through gestation is a given, and the mother is expected to be the passive handmaiden of the baby (I borrow the term of "handmaiden" from Margaret Atwood's dystopia of childbearing, *The Handmaid's Tale*). Liberals insist that the mother in this process is not, in New York parlance, merely chopped liver: The mother creates the baby; she is not merely the receptacle in which it fulfils its foreordained developmental process.

Conservatives require a black-and-white answer to questions of the state of things so they can return to their rules of action. Thus the mother cannot be partly one thing and partly another, perhaps in varying ratios as the pregnancy develops. If we do not have an *a priori* answer independent of circumstances, the conservative cannot appeal to the external rule. At their most doctrinaire, conservatives do not even see a close fight between the rights of the mother and the rights of the fetus: The fetus, an "unborn child" in conservative parlance, always wins. To liberals this seems counterintuitive: The mother already is, and the fetus isn't yet.

To conservatives, saying that the mother has rights that can trump those of the "unborn child" gives in to the self-indulgence that's ruining the world. Unborn child, then mother, in that order. Yet interestingly enough, as soon as the unborn child becomes a born child, it can compete on something like the same plane as the mother, and even conservatives do not immediately say that its rights trump those of the mother. It's only because it isn't yet that, paradoxically, it can be held to be the thing to which all those who are, in the ontological sense of "are," must defer. It isn't an individual, so it can't be sacrificed. The mother is, so she can be.

Self-sacrifice is its own point, because that acknowledges the outside rule. Less important is the question, whether the thing to which the self is being sacrificed deserves this deference. Because of the way conservative ethics couches rules in terms of Absolute Actions, the individual—here the mother—takes second place, if he or she is considered at all. In positive terms, this is expressed as the great conservative virtue of devotion to something beyond the self. For those unwilling to sacrifice themselves, pure conservatives have nothing but contempt.

Thus it is liberals, defending the rights of the mother, who see the fetus as having greater reality than conservatives, for whom it isn't an individual but something to which the individual, the mother, must defer in pursuit of the Absolute Action. It is liberals who actually see the fetus as being something with enough substantiality to be able to compete with the mother: Sometimes, under some circumstances, the fetus wins; sometimes, under other circumstances, the mother wins.

To conservatives, "choice" seems like a death threat. Virtually all conservatives say things like, "What if my mother had 'chosen' not to have me?" "But," the liberal will respond, "so what if she had made this choice? Perhaps another child would have been born, one who cannot speak for him- or herself because it was never allowed to be conceived. What about this person? What if another sperm had gotten to the egg first? So what if it had? What makes us think we as individuals are so necessary in the world?" The world without us is perfectly thinkable.

Thoughts like these typically cause conservatives to suffer vertigo. Me not be? Conservatives begin with what is, not what might have been. Yet this puts them at a disadvantage for talking about edge situations like the development of something that will be: They must have this already have happened, when in fact it hasn't. This is why liberal thought typically sees the fetus from the mother's point of view, which includes the time before implantation took place. The conservative view is, in a structural sense, the outsider's view, which usually means, the male's. The beginning of things is when there is news to share.

4

MALE THOUGHT AND CONTROL

Although control can be achieved, it is always achieved at a price. The price is that you have to deny the existence of the things that cannot be controlled, or at least fail to consider them. The need for control is more a conservative need than a liberal one.

People who drive SUVs don't want to hear about the deleterious effects wrought on the environment by their vehicles. Indeed, conservatives don't want to hear about global warming at all, and usually scoff at "alarmist" liberals who talk in terms of things whose effects won't be felt for decades. The military, similarly, wants to talk about its own troops and kill ratios, not about the widows and orphans on the either side that the war produces, or the devastation to the economy of the invaded country, or for that matter the economic costs to the country doing the invading.

It might seem that this is so because nay-saying liberals are, after all, saying "nay" rather than "yea"—liberals invariably point out the negative consequences of conservative action. The army, it is clear, doesn't want to hear about any negative effects of their actions or anything that could harm them in political terms, and wants only to talk about the dead enemy. And it's the negative things the liberals will be emphasizing; if they are out to emphasize the ways in which they diverge from the conservatives, they will, of course, avoid another litany of the positive consequences like that offered by conservatives.

But if we look more closely at conservative responses to such liberal retorts, we realize once again that conservatives don't want to debate these things on their merits. The deep-structural point is that they don't want to debate them at all. Liberals extrapolating from current trends regarding greenhouse gases meet with conservative opposition not primarily on the grounds that their arguments are wrong, but that the mere extrapolation into the future is ridiculous. Conservatives like arguments such as that pointing out that in 1890s New York, disposing of horse manure was a big problem. Someone extrapolating population from the situation then would have concluded that in 1950 there would be no room for the people, so huge would be the piles of manure.

Conservatives are always happy to dismiss, with a snort, liberal "worrywarts." Thinking about consequences, at least past a certain point, is not compatible with the conservative emphasis on action for its own sake. Conservatives thus tend to deny the point of trying to list consequences. Everything is in God's hands. Besides, miracles, conservatives insist repeatedly, are always possible. Of course they are, the liberal might respond, but what makes them miracles is that they aren't what we expect. Being possible doesn't mean they're going to happen. This is typically not the way liberals respond, however; instead, like a dog in a cage biting at the stick shoved at it, they typically argue back that miracles aren't possible.[1]

Conservatives have a strong sense of entitlement of the real. What you don't see has exponentially less value for conservatives than it does for liberals. The people who are born are the people who should have been born because we infer purpose from seeing what, in fact, is the case. There's no point in speculating about being another person, or someone else having been born in our stead.

Conservatives quickly become exasperated when liberals want to talk about secondary and tertiary effects of their actions, because the conservatives are being required to acknowledge the existence of things they don't control. Conservatives confine their attention to things within their ken because these are the things amenable to their control, or at least the sense they have of their control—a sense attainable only by limiting their view to a relatively small part of things. We don't make an absolute increase in the amount of control in the world when we limit our attention to the things we control, only fill our lives fuller with the things that an individual controls and turn away from the things that an individual doesn't control.

Conservatives therefore don't deny the existence of things that they don't control. But they do avoid focusing on them. And this denies such things any ontological weight. For conservative thought, the question is closed when we, e.g., defeat our foe, effect what change we as individuals can effect. For liberals, this is only the center of a series of concentric ripples of extended effects. Conservatives don't deny there are ripples. They just don't find them legitimate objects of attention.

This refusal to focus on ripples beyond our immediate control, or even acknowledge them as being of primary importance, is the source of conservative individualism. Conservatives are individualists because that's the realm of things they can control. This emphasis on the world of the individual and what that person controls is part of the structure of conservative ethics. Since each person is linked by his or her own thread to the Absolute Action, there are no intermediate structures of any ontological importance.

Conservatives fiercely resist the argument that qualities they take to be secondary, such as your economic status or your skin color, determine much of anything. We are always free to do the right thing. "Just say no," as Nancy Reagan famously counseled regarding drug use. We control these, insist the conservatives, not they us. Similarly, conservatives refuse to consider the ripple effects of their actions which they cannot control. The war may be won, say the liberals, but what about the effects of the peace? Or on civilians? Or on the economy? For conservatives, this is speaking a foreign language.

The conservative need to focus on situations of control leads them to insist that many distinctions are more clear-cut than they seem to liberals, not just the ontological status of zygotes. These are always the situations where it's possible to assert control, the ripples closest to the stone's fall. The further ripples are too far for conservatives to try and bring within their ken, so these are the ones conservatives simply will not debate.

Conservatives always compare this area just outside their walls to their own controlled world and find it in need of being controlled. But, as I noted earlier, if they were to compare it with the even larger ripples that are, in fact, beyond their area of focus (and so not available for comparison), they would find this area the most congenial part of the outside world rather than the least congenial part of the inside one. Even if all liberals gave in today to all conservatives, the degree to which the conservative domain of control would have been expanded is minimal, at least in the first round.

Samuel Huntington famously claimed in *Clash of Civilizations and the Remaking of World Order* that "Islam has bloody borders."[2] In his view, Islam is always pushing outward bit by bit. In the same way, conservatives are always trying to colonize the areas closest to their own borders, bringing them inside. Krugman, cited in the Introduction, is not wrong in his intuition that the culture wars are largely the invention of conservatives. Liberal thought lacks the same all-engirdling sort of border; the borders are within, and fainter.

The reason it's not liberals that start these arguments is that the conservative is always at the position of the stone at the center of the ripples, moving outward to expand his or her grounds. Liberals come from somewhere in the multiple ripples and work inward to the stone. Liberals do not deny the stone; however, the impulse of the conservatives is to deny the ripples, or to incorporate them into their ken.

The conservatives' viewpoint ends at their own borders, so the area right on the other side is always the most tantalizing. This, again, is what leads to such conservative fervor for apparently small issues: keeping "under God" in the Pledge of Allegiance when the world has so many other much more pressing issues; naming something in every county after Ronald Reagan when children don't have enough to eat; making sure that all fetuses are born when the world, at least arguably, has too many people already and those who are born end, in many places, badly. Conservatives typically oppose the social programs that would help ensure that these children do not end so badly.

The fact that conservative thought is most interested in the tiny border area just outside its walls and is completely unconcerned with the fact that what is outside may be much larger explains why the greatest amount of capital is expended by conservatives on the least strategic ground, much as World War I trench warfare reduced men to taking and retaking the same few yards of completely useless bombed-out terrain.

It never discourages conservatives to be told, as liberals tell them, that their principles only end up affecting a small number of people—e.g., through a ban on so-called "partial birth" abortions—where there are problems of different sorts (e.g., malaria and schistosomiasis) that affect large numbers of people, problems in which conservatives are resolutely uninterested. Conservatives are unconcerned with numbers. The structure of conservative thought is based on the individual and his or her absolute principle, not groupings of individuals.

In this sense, liberal, rather than conservative thought, is the more pragmatic. The sense in which conservative thought is more pragmatic has been sketched above: Conservative thought waits to see what happens, or who is born. This is clearly what was "meant" to be. It doesn't deal in hypotheticals.

Thus we can't say, definitively, whether liberal or conservative thought is more pragmatic—which usually means, more realistic. Conservatives pride themselves on being hard-headed realists: They insist that there really are Enemies. At the same time they are quite (liberals would say) unrealistic. Only the principle matters, not the extent to which it actually affects the world.

The Wall

Postulated structures are what establish the boundaries of our worlds. Sometimes the geographical boundaries of our world are clear as well. When I lived in West Berlin during the Wall years, I was initially fascinated by exploring the pockets of the boundary, sometimes rather oddly shaped, of the western part of the divided city. On the other side was the East, an area guarded by watchtowers, soldiers with guns, and—we were told—mines. (In fact, this turned out to be a myth propagated by the East to deter would-be escapees.) I would go running along the Teltow Canal in the West, fascinated by the point where the Wall appeared on the other side and the guard towers. That was the East. A cluster of about twenty houses called Steinstücken was attached to the rest of West Berlin by a road—on both sides of which rose the Wall, which cut through backyards of this little plot of land otherwise orphaned in the East—to include it in the West. I found this fascinating.

I was fascinated, too, by the Glienicke Brücke into Potsdam, painted and cleaned on the Western side up to the middle, where it turned as unpainted, rusted, and gray as the decrepit Potsdam that continued beyond it into the rest of East Germany. Blocked off at both ends, East and West, the bridge was used for the exchange of spies. The people being traded would start off at the foot of the bridge on what for them was the wrong side, meet in the middle, and continue walking to safety. I would stand in front of the Glienicke Castle and look into the fascinating world beyond.

One day, visiting East Germany, I went into Potsdam from the East, arriving via a giant loop that went into East Berlin and then around back to the other side of West Berlin through East Germany. I saw this bridge from the other side: Instead of a bridge into a mysterious world, it was merely a nonfunctional way to get back to reality. The bridge itself lost its ability to define another world, and became merely a bridge again. This is how liberals see conservatives' expansionism. It's as if either side tried to take a few inches past the middle: Seen from their own side, this would have been a few inches of progress, and so worth fighting for. Seen from the other side, it would have been trivial—though, of course, hotly rebuffed simply to avoid the possibility that some day the territorial grab would be measured in thousands of miles rather than in inches.

Now, with the Wall gone, people pass daily through what at the time seemed absolute limits. I walk through the Brandenburg Gate; the ghost of the division that is no longer a division rises to meet me. I've now driven over the opened and completely painted Glienicke Brücke, and wondered at how uninteresting it seemed.

Liberals are like Wall-jumpers, people who pass through boundaries that for conservatives are absolute. The intensity of conservative interest in the no-man's-land immediately abutting on their area of control seems misplaced to liberals, who see that this is only a tiny sliver, and that there is a whole other world on the other side. Conservatives, in turn, think liberals are simply vague if they cannot see the intrinsic interest of this area.

Liberals are not, generally speaking, too concerned with clear borders. Generally speaking, conservatives are. Liberals would say: You don't need an Absolute Action with respect to, e.g., abortion; sometimes it's more justified, sometimes less. In terms of borders, this is expressed by saying that developing human beings are part of other categories entirely outside of the jurisdiction of the human. Conservatives can't allow another category, a sort of half-and-half, or Unknown category: Either it is or it isn't. Thus conservatives insist that "the unborn" have to be exactly like living breathing adults in any way that counts. To liberals, this seems so untrue as to be ridiculous.

Because underlying structures can only be described, not debated, the debates take place between liberals and conservatives over the precise location of the borders. If liberals would say more clearly than they do that absolute borders at all are neither possible nor desirable, they might at least get some respect from conservatives, who as it is get to pat themselves on the back for the certainty of their position. To conservatives, liberals merely look weak.

Conservatives don't deny that some people are controlled; they just aren't fond of acknowledging them to the extent of having anything to do with them. It's the liberals who man soup kitchens and set up welfare systems, not conservatives. This is the reason why conservatives are uninterested in "losers."

The military is all about control. Everyone in the military is at the behest of someone else, indeed of many someones. They do not have the freedom to choose what they will do with their days. But because they have voluntarily submitted to the system, and the control is control by a system rather than by unpredictable individuals, they can forget what is so evident to someone looking on from outside: that very little of what they do is up to them. In their minds, they are acting like free individuals. By making the control they submit to predictable control, it itself is in a sense controlled, freeing up the rest of the world for the illusion of autonomy. For the rest of us, our servitude isn't so clearly external, nor so willingly embraced. It's stirred through our being, so we can't escape it so easily.

This is why, in the same way that self-made millionaires invariably insist that anyone can do what they did through effort and determination alone, midshipmen tell me that they got where they are through their individual hard work. I have to point out to them once again that they are the result of many factors beyond their control: their parents, their socioeconomic status, the schools they attended, even their skin color. People who aren't physically healthy never get in. Truly stupid people don't get in, though the fact is that we lower our ostensible minima to accommodate the groups we give special treatment to: racial minorities, team members, and prior members of the Navy and Marine Corps. Yet from their perspective, they have done it all themselves.

To a liberal this seems ridiculous. From the students' point of view, it makes perfect sense.

Austen and Annapolis

The way midshipmen see themselves, as rugged individualists, has its effect in the classroom. I long ago gave up trying to teach the novels of Jane Austen at the Naval Academy: The situation of Austen's characters is simply too far from the way my students see themselves. Austen's heroines are extraordinarily controlled. They are controlled even more than most people by the aging of their bodies, being marriageable for only a few years after about the age of sixteen. They are constrained geographically, being forbidden from striking out on their own in the world, and kept within the confines of the house where they were born, which they typically may leave only to marry. They cannot even set about to broaden the pool of eligible young men from which they must choose, and of whom one may free them from their prisons. Instead, they must wait patiently in the house that fate has put them in for a marriageable man to arrive at one of the dispersed houses of the other "ladies and gentlemen" in their small corner of their county. If fate brings them no such young man, they are destined for spinsterhood. They are also constrained in what they are allowed to do to make marriage happen. The actions permitted them consist of being receptive and waiting for the young man they have set their eye on to speak. They themselves cannot of course "pop the question," or even suggest they want it popped.

From the liberal point of view, the control of the military is in a sense much more absolute than the control to which Austen's heroines must submit. At least the women in Austen's novels have largely free rein over how they will spend their time. But, as I suggest, our students submit to the fact of an external, predictable structure so that they can preserve the illusion of autonomy in the rest of their lives. This is why, I have decided, they will not respond positively to an outside view of someone else's servitude that forces them to acknowledge their own. Midshipmen at any rate apparently find it well nigh impossible to identify with Austen's heroines, who sit with their sewing, listening to the clock tick and watching the shadows grow longer, wondering if Fate will sing an eligible man up to their door.

Besides, it's just too difficult for male midshipmen to identify with women, at least the women of Austen's world. Frankly, who would want to? In Austen's world, only men are conceived of as the free agents—though they may be subject to other forces invisible to the women. The man can propose, or not, as he chooses; he can leave the neighborhood or stay, as he chooses; he can visit or not, as he chooses.

At twenty, I too found identification with Jane Austen's world difficult, thinking as I did at the time that I alone could determine my future, and that anything was possible. A disastrous marriage and some decades later, I realize that there are many things we do not foresee and cannot control. To me, the differences between Austen's world and the midshipmen's seem slight. I can understand they can't afford to see this.

The Birthmark

The military tries to colonize death as part of its sphere of control: Death on the battlefield is achieving immortality. In some way it's a thing devoutly to be wished for. Glorifying death is one way to bring it into the realm of the known. Some religions engage in the same project. Islam celebrates death on the battlefield in a religious cause.

It guarantees entrance into heaven. Christianity has at various times in its history claimed the same.

But this is death in battle: It is something we control by making it the centerpiece of our consideration. Far less talked about is natural death, or death that comes gradually rather than in a bang. Wounds in battle are not things the military talks about gladly: They happen, but simply take the soldier off the field. What the effect on the soldier's life might be is not something the military wants to think about.

I noted above that the colonizing efforts of conservatism are by definition always in the area just outside the wall around their positions. Compared to the things conservatives do not and cannot attempt to colonize (such as death itself, fear, uncertainty, other people, the Other Sex, the fact that we rarely get the things we really want), what conservatives make the center of their attention is very limited indeed. To liberals, conservative obsession with close-to-them topics like the ontological status of the fetus/unborn child, or pornography—almost within the untouchable realm of the private, but with a toe in the realm of the social that ethics can regulate, as I have argued in *Sexual Ethics*—seems an example of the fact that topics become important because we make them important. They're like flaws on our skin that we can either pick or leave alone. From the liberal point of view, conservatives allow themselves to be bothered when they could very well walk away. Because conservatives are comparing their expansion outward from their wall to the wall, and not seeing it from the opposite direction, as a tiny fringe at the edge of a much larger Great Unknown, it seems to them they are fearlessly conquering new territories.

To liberals, conservatives seem puzzlingly unable to take their own advice to "just say no" when given the opportunity of routing out an anomaly, not leaving it alone. Nathaniel Hawthorne's short story "The Birthmark" shows this process. The husband becomes obsessed with a tiny hand-shaped birthmark on his wife's otherwise flawless face. Perhaps because he sees it as a hand, it seems to him the mark of another man; perhaps it stands for some other, perhaps invisible, sort of "stain" he fears marks the wife. The birthmark seems bothersome only to the husband; Hawthorne suggests others like it. In any case, the husband subjects his wife to various treatments to rid her, and himself, of the mark, until finally, the treatments kill her. The husband's personal regret at having to do without his wife aside, he can at least console himself that he has done the "right thing."

From the outside, it is easy to see, and to say, that the husband was the one who created this problem. The reader isn't the husband, and so is able to weigh what the husband gains for continuing his crusade against what he loses. To the husband, of course, such a point of view is unavailable; it seems clear to him that the birthmark must be eradicated regardless of the cost of this victory. To himself, he seems principled and self-sacrificing. To the reader, he seems cruel and destructive, not only of another but of himself as well. The reader has the liberal viewpoint, the husband the conservative. To the husband, "is" does imply "should"; once you identify the problem, you are already on your way to solving it. Someone on the outside not similarly involved in the vector of action will say that this "is" does not, and indeed cannot, imply "should."

From the husband's perspective, what he saw as a flaw on his wife's face ruined his postulate of a smooth complexion. An outsider would have seen it, if at all, as part of the wife, not imagining or postulating a cheek without it. The conservative won the battle of eliminating the birthmark, but at the price of eliminating the wife at the same time. Even if this had not been the result, an outsider would have seen the husband as obsessed. Such a small thing to devote your entire attention to! For the husband, focusing on the area just outside his control to try and control it, this is the only thing that mattered. From the perspective of someone on the outside, this is pointless since, this control, even if achieved, is of something so small.

Hawthorne is reminding us of the potentially deleterious effects of completion of structures that are such only to the perceiver. Yet the fact is that completing structures is a familiar action for all of us, the motor behind many of our quotidian actions. We can all understand this need to complete a structure that is behind the conservatives' itch to rectify the uncertainty in those parts of the world immediately abutting their area of control.

It's this need to fill out structures whose very existence may be invisible to outsiders that, for example, fuels the mania of collectors. Stamp collectors start out with well-defined matrices that they fill in: the urge to "complete a row" in an album or to get the last remaining whatever can become so strong it leads, in extreme cases, to socially unacceptable behavior—lying, cheating, and stealing to acquire the precious scrap of perforated paper. The oddest things become the Holy Grail of a certain subworld: a stamp of an airplane with the airplane printed upside down, for example. Bottle collectors spend hours searching for the one bottle that provides what they see to be the missing link in a collection. Yet no one but a fellow bottle collector would know that the one bottle the collector finally holds so triumphantly aloft should be coveted as the one that completes the structure. To outsiders it's merely another bottle, as a rare stamp is only another piece of paper. Museums, as another example, look for a specific sort of painting by a specific artist that fills a hole in their collections. A painting whose acquisition would be a coup for one museum might merely be another X for a museum that has many of this subject by this painter.

So, too, for our daily actions: We aim at completing structures. We continue taking courses toward an academic degree because that means filling out what we have come to see as a structure. But if we can define where we are in the degree program in terms of some other structure that does not require such filling out—e.g., developing our interest, or keeping ourselves occupied—suddenly the impetus to do more disappears: We are merely adding 1 + 1 + 1, no longer approaching an external limit. We go on vacation in the same spot because we have always done it this way, so we are continuing to fill in the same structure. Going somewhere else may feel like abandoning our responsibilities. If suddenly it seems to us that it doesn't matter where we go on vacation, we are released from servitude to this responsibility.

Most long-term goals and structures of life rely on this sense of "filling in" a structure. This fact gives us a sense of the undeniable advantage of conservative thought over liberal: It allows for much greater intensity of action. I have to get this bottle to complete my collection! I have to make sure people aren't getting abortions! I have to make sure two men aren't getting married! Liberals fail to see actions implied in these things.

It is a misrepresentation of the conservative position for conservatives to say that the mother is being called upon to sacrifice herself to the unborn child. She isn't. The sacrifice called for is to the external action of Childbearing: There's no reason why this particular child had to be born rather than another. One day we may simply walk away from the abortion argument as we have walked away from the theological discussion of angels—difficult as that is to believe for those obsessed with it. Human history is littered with abandoned questions—which is not to say questions that have been answered. The husband in Hawthorne's short story could very well have decided not to focus on the birthmark. Had he done so, his wife might have lived to a ripe old age.

Male Thought

Because there is such a tight correlation between conservative thought and the need for control, conservative thought overlaps to a great degree with male thought. This is yet another reason why the Naval Academy, conceived by and for men and still largely populated by them, is so intensely conservative. Men are taught to limit their consideration to situations they can control, and then to control them. Men see themselves in the way the conservative worldview conceives of individuals, as active agents aiming at an Absolute Action. Opposition is always outside of their worldview, not inside. Control is achieved through actions, and this is control of an external world.

Not all action by men is "male action" in this sense; if it were, men would not be capable of being liberals, since liberalism builds conflict into the realm of the allowable, rather than banishing it to the outside. A biological male can act as other things than a man. Yet it means that biological males will have a tendency to act, at least as a default, as men.

Men acting "as men" are nodes of one. In the recruiting phrase thought the most suitable by taxpayer-supported advertising executives to entice young men into the United States Army, where they lose virtually all autonomy at least when seen from the outside, they are an "army of one." Each man acting as a man regards himself as alone against an undifferentiated cosmos. Because each of many men sees himself as acting independently, the visual result to someone on the outside is the same as a jar full of tadpoles or a pen full of puppies: a great deal of wriggling about is visible, and many things butting heads with each other.

The reason this recruiting slogan makes sense at all is the same as the reason why midshipmen don't like Jane Austen. In both cases, members of the military separate the control in their lives from the uncontrolled part; they then offer up the control and hence can afford not to focus on it. What's left is the view of themselves as Rambo, an "army of one," and utterly unlike the agonizingly controlled females bent on marriage of Austen's world.

Male actions when seen from the outside are largely predictable, though each individual male may be unaware just how predictable they are. We have only to watch two male motorists in a Latin country who are involved in an accident with each other to see this. Testosterone requires that they immediately threaten each other and that the encounter end in fisticuffs. There's no way to avoid this, and the incident must simply be allowed to go its weary way to the inevitable scuffle. Should one of the men want to short-circuit the tiresome prayer-wheel-turning of vituperation he saw coming, he'd be vilified as a wimp.

Conservatives see all relationships as larger versions of that of one man (not person) against the world. Each man focuses on a series of single other men; no man need see further than the man opposing him. The only thing he need think about is defeating this single opponent. Looking further than this one encounter is not part of the masculine mindset. And of course, it's downright unmanly to spend too much time thinking things like, "What happens if he defeats me?" (This is "cynical" thought.) Or: "What do I do with him if I defeat him?" (This is asking something beyond the moment, which might take away from my ability to act here and now.) Or: "Is there any real point in defeating him?" Or: "What of all the people that will suffer if I defeat him?" (Both of these clearly leave the realm of control.)

Countries, if run by conservatives, tend to engage in actions that are forms of male actions writ large: Action is its own end; moving forward at any cost is its own justification. This means that avoiding mistakes is not very high on the list. You do something then ask questions later, if then. At least you've made a decisive action, and decisive action is the lingua franca of men.

The conflation of nations with individual males is one reason why nations make mistakes in international affairs, refusing to "learn from history." Barbara Tuchman's *The March of Folly* gives numerous examples, from the Trojan War to World War I and Vietnam, of countries resolutely and over long periods of time doing the wrong thing. For her this means doing things that had deleterious effects on their countries. Her question is, "How can this happen?"

Tuchman is working from an intrinsically different point of view than the societies she criticizes. She is working from a liberal point of view, the societies from a conservative one. It's not chance that most of these follies, as the liberal is bound to see them, are committed by men. More to the point, they are committed by men banded together into groups that allow them to ram home the male, which is to say conservative, point of view, with no fear of anyone objecting to their doing so. Their conservatism seems self-evident to them. The clearest form of action for men is action directed outward, toward an external foe. The clearest form of action outward against an external foe is war. Hence the love by conservative societies of waging war, and the problems Tuchman sees attendant upon this.

Chris Hedges, in his affecting book *War Is a Force That Gives Us Meaning*, offers his title postulate that war gives a purpose to life that otherwise lacks it, horrible though war undoubtedly is. He's trying to answer Tuchman's question: "Why do nations seem to love war?" I'd say it's something men do the same way they get in fistfights in Latin countries after an accident. So long as the point of view remains that of the individual man alone against the world, or his multiples in organizations like the military, there's no way around it. It's not something you can think your way out of; thought is a liberal thing.

Men act. Just because other men have shown how pointless this is in the long run, no single man, or his multiple, is acting in the long run. He's acting in the short run if he acts like a man.

Being male means limiting your point of view to what you can control. And then you act. Of course, by acting, you'll probably initiate events that you then can't control. But because you don't consider them, you never lose the sense of being in control, even when you aren't. You can always say, "I was blindsided," and retain your dignity. So what if there are people screeching in the streets, "We *told* you so!!"? You don't have to listen to them. You've stayed the course, acted like a man. Or here, like a conservative.

Military thinking, like the male thinking that overlaps with it, is unitary: it focuses on one thing, and then the next. It only focuses on the achievable, the controllable, not the uncontrollable. The insistence of the Prussian theorist Carl von Clausewitz that war is intrinsically unpredictable—you can go in with a plan but it gets blown to bits in the first few minutes of fighting—is something military people can contemplate in a classroom, like the possibility that God doesn't exist.[3] But it cannot be allowed to influence their actions. For the military, the only permissible direction is forward, except when it's backward: Both require decisive action.

The insistence on decisive action has led to the somewhat comical nature of U.S. Naval Academy ethics courses, instituted in a hurry in the wake of massive cheating scandals in the 1990s, and of Academy-wide "Character Development Seminars." I've taught these and know how disoriented our students become when I tell them I want discussion and don't care how it turns out. First they set their jaws: I have to be lying to them. Just give us the bottom line, their clenched jaws say to me, and stop the charade. As it dawns on them that I really didn't have a bottom line, they became angry, smelling the rank scent of "relativism." They want to know what to do, a conservative demand. I'm giving them a liberal response. They don't like it, not one little bit.

This male need for control is the origin of the societal structure we usually call "the patriarchy," the notion that the king of all units involving both men and women, from the household on up, is a man or men. Every man is king of his own household, ran the Anglo-American mantra. "But why does a household need a king?" ask feminists—and, nowadays, many others. From the perspective of the family, perhaps it doesn't. But men do sense the need to control; only control allows action, and being a man is all about action.

The Binds of Maleness

Journalism sometimes captures the nature of fundamental truths better than more thought-out treatises—usually by trying to do something else entirely. An article in the Style section of the *Washington Post* called "Vanity, Thy Name is Metrosexual" by staff writer Alexa Hackbarth allows us—though the author's intent is certainly elsewhere—to examine the close matchup between conservatism and maleness.[4]

Hackbarth is writing primarily to describe and critique something that's been dubbed the "metrosexual"—roughly, a straight man who spends time and effort on his appearance. (As I write, the term seems already to be going out of circulation.) The assumption that "regular" guys don't do this is what the author shares with those who coined this term to begin with, and undoubtedly the reason she is drawn to it. In describing metrosexuals, Hackbarth expresses with great clarity the qualities women have typically expected from pre- or nonmetrosexual men. We may call these, for the sake of brevity, male qualities since, at the same time, these are also the qualities men expect from other men, and from themselves.

What is so striking is that these qualities, male qualities, are also quintessentially conservative qualities. Because most men, excluding so-called metrosexuals, define themselves by respect to outside criteria, they are natural conservatives.

The point of Hackbarth's article is to complain about metrosexuals, presented by some as a new understanding of what it means to be a man. We might, therefore, initially say that her piece is conservative by definition: It rejects the new in favor of the old. Yet here as elsewhere, holding to the old doesn't, in itself, make one conservative, and cleaving to the new doesn't make one liberal. It isn't the old-fashioned nature of the maleness she praises that makes her view conservative. It's the fact that the male worldview jibes to a great extent with the conservative one. Metrosexuals are more likely to be liberals because they are likely to see themselves as an alternative to something—not because they are the more recently defined type of men. Real men, in Hackbarth's view, will see what they do as the only possibility. This is what makes them conservative.

Hackbarth offers a brief history of the term she's focusing on. A metrosexual, she tells the reader ("in case you didn't catch any of several newspaper articles about this developing phenomenon"), "is a straight man who styles his hair using three different products (and actually calls them 'products'), loves clothes and the very act of shopping for them, and describes himself as sensitive and romantic." She then lets off the zinger: "In other words, he is a man who seems stereotypically gay except when it comes to sexual orientation." Clearly, for Hackbarth, metrosexual men aren't just another sort of men, they are men to a lesser degree, feminized men. They are like gay men in virtually all ways except that they want to have sex with women.

They won't be having sex with her. Hackbarth makes clear that she finds metrosexuals unattractive. "I lose interest in men," she tells us, "who not only won't make the first move, but hesitate to make the second and third." Part of being a real man, in Hackbarth's view, is being sexually aggressive toward women in a way that metrosexuals aren't.

Hackbarth's more basic objection to metrosexual men is not, however, that they're too much like gay men, but instead, that they're too much like women. Manly qualities are the qualities that distinguish men from women. Manly is what isn't feminine. That means that someone who's biologically male has to aim at something outside himself; he doesn't just have it. Being a man is a perennial process of becoming, defined through his actions. This is the quintessentially conservative aspect of Hackbarth's consideration, the presupposition that individuals define themselves by seeking to attain an external definition, a set of actions.

What, for Hackbarth, are manly actions? She grew up in a "small western ranching town," where, we're informed, "men wrangle cattle before sitting down to a breakfast of bacon and eggs. They're the strong and silent type, capable and calm in a crisis." Presumably such crises include the "leaky faucet" or necessity to "rewire an electrical outlet" she immediately goes on to consider. It's a bit unclear whether the fact she shares just after this that "they drive pickup trucks" is meant only as local color or whether it's another of their virtues. What's clear, however, is that it's good that "when they cook, it's steak and potatoes, not wine-braised duck." Real men don't eat gourmet meals, they merely tank up on grub to keep moving. The reader clearly isn't supposed to be salivating over the duck she evokes, but despising it as Hackbarth does.

We can tell she despises it because this information is followed in the same journalistic breath by the following "gotcha": Real men "sure don't spend hours in front of the mirror only to emerge with prettier hair than mine." The reader probably already knows that "pretty" isn't good for men. Even if we substitute for it something more masculine, or even neutral, like "good-looking," it's clear that hair is something men aren't supposed to be fussing with. Probably they aren't meant to have enough of it to fuss with. The men Hackbarth despises, the metrosexuals, are worried about how they look rather than focusing their energy on doing things, just as they are concerned with the taste of what they eat.

Hackbarth is evoking in many ways the male/female dichotomy of being vs. doing, articulated by many writers, perhaps most evocatively by the novelist and theoretician John Berger in *Ways of Seeing*.[5] Speaking of art and what we now call "the gaze," Berger suggested that "according to usage and conventions which are at last being questioned but have by no means been overcome—*men act* and *women appear*. Men look at women. Women watch themselves being looked at." The problem with the man Hackbarth was having dinner with—a man who, as she describes it, "rais[ed] an eyebrow at my chicken alfredo selection after he had ordered a salad"—is that, she reveals, "I saw him check his reflection in the silver water pitcher three times."

Clearly salads are bad, because they aren't red meat (which is manly, because it indicates killing large animals, in contrast to a veggie burger) or perhaps betray that the man is conscious of what he eats. Being critical of high-fat alfredo sauce is bad, too: Remember those men back home cooking steak and potatoes, though presumably also dying of arteriosclerosis at an early age. (Hackbarth doesn't want to consider these side effects any more than drivers of SUVs want to think about global warming.) Both indicate concern with appearance and longevity rather than with the quintessential masculine currency, action.

We can tell that for Hackbarth, being aware of how you look isn't masculine because of her claim that if a gay man were to come on to her "metrosexual" dinner companion, he is "more likely to thank the gay man" for the compliment of being approached sexually rather than "punch[ing] him in the face." Hackbarth pretends to seriously consider the possibility that this means "metrosexuals are more accepting of other people's sexual preferences." We know she's just kidding, however, when she goes on with her joke: "Either that or they're afraid of breaking a nail when their fist makes contact."

Real men, in sum, aren't "pretty," don't mind getting dirty, and take minor physical harm as part of a day's work. They punch out fags who make passes at them. Men don't like being looked at or admired, and they don't worry about how they look or what condition their nails are in. Nor, according to Hackbarth, are real men articulate (she evokes dreamily the "strong and silent type") or too aware of how they feel. As she puts it: "I don't want a man who pours out his heart on the fourth date." She plays at taking the blame for her reaction on herself ("perhaps I'm unusually insensitive"), but the reader knows she doesn't mean this either. Instead of coming on to her, perhaps throwing her to the ground and having his way with her, he's talking to her. Talking, we assume, is something a girlfriend does. From the man other things are expected. Of course, as nonmetrosexual men will say.

Hackbarth takes her own reaction of derision toward metrosexuals as the one to be emulated; she's not confessing a fault on her part. She echoes Paula Cole ("where have all the cowboys gone?") to summarize her disdain for the citified wimps she finds herself dating so far from the ranch. Thus country vs. city is another of Hackbarth's so-absolute dichotomies, second only to doing vs. being, where one of the two contrasts is the positive pole and the other the negative. Here, as we might expect, "country" is the positive pole. Indeed, her whole article seems ripe for a 1950s-type semiotic analysis such as that of Lévi-Strauss, complete with contrasts set up on opposite sides of a "semiotic square."

Ultimately the article is rather sad, as Hackbarth clearly feels isolated in the big city. She rages (or sobs?), "each of the nearly two dozen men I have dated over the past eight months has displayed metrosexual traits." Maybe, the reader murmurs to him- or herself, they thought her a bit of a hick. Besides, without a photo—there is none accompanying the article—we can't even tell if she's attractive.

Closely allied to the country/city dichotomy in the article is another positive/negative contrast, that of inside/outside. Here the positive pole is that of outside. As Hackbarth puts it, "There are just . . . too few men who associate sweat with hard work instead of a stint in the sauna"—these are the same sort of men "who know all the soap opera story lines and designer labels." Men ought not to know about clothes, or be interested in them, nor in shopping. Masculine means one pair of muddy boots and no interest in consuming any form of the arts, much less in producing them. Hackbarth is as turned off by "poorly-written poetry and a closet full of shoes" as she is by "plot-line knowledge of 'The Bold and the Beautiful.'"

Hackbarth shares Marx's nostalgia for the autarkic life, explaining the corruption of men as being the result of too great wealth. Money renders men less masculine, because it allows us all to buy specialists when we should be doing things ourselves. Hackbarth states, "A man with money doesn't need to know how to install a water heater. He doesn't need to know his way around a sawhorse; he can pay someone else to build his cabinets." Hackbarth waxes positively communist when she speaks of "a visible connection between hard work and the fruits of labor," though she is modern enough to think a men merely has to know how to install his water heater, not build his own log cabin.

It's easy to make fun of Hackbarth, but what she describes is the way most men who cultivate their masculinity see themselves. I put it this way to avoid entering into the fruitless discussion about whether there are different kinds of masculinity or only one. Hackbarth presumably would claim the latter, that the only real man are the taciturn cowboys she describes; defenders of metrosexuals might well claim that they are simply being masculine in a different way—one more appropriate to the urban milieu in which they find themselves than wrangling cattle before a breakfast of ham and eggs.

Saying that masculinity, by definition, isn't femininity, doesn't answer the question of how much the individual will, or even should, achieve a pure form of either. Followers of Michel Foucault have tried to express this intrinsic slippage between the individual and the pure end of a spectrum by making a distinction between "sex" and "gender." Sex is the biological fact and gender is all other things. Usually this distinction is expressed in the clumsy language of "societal construction," the insistence that whatever you're born with to begin with, gender is constructed. It also effectively demotes sex as a quality: Gender is all.

The insistence that gender is "constructed" is necessary in Foucauldian theory to justify the decoupling of sex and gender. But it turns out unsurprisingly to be almost impossible to prove that many aspects of gender are in fact constructed. Claiming that they are puts the onus of proof on those who would show this. Far better would be merely to make the distinction between a concept (here, masculinity) defined by contrast with another, and (on the other hand) a living individual. This makes unnecessary an assertion of "construction" but leaves open how much an individual should define (here) himself with respect to the absolute Other.

It's not only Hackbarth but also most men who see being masculine as being about doing. Masculinity is a code of action, which is why its worldview overlaps to such a degree with the conservative worldview. This is the reason there's such a strong compulsion for men to be conservative. According to men, the individual male's function is to pursue and achieve to the greatest degree possible the Absolute Action outside.

Male is to female as conservative is to liberal: The first terms of each of the analogies have a similar structure, as do the second terms. This means that femininity doesn't have the same structure as masculinity at all, which is why women are more likely than men to be liberal. Being a Smurf in a universe where living beings divided into Smurfs and Smarfs need not necessarily imply a rejection of Smarfs, only not being one of them. Being a woman isn't all about not being a man, whereas being a man is all about not being a woman. Being a woman in a universe that divides into masculine and feminine is taking what's left when the man has taken what he wants: Men define themselves, as a result, with respect to a structural negative. This is why men are the doers and women the be-ers, why the man is the one who gazes and the woman the one who feels herself in the man's gaze.

An important aspect of the masculinity that Hackbarth is describing is precisely awareness of masculinity as a thing to be cultivated, the goal of being opposite to the alternative part of the nature of masculinity. Metrosexuals may for some thinkers be just as valid a sort of man as cowboys. But they're not defining themselves against women. Cowboys would feel wounded (or punch you in the face with no fear of breaking a nail) if you suggested they weren't men, and metrosexuals would probably just shrug, or look at you puzzledly—or, in Hackbarth's telling, go back to talking about soap operas.

Hackbarth's man can fix things, he makes a woman's life easy (except that she might be expected to put all that food on the table), and he's paying attention to her rather than asking that she pay attention to him. The man is there to take care of things, including the woman. The man does all the heavy lifting, leaving the other stuff for women, the girlie stuff. When challenges arise, it's the man who has to rise to them. When someone knocks at the door, it's the man who goes. When it's the wolf, the man makes sure he stays away, or kills him. "My hero," sighs the woman safe inside.

Being a man, in Hackbarth's telling, is hell for the man and heaven for the woman. Only the woman can *be*, lounging at home in her negligee eating bonbons. The man, by contrast, *does*, going out to kill the wolf, or the mastodon, or staying at home to install the water heater. Being a man is hard work, and Hackbarth likes it that way. Men do, too, because we think we're being good men. Being masculine is a thing done, not a thing achieved. Men who like being men embrace the process, accept that we are the doers, not the be-ers.

Masculinity as an endless struggle is, in fact, the life most men know. It's rough. We spend our childhood identifying with our male role models, our adolescence rebelling against them, a few decades being someone else's male role model (if we're lucky), and then a few decades more being merely useless. It's not for nothing that Jack London's *Call of the Wild* was popular with a generation of boys: It shows in naked form the fact that only one wolf gets to lead the pack, a position he has wrested from an older one, in turn defending his hegemony against challengers with the full knowledge that one day he, too, will finally lose one of these fights and be bested. If you complain, you've lost the battle for your masculinity. Admitting weakness before the enemy, in this case other men, means you've accepted no longer being lead dog. The lead dog always says that things are "outstanding." Or perhaps growls menacingly. Or makes no noise at all, simply lunging forward once more in the traces.

Paradoxically, the "real" man, the one Hackbarth admires, is even more self-aware than the man who keeps checking his hair in the pitcher. But his currency is action, not talk—things done, not their appearance. Being a man, at least in the sense that Hackbarth imagines a man, involves a life of constantly shoring up the structure from within, plugging the dikes. Because the man is the one whose attention is focused on plugging the dikes as they spring leaks, his field of focus is circumscribed. He cannot concentrate on things beyond the dike; he waits for them to come to him. In this sense he is weakened; he can never see the big picture. Only women and liberals can see the big picture; this is the nature of their structure.

Sexual Identification and Control

One major unsolved problem for men, who carry the nodes of their individual worlds with them, is the relationship with other men. If you are an "army of one," as most men see themselves, how can you relate to another "army of one" except by fighting him? The flip side of this is what men call "bonding," the second-step alternative after the aggression that is primordial. (I have considered these two steps in greater detail in *Sexual Ethics*.) Men, at least in Hackbarth's sense, are intrinsically unitary, and can only relate to each other at the other extreme in bonding, the warm bath of sameness. Thus they are natural conservatives. You're either with them or against them. The demand that other men be hetrosexual is a way of achieving control over the world, something central to both the male and the conservative worldviews.

Most people fail to analyze sexual desire. We feel it and articulate it, but we don't ask why the desires are what they are. We see a woman, or a man, as attractive, perhaps visualizing what we want to do with or to that other person. If we ask, "Why do we sense what we do?" it seems our desires are related to the larger issue of what we want to do with whom. And this is what most of us understand by sexual orientation. Straight men, most of us would say, are those who would never consider, e.g., sucking another guy's dick, or be repulsed by the thought. But this gets the causality backward. In fact, "straight" is just the way we express the fact that they don't and wouldn't consider it. And to this, we can ask, "Why not?"

The answer is probably something like this: Men who are, individually, an army of one, are not typically willing to engage in a relationship of domination and submission such as sex with entities that are at the same level as they are themselves. Because this conceptualization of other men as fellow armies of one is so widespread, we have given a name to the fact that a large number of sexual situations are decided by it, one way or another. Saying that a man is "straight" is like a shorthand version of saying, he conceives of other men as being on his level in the power grid. You can be buddies with such entities, or the reverse, enemies. But you can't be involved in the complex symbiotic game of giving and taking power that is sex. Gay men are those who, by contrast, can be involved in such a game.

Such men want the assurance that other entities on the same level of the power grid see things the way they themselves do. Being heterosexual is thus something, I'd say, men are intrinsically more interested in for its own sake than women are, and for themselves rather than for women. It's common knowledge that straight men find lesbian sex arousing, if the two women are women they themselves are attracted to. But having an assurance of another man's straightness allows men to predict that a being who looks like a man will act "like a man" as well. The man knows how things will unfold. If men who were not expected to act like a man clearly looked different in some

way, things would be at least predictable; this may be why a generation ago the only kind of homosexual recognized was the feminized
"nelly boy."

Research into attitudes toward homosexuality of the Greco-
Roman world has revealed solutions of other societies that are, if different in detail than ours, then at least seem similar in spirit. The
Greeks sang the praises of sexual relations between freeborn men and
freeborn adolescent boys, which had to end when the boys themselves
became mature, married, and presumably themselves began relationships with boys. Both the Greeks and Romans accepted that freeborn
men would, could and should be able to have their way with male and
female slaves. In relations between mature freeborn men, the "top"
was held to be the masculine one, the "bottom" the effeminate and
hence reprehensible one.[6]

Foucault

The single most influential thinker for our time on the subject of sexual definition has been Michel Foucault. Virtually all work on sexual
definition in the last several decades begins from his oft-repeated
claim that in the premodern world, people were not divided into types
based on their sexual practices, whereas in the modern world they
are.[7] What he apparently means is that men who had sex with men (as
we sometimes say nowadays, trying to move away from the seemingly
absolute modern categories of "homosexual" and "heterosexual") were
not for that reason a separate type of man. But from this we cannot
conclude there were no types in the classical world, only that their
types weren't quite the same as ours.

It's clear that we in the modern world are different in some ways.
Unlike the Greeks but like the Romans, we frown on men having
their way with teenage boys. Indeed, mainstream society tends to
frown on any male–male coupling, rather than focusing on who is a
"top" and who a "bottom," as the Romans did. But the reason we're
different is that our society has diluted the absoluteness of other types
of people that allowed the classical world to achieve the same predictability men seek nowadays as well. The problem posed by the modern

world for the male sexual map of antiquity is that, in something close to true democracy—a world without slaves, a world where adolescents aren't seen as entities of a different sort, and without the ingrained notion of hierarchy that made it all possible—the number of evidently differentiable categories available for sexual domination has been reduced to one: women. Feminism, according to some men, reduced even this last category to something smaller than it used to be.

In both the classical and the modern worlds, I'm suggesting, it's plausible to say that men want to know beforehand who is available for domination. The classical world allowed more types of such phallocratic self-assertion because it contained more absolute types of people. In a democracy, where each man is an "army of one," where each man must be treated with the respect that in a hierarchical society was reserved for those at the top of the heap—whether freeborn males in classical democracies or the king and nobility in the European monarchies—all men are equal. This means there are no groups that can be separated off *a priori* as available for sexual domination. In conservative thinking, indeed, people are not separated *a priori* into groups at all.

This doesn't mean that subgroup or one-on-one negotiation for such relationships can't go on under the radar. Having something as a default doesn't mean it has to be observed all the time. But in a world where each man is assumed to be a self-sufficient top dog, the only thing that another top dog can offer is initially hostility perhaps leavened with wary respect, or jumping across the quantum leap, if circumstances allow it, to what we call "male bonding"—where the erotic charge is, so to speak, stirred through the relationship, and so is diluted to the point where it can never be expressed in specific actions: it informs, instead, the whole relationship.[8]

The last gasp of state-sanctioned slavery in the West, that of the American South, took place during a period of otherwise widespread democracy: For this reason, I suggest, we hear a good deal about Southern slave owners having sexual relations with their female slaves, but, unlike slaveowners in the classical world, very little if anything about relations with their male ones. Though an anachronistic subsociety, it was still part of the modern world and influenced by it.

Nowadays all men are considered as being members of the classical category of freeborn adult males.

Thus I propose that the question of who's gay and who's straight is quintessentially a male question. It arises because our world, unlike the classical world, doesn't have the clear types of other people that would make such questions unnecessary. Sexual definition is an outgrowth of the power position we assign ourselves, and of what power position we assign others. It isn't "object choice" that's the criterion of the definition of straightness, as Eve Sedgwick and many others influenced by her have claimed, saying that a man is heterosexual if he wants to have sex only with women.[9]

Object choice isn't very helpful. Saying that 100 percent of a man's sexual partners are women still doesn't tell us much about his sexual partners, only the ones who aren't his sexual partners. We still can't tell if he'll want this woman, or that, or what his "type" is. It's not telling whom he'll want that's the point of speaking of sexual orientation, only telling whom he won't want. And this is the point for men of certifying another man's heterosexuality.

No man is attracted to all women, except perhaps Don Juan, who, in Mozart's opera, had a compliment for every size, shape, and age of female. And that fact was what makes him so strange: He seems to have wanted The Female, not specific women. Most men do have a "type" they're attracted to. Evidently not Don Giovanni. To say that a man wants to have sex only with women doesn't mean all women. He can't know when he meets a woman whether or not she'll be his type at all. Sometimes he'll want a woman who isn't his type, or he may not have figured out yet what his type might be.

Even if 100 percent of the people a man wants to have sex with are women, this doesn't explain why he is drawn to a certain type of woman, or why someone he has regarded without registering her (probably because she belongs to a "forbidden" category, such as women under our protection, daughters or relatives or women we have to obey—the boss, for example) can suddenly change status and become a possible sexual object.

Thus the problem with using object choice as the criterion of sexual definition is there's nothing permanent about sexual attraction to our object choices. One day, after some decades of marriage, the husband realizes he's no longer attracted to the wife, and starts playing around. Or he may marry a trophy wife. Alternately, we can work around someone comfortably for years without having a sexual thought regarding that person. One day, for reasons we cannot explicate, we "see" him or her differently, as sexual, interesting, and suddenly available. This sometimes happens when a woman we have seen only in a uniform takes down her hair, puts on makeup and a short skirt. Suddenly we are interested.

Being straight is not primarily about a relationship with women, but with other men. It's about acknowledging other armies of one to be such. Men want to get their relationships with other men into the predictable zone. The need to do this may be more intense because a man can't determine his relationship with all women the way he can, by enforcing a demand of straightness from men, determine his relationships with men. Some women are unattractive to him, some are attractive but off limits, and some are so completely off limits he never asks himself whether they are attractive or not.

Men act. They throw themselves into the void relentlessly, moment after moment, day after day. It's merciless, bruising, fun, and wearing, all at once. Men don't mind playing the game if everyone has to play it; in fact, it's exhilarating. But men are constantly making sure that other men are playing it, and not getting away with something. You're on your own, buddy. No pairing up. That's not fair. To straight men, it seems as if gay men are getting away with something. What the straight ones express is their disdain of the gay ones. But at the heart of this is a certain degree of envy.

This is consistent with, rather than contradicted by, the fact that nowadays many more straight men are accepting of gay men. It's only when straight men see gay men as an imperfect version of themselves that their attitude becomes one of scorn. If gay men are simply another category, that's the way it is—they do things their way; there is neither a threat nor a sense that "we" have to change "them." Modern straight men can have gay friends and not be bothered by this fact.

But the straight men who achieve this acceptance do so by delineating a separate category of men, as in the classical world. Foucault may not like there being a separate category for "heterosexuals" and another for "homosexuals," but in fact these categories are just what let each side accept the differences of the other side. Being a straight man means being condemned to fighting other men, or making peace with them, and competing for women. It's an edgy position: It's hard work, and it leads to physical damage and early death. It's only tolerable if everybody who looks like us has to be there. Otherwise it doesn't seem fair that we should do it. It's only when we make a separate category of men not subject to the same rules that straight men can cease to make the same demands of gay men.

None of this chapter will convince a conservative determined not to let go of his or her conviction that we may not arrive at the conclusion that homosexual acts are anything but forbidden. My very means of considering the subject is liberal, not merely the conclusion. It's losing sight of that fact that leads to our culture wars.

5

CONFLICT OF WORLDVIEWS

The Conservative Void

There's nothing in the conservative structure between the individual and the external action he or she is aiming to achieve. Weirdly echoing existentialists such as Sartre, conservatives insist we are primordially free because we can always "just say no." They do not, indicatively, claim we can "just say yes." Our only power is refusal.

What this means is not that limitations don't exist, only that they can't be generalized and calcified. They're absolutely individual. Nor does it mean we always achieve the Absolute Action we're aiming at, or even that we necessarily want to. Conservatives are well aware that there may be reasons why we wouldn't want to do the right thing. All these things are lumped together under the rubric of "temptations" or "weaknesses." We just have to try to overcome them. As the Marine Corps T-shirt I sometimes see in the weight room has it, "Pain Is Weakness Leaving the Body." Denying that they're there doesn't have to be accurate; it's a rhetorical ploy to make them seem less daunting. What we say can be part of the action. Whether or not it's true in some objective, removed-from-the-fray way is secondary.

Because conservatism is a thing done rather than a thing said, conservatives tend to conceive of everyone, including liberals, as being primarily doers rather than sayers. Hence what for liberals is the odd use of "lifestyle" in the phrase "homosexual lifestyle," the way conservatives refer to people whose sex is with people of the same sex. For most gays and lesbians, the sort of person you have sex with doesn't determine your lifestyle. There are promiscuous gays and boringly domestic ones.

Conservatives insist that sexuality, and virtually everything else, is a "choice" as a way of saying that in their worldview there's no way to codify constraints. To liberals, it seems as if conservatives are simply denying facts when they insist that everyone is an individual and people are free to choose their actions. People with no education or a skin color that has made them the object of racial prejudice, liberals will point out, will not be able to "choose" their action in the way someone without these impediments may well be able to. But there is no fight once it is clear that both are asserting different things. There is deep-structural divergence.

Liberalism, for example, may insist that college applicants who are black (or African-American, as we say puzzlingly nowadays, mixing a passport with a continent of origin to create what is really a physical description: Do we distinguish these from, e.g., African-French? African-Haitian? Arab-African-American? White South African-American?) may legitimately be given advantages that their fellow applicants who are white do not get. The liberal accepts that rules will be about groups, since that is the form that liberal ethics takes.

From the perspective of liberal thought, saying that people may well be disadvantaged because they are, e.g., black and/or poor, is merely summarizing what we know to be true. It's summarizing a probability. Because conservatives operate in a worldview that contains only two units—at one end, the unit of the individual and, at the other, that of the Absolute Action—they interpret this causally, believing the liberals to be saying that because someone is black, he or she will always be disadvantaged. To make things more confusing, liberals (usually reacting against conservatives) are sometimes saying just this—assuming that because a person is a member of a certain group, the person has certain qualities and must be treated in a certain way.

For the conservative, a single case of "misclassification," a person ostensibly in group X who doesn't have the qualities that produced the notion of this group to begin with, is enough to show the whole enterprise is flawed. One "Welfare Queen" (President Reagan's favorite example) is enough for conservatives to demand that the whole welfare program be scrapped. For liberals, it only has to be more or less true that, e.g., black people have been disadvantaged to turn around and attempt to give advantages to all black people. If we give preferential treatment to all black college applicants and only most of them in any way need or merit it, that's fine with liberals because the ethics were expressed in terms of groups, not individuals. The whole thing seems a general step forward. For the same reason, liberals typically approve of social programs that target groups: It only has to be more beneficial than not to most of the members, not absolutely beneficial to each one. Conservatives see programs based on such groupings as intrusions in the postulated void between the unit of the individual and the Absolute Action.

Ping-Pong Balls

Individuals for conservatives are ping-pong balls with hard shells. The area around them is simply empty; this means you can fill it any way you like—it's up to you. Liberals lack this already-determined shell. For liberals, the definition of who they are involves precisely figuring out their relationships to others. Filling the space around the individual defines that individual, which lacks the ping-pong ball-like shell. It's precisely what people have to talk about; it's not a trivial thing, left to individual whim. It's the very nature of ethics. And so liberals set about to fill this space with postulations of groups, probabilities, trends, and the facticity of life. This is part of figuring out who they are. Conservatives don't have anything to figure out. For this reason both liberals and conservatives are right when they say they privilege the individual.

Because conservative ethics leaves empty the space between the individual and the Absolute Action, it's trivial how that space is filled—which means, it's up to the individual. Nor does the particular fill-in have to be justified. Liberals will ask for justification for such fill-ins, because the nature of their ethics is precisely to regulate relations in this part of the structure. Because liberal ethics are general rules, and these general rules define the relationships between individuals, a diehard liberal will insist that there's no more reason for me to defend my own child than to defend someone else's child. Personal relations in the liberal worldview are replaced by generalizations about subgroups of people. What, liberals ask, justifies me giving preference to members of my family over strangers? All should be treated alike.

For a conservative, it is both ludicrous and pernicious to say I do not have any greater justification for defending, e.g., my own wife and children than someone else's wife and children. Indeed, defense of our particular turf is a hallmark of conservative thinking—and male thought. For the conservative, there is simply no reason not to acknowledge these concentric circles going outwards from the "me." This is so because the locus of conservative ethics is elsewhere completely, in the action that each person must aim at attaining.

Yet this means that devotion to the rings around each of us isn't an intrinsic part of the conservative worldview, only a corollary. To conservatives, liberals are infringing on conservatives' liberty by drawing ethically binding relationships between people. For conservatives, they're part of the realm of the unregulated, which is labeled personal choice. So long as I refrain from, e.g., committing adultery (an Absolute "Thou shalt not" Action), I am free to give a job to my own son over someone else's son. No rules about specific individuals exist, only the general ones. And it goes without saying that I will defend my own family.

This corollary in conservative thought—that if the area around me isn't regulated, I can do with it as I alone choose—is ultimately the source of the conservative devotion to gun ownership. A poster seen frequently around the U.S. Naval Academy says smugly, "Gun Control Means Hitting Your Target." Conservative devotion to guns does not arise because the "right to bear arms" is "guaranteed in the Constitution." Conservatives make so much of the "right to bear arms" in Amendment II of the Bill of Rights because they want the guns, and of course reject the clear suggestion of the Constitution that this is to be in the context of a regulated militia. They are completely uninterested in liberals arguing that if everyone has guns the homicide rates go up. Such attempts to create generalizations in the area between the individual and the Absolute Action are simply foreign to them, and must be repulsed.

If conservatives didn't want the guns, this amendment would go as unremarked as, e.g., Amendment VIII prohibiting excessive bail. Indeed, being "in the Constitution" hardly suffices to create conservative devotion for something. Amendment I prohibiting any "law respecting the establishment of religion" is one that many conservatives might like to see disappear. Conservatives make so much of this particular amendment because they feel liberals are trying to regulate their actions as individuals, trying to insert ethics into a realm where there are no general rules, and where as a result each individual is free to do as he or she chooses.

The reason conservatives are, so to say, up in arms about this issue is that the liberals have made it one by, as the conservatives see it, threatening them. The threat would be at least as strong if it were against any other aspect of their lives not regulated by the Absolute Actions they seek to attain. But guns hold a special place in the conservative heart because conservatives can imagine themselves holding a hostile world at bay with them, protecting their own women and children. What may have been reality on the frontier correlates to the conservative worldview, and so is defended even now.

Conservatives, therefore, feel that liberals are out to take away their freedoms. This is so for structural reasons. For conservatives, ethics is not a codification of the area between individuals, but a linking of each discrete individual to the external Absolute Action. It's paradoxical, therefore, that liberals feel in return that conservatives are out to limit personal freedoms as well. For instance, by reaching into the bedroom when they demand that everyone have sex in certain ways, or not have it—which for liberals is tantamount to threatening personal liberty.

For conservatives, however, this is merely ensuring that everyone does the external Absolute Action. The reason liberals want to regulate guns is quite different: It's not because it's immoral to own guns, but rather for practical reasons, horizontal justifications rather than vertical ones. If liberals produced a Holy Writ that said it was immoral to own guns, conservatives would certainly understand the logic. They would of course resist it, in the same way that claims for rival Holy Writs from, e.g., Muslims always infuriate evangelical Christians. But at least they would hear the same language they are used to. Liberal reasoning, that having guns leads to more murders and so on, does not seem to conservatives to be part of an ethical framework at all, and so not amenable to regulation.

You won't leave a seminar on liberal ethics knowing what to do, just knowing how to discuss or think about what to do. To conservatives, this means liberals have no ethics because they don't have ethics of the "Thou shalt not" sort, and are confirmed yakkers to boot. And so they are, because this is necessary for describing the landscape between particular individuals. Conservative ethics is utterly uninterested in this landscape, except as something to be filled with personal choice. It's part of the no-man's-land between the individual and the Absolute Action. Conservatives don't see the point of liberal yak-yak, so essential a part of the undertaking to liberals. To conservatives, it's all just hot air.

Do Unto Others

Just as the backbone of conservative ethics is always an absolute rule for action, typically a "Thou shalt" or, even better from the conservative point of view, a "Thou shalt not," so the backbone of liberal ethics is some form of the golden rule. Thus thinkers as diverse as Jesus, Kant, and John Rawls make it the centerpiece of things. Instead of telling us what to do and what not to do, which is the form conservative ethics takes, the golden rule couches what it enjoins in terms of the actor. We are to think of other people as if they were ourselves, and do to them what we would have them do to us. At least this is the liberal point of departure: the result may well be the person decides he or she is unable to do this. But at least he or she tried.

All such liberal talk produces is, as always, conservative exasperation. Liberals may find conservatives incomprehensible or threatening, but they do not find them exasperating. For conservatives, by contrast, liberals are in the way: They talk to no purpose about irrelevant things (like guns leading to more murders), and prevent conservatives from doing what needs to be done. Conservatives resent the fact that they must over and over shake off the yipping dogs of liberals. They begrudge the time and effort it takes to beat them off.

The sophisticated communitarian (conservative) thinker Amitai Etzioni proposes a "new golden rule" in his book of that title.[1] His golden rule is a compromise between what for my purposes are the givens of liberal thought and those of conservative thought. Paraphrased in my terms, it's that liberals and conservatives should treat each other as they would wish to be treated. In Etzioni's formulation, playing off between the conflict between liberty and order (prime values, respectively, according to Etzioni, for liberals and conservatives), it's this: "respect and uphold society's moral order as you would have society respect and uphold your autonomy to live a full life."

Etzioni can sketch this fusion because he sees each side from the point of view of the other. Liberals only stress liberty, for Etzioni their primary defining characteristic, when they're trying to say why they're not conservative. Conservatives only stress order, which is comparably central for Etzioni in understanding the other group, when they're trying to say what they have and the others lack.

Etzioni's fusion is as plausible as it is because it's aimed at liberals, using their currency of talk. He's responding to a situation he perceives where we have drifted in the direction of too-great liberty. He's trying to reassure liberals that they can trust conservatives. A comparable attempt to move conservatives toward liberals is not likely to succeed. It would ask that conservatives accept that their absolutist views admit of being adopted in percentages rather than wholesale. This won't happen for the simple reason that wholesale adoption is the nature of absolutist thought. This is why someone like John Rawls, with his attempt to show that logic demands everyone should be treated equally—in *A Theory of Justice* and its spin-off works—met such opposition from communitarians.

An attempt to derail the sex-ed curriculum of Montgomery County, Maryland, in suburban Washington, D.C., led by a Mormon mother of four named Michelle Turner, offers an example of a less sophisticated attempt than Etzioni's to use liberal givens to argue for conservatism.[2] It in turn echoes the confrontations taking place across America on the subject of teaching evolution.

The county's curriculum has as one of its goals to "foster discussions of homosexuality, portraying same-sex attraction as natural and involuntary for gay people, as something that is common and acceptable." In response, Turner and her fellow members of "Citizens for a Responsible Curriculum" say, as the *Washington Post* summarizes their position, that "science has not proved that homosexuality is genetic, that more likely it's a choice." And the *Post* summarizes their reaction, "that the curriculum ought to present their beliefs, as well, and that students should be taught that it is possible to avoid, or to get out of, the gay lifestyle." Turner is quoted as calling the curriculum's view of homosexuality "unbalanced" and "one-sided."

This encapsulates neatly the asymmetry of the two positions, liberal and conservative. For conservatives, here represented by Turner, any position that fails to valorize his or her own will be "unbalanced." There's no such thing as a meta-position that is somehow neutral, the claim of liberals, who say: "We teach only science; belief is up to you at home." If science contradicts belief, then science has to be opposed. It's simply come up with the wrong answer. This seems ludicrous to liberals, and completely reasonable to conservatives. Science believes it's proved that evolution is the correct explanation; this doesn't stop the creationists from saying, "If your end result isn't my end result, you have to teach mine, too."

Liberals point out that this view has already been considered in the process of arriving at a scientific bottom line, and rejected as lacking evidence. At this point those whose view has been rejected reject the claim that only things that have adequate evidence are true, or should be accepted: Saying that this is a necessary condition is a "bias."

Let's say Turner achieves her ostensible purpose of having the view that homosexuality is a "lifestyle" choice taught "alongside" whatever it is that science offers. Why should Turner accept that her children be taught half the time that homosexuality is inherited and that the "gay lifestyle" is not a "choice"? Half the time is better than none, but it's still not as good as all the time. Absolutisms are just that: absolute. They don't admit of being reduced; they can't, and still retain their viability. Indeed, Turner objects to having any teaching about homosexuality. She evokes the standard conservative devotion to purpose in knowing what to do: "As far as the homosexual issue goes, our bodies are not meant or created to be used in that way." A liberal would say, that's Turner's belief; she's entitled to it, but don't force it on others. Turner would presumably say it's the truth. And that means the truth for everyone, not just for her.

Advantage/Disadvantage

Each worldview has certain intrinsic disadvantages. In a world where each worldview must accommodate itself to the other, the slack created by the disadvantages of one worldview is taken over by the other. This is what I conceive of as a healthy situation, or at least one that bodes well for the future of American democracy. In a world where each goes its separate way, by contrast, each may well produce what I call a calcified version of itself, an extreme. Calcified versions of both worldviews have produced the current American culture wars.

The disadvantage of the conservative worldview is that, with its rules expressed in terms of actions, it does not have any means of integrating differences between individuals within its framework in a nontrivial way. Indeed, typically it denies difference, since the individuality of the person acting is of no importance with respect to the outside action: Everyone can do as he or she likes, so long as everybody achieves the Absolute Action. Because its worldview lacks a space to put a concept of the group in theory, this is replaced with a heavy reliance on the group in fact, things like individual family, town, football team, religious beliefs, or nation.

The result is that conservatives form subgroups like the military as a whole, or the Naval Academy in particular, where they can live among like-minded people and express their conservatism by what they do rather than what they say. This isn't saying that there are a priori groups of people, as the liberal may say: It's saying this is the only kind of people. Outside are only barbarians.

A world of people constantly ensuring conformity to a common code, such as the Naval Academy, is the calcified form of conservatism.

The disadvantage of this world is that there are no different drummers to march to; someone not marching with the rest of the brigade, the student and military body, is simply out of step, and will be hounded until he or she gives in or gives up. This is the aspect of conservative thought that liberal thought sees as proto-fascist, a world where everyone does the same thing, a world with no room for difference.

The disadvantage of liberalism is that it doesn't tell people what to do. Liberal thought is a grid like the lines on graph paper—or, in another analogy, the metal grating sometimes laid over areas where people want to walk but where the caretakers still want grass to grow: The people walk on the raised grating, and the grass grows between the squares, almost covering it. Liberal thought sets up the rules for action, the grid, but not what's inside them. The holes in the grid remain to be filled. For liberals, individuals function like patrons of a library. Each person may choose a different book; the only concern of the system is that they check them out, refrain from talking, and so on. These things constitute the liberal grid, operating like a traffic light that all must respect.

Democracy, a self-consciously artificial form of government that prizes stability over other goals, will of necessity be a grid, and hence a liberal structure. Yet within that liberal structure people will be free to hold to their absolutisms, so long as the grid always trumps any particular absolutism. This necessity is the source of the eternal dissension that is the hallmark of democracy, and the reason why we will never achieve the consensus that some people hold out as its goal.

Because liberal ethics does not tell people what to do, a conservative is left scratching his or her head, and probably finding the result very messy indeed, not to mention frustratingly imprecise. That's the fill-in-the-grid aspect of liberal thought. It's exemplified by the notion in the United States Declaration of Independence that one of mankind's fundamental rights is something this document calls the "pursuit of happiness." It purposely leaves out telling us what this happiness should be, or how we are to pursue it. Indeed, the implication is that there may be as many kinds of happiness, and as many pursuits, as there are individuals.

In the image of the graph paper, the squares remain to be filled, but in absolute terms, they are quite small. Thus there is no entry possible for large squares, individual absolutisms, and the absolutisms that remain will have to limit themselves severely. They are allowed to flourish, but only if they agree to cover only a small amount of ground. Their edges are, so to say, ground down.

To a degree, this grinding down the edges is what has happened to religion in America, at least until recently. People still interact and work with and greet one another, though they go to different houses of worship. People respect, as we say, others' rights to worship as they choose; the rest of life is unaffected by the particular choice of a house of worship. Religion doesn't end up, we might say, really mattering; it's a matter of personal choice on the order of whether to wear a black or brown suit.

But this is precisely what changes when a single absolutism senses the wearing away of its edges and refuses to accept it, the situation on the current American scene.

Conservative Excess

If one absolutism grows up stronger than the rest, as American Christian conservatism has done—America has no internal form of extremist Islam, or militant Hinduism —liberalism will find itself in the position of having to limit it. We might think of introducing other expansionist absolutisms to curb the one we have, as James Madison might suggest (*Federalist Papers 51*), but what if they proliferate in their turn and eat everything else up? What will we introduce then? And this limitation by the system will of necessity be perceived, as by Michelle Turner, considered above, as an affront to the givens of the absolutism. As of course it will be. There is no way out of this paradox, no way that honeyed, nuanced tones such as we hear from intellectuals such as Etzioni or Rawls can create a unity where in fact there is asymmetry.

Any given conservatism can live quite well within democracy, until it begins to dwell upon the fact of its intrinsic limitation, the persistent itch, inexplicable in the conservative worldview itself, of the fact that there are things not mentioned in the worldview that clearly exist. There is no intrinsic contradiction, for a conservative, in the fact that the notoriously conservative Ayatollah Khoumeni lived for years in Paris, home to a good number of Western vices. The structure of Western democracy is a liberal structure, which allows many conservatisms to flourish within it. Yet while they are within it, they must sense themselves to be biding their time, for while they are in the West, the one condition they may not break is the condition that they accept being only one of many absolutisms. And this means, accepting the yoke of the liberal overstructure.

Accepting the intrinsically paradoxical state of relative absolutism means compartmentalizing the influence of the absolutism. You can go to any church you want, but you have to accept the lineup of churches that will result. For most conservatives, living in a democracy means adopting a constant low profile, accepting hypocrisy. For if what they say is true, why is everyone not doing it too?

For the Ayatollah, the West must have felt like a tree nursery: It was fertile soil, but being part of a lineup was constraining. How he must have despised this decadent West, nurturing him in his exile without understanding that one day he would rise and slay it! In the case of the Ayatollah, in order to grow any bigger, he had to leave the neat rows of different plants and go somewhere where he could be the only one.

From the perspective of any given absolutism, those absolutisms that have agreed to the grid are in some sense toothless. The Ayatollah Khoumeni would certainly never have accepted to willingly live out his life in Parisian exile, his world-covering view transformed, in Paris, into one more flavor to make the capital city "exotic" and "culturally rich." This is the way liberals conceive of the world, which is why there is some justice in the conservative charge, articulated in the Introduction, by Krauthammer, that liberals think everyone is a "nice person."

There is no way to say merely by looking at a conservative structure operating in the context of a liberal democracy whether it will be a "good citizen" and play by the rules of that democracy, or whether it will attempt to expand and take over the show. A theocracy within the American framework, e.g., an enclave of orthodox Jews in the

Catskills, or one of the now-defunct Shaker communities, is not structurally different from a theocracy that opposes American democracy from without, e.g., fundamentalist Islam. The two domestic theocracies mentioned, in fact, really only want or wanted to be left alone. In this sense they are "good citizens."

Indeed, most American conservatives are "good citizens." They place their allegiance first of all in the system of which they are a part, and only secondarily in their conservative structure. They're liberals at the most general level and conservatives at all others. American conservatives get hot under the collar when liberals place them in the same continuum with Islamic fundamentalism and Adolf Hitler. Usually liberals only reach for this most extreme comparison when tempers are running high. It never fails to get the attention of conservatives, and their goat: It's not that the comparison is invalid for reasons X, Y, and Z. It's that the comparison itself causes problems. Once again the two worldviews are shown to be asymmetrical.

A recent example of conservative indignation at liberals pointing out their conservatism was that of the alleged 2002 jibe by Germany's then-Justice Minister Hertha Däubler-Gmelin comparing the Bush administration's tactic of vilifying a foreign regime before attacking it to Hitler's demonizing of Poland before his attack on that unhappy country.[3] For liberals, it seems legitimate to be able to separate out some of Hitler's actions and identify them with policies of a U.S. president. For conservatives, pushing the Hitler button is like pushing the Jesus button: It's absolute and implies all of the qualities of the individual in question, not just some of them. "Hitler" functions as a public entity in the same way "Jesus" does: The point isn't analysis, it's invoking the public show of respect or vilification.

This use of proper names as opportunities for public exhibitions of approval or disapproval is a feature of conservative thought, whose currency is action in the public sphere. In the same way that it's impossible to be a little bit pregnant, for conservatives it's impossible to be a little bit like Hitler. In the same way, you don't reason about Jesus, because the very name is a public absolute. For liberals, this seems tantamount to stupidity, this inability (as they see it) to make finer distinctions, to separate out individual qualities.

The German minister wasn't saying that President Bush was setting up death camps or operating on prisoners. Being in the same continuum doesn't mean all things that are part of this continuum are identical.

The conservative worldview is intrinsically without nuances, given the nature of action in the world. To convey a public message you either stand up to support the speaker or sit down to show your lack of support; there's no time or room for lengthy explanations of in-between positions. That's why conservatives after the initial United States invasion of Iraq were so angry at liberals who questioned George W. Bush, a "war president." Doing so, some hold, is tantamount to giving aid and comfort to the enemy.

Liberals point out that, if conservatives were to engineer things so that suddenly they were in power (Adolf Hitler was after all democratically elected), nothing in the conservative worldview would prevent them from trying to impose that view on the world. What liberals want from conservatives in these circumstances is an explicit renunciation of the absolutist nature of their worldview. Of course, that isn't something conservatives can offer. Doing so would mean they would cease to be conservatives.

Even an assurance from conservatives that "Oh no! *We* wouldn't impose our views on other people!" would of necessity be external to the conservative worldview itself. And what kind of assurance would be assurance enough for frightened liberals? An assurance from conservatives that they wouldn't make people do something they didn't want to do would of necessity ring hollow, since it would be offered only by certain individuals and could be rescinded at any time. Liberals would point out that it could be an assurance from the wolf that it was only a lamb, as liberal commentators saw the preelection assurances of the Bush administration of 2000 to 2004, in order the better to grab power, at which time the pretense could be thrown off.

Liberals might accept as reassurance a conservative assertion of adherence to the tenet that, even though voluntary conversions might be the goal, there was no value (theological or otherwise) in forced conversions. Orthodox Judaism, for example, is utterly uninterested

in converting Christians. But even if this particular group of conservatives sincerely believed there was no value in forced conversions,
who's to say where the limit would be drawn on "encouragement" to
make the conversions voluntary? Or that their successors would feel
the same way? This would seem to be saying that though the Absolute Action is valid for everyone, actually it isn't. Such a position is
consistent only if the Absolute Action is only valid for X sort of people (chosen, good, enlightened).

In its more tolerant phases, Islam renounced conversion by the
sword. Yet in domains controlled by Islam, it was perfectly clear that
non-Muslims were second-class citizens; Islam was the only true
faith. In a similar way, the Catholic Church under John Paul II reiter-
ated that ecumenical gestures stopped short of saying that there were
other versions of truth than that of the Catholic faith.

Still, there is nothing impelling conservatisms to expand in the way
the Ayatollah expanded his own. They can equally well live side by
side and abide by the traffic light. The question has been hotly
debated whether Islam is capable of giving up its demands for control
of secular law, or even of making distinction between secular and
sacred law. Is there such a thing theoretically as liberal Islam? The
answer surely is that if Christianity can do it, Islam can do it too. But
will it do so? The question itself seems off-kilter, implying that it's
Islam itself that will change. It's always people who change.

By the same token, there is nothing in an absolutist, or conservative, structure that guarantees or even makes probable peaceful coex-
istence with a relativist one. In this sense, the relativist is right to be
afraid. Still, a conservatism, for reasons peculiar to itself, not as part of
its conservative essence, may come to terms with the liberal overstructure. As I suggested above, it may realize that it is bound to remain
weak, and so needs protection against other conservatisms. Or it may
reason that even if it managed to take over for a time, it would be perennially defending its position—rather as if Macbeth had been able to
turn away from being king, and so avoid all the bloodshed his ambi-
tion caused both himself and those around him. Or, when it accepts
being part of Western democracy, it may simply have decided that
things are better if it does.

There's always the danger that hot-headed younger members of the group will see the compromises made by the older generation in the name of realism as pusillanimous and call for a new commitment to whatever their faith might be. This possibility is written into the conservative worldview.

Currently we see evangelical Christianity flexing its muscle on the American scene, as if newly awakened to the delicious possibility that if it only pushes forward it may win. What would make expansionist conservatism slow down in America is the realization that it has no way of communicating with other expansionist conservatisms save through force, and if this cannot be limited to the world outside, it may not be the best choice. There is after all a point to the "let's talk about this first" attitude of liberals. It's not just spinelessness—as conservatives are convinced is the case.

Liberal Excess

For traffic to flow and people to stay alive, everyone, even people in a hurry, have to agree to stop at a red light. In order to live with each other, conservatives and liberals must acknowledge, as a good independent of either worldview, that neither side should aim at the extermination of the other.

Liberal thought has a greater affinity with the traffic light than conservative thought does. After all, democracy is a liberal structure. But in order to have a point, traffic lights presuppose cars going somewhere that the traffic light doesn't regulate. Sometimes the traffic light forgets this. The result is what is frequently the liberal lack of sympathy with the point of view of the drivers of the cars, who must perceive the traffic light not as a necessary regulator they should be thankful for, but only as an impediment, especially when it is red. And when it is green, it is redundant.

Liberalism thus may seem to suspicious conservatives to have a strong tendency, if unchecked, to achieve its extreme form. To the extent that liberalism moves toward its logical extreme, it becomes increasingly intolerant of the absolutisms within the relativist grid. In this extreme form, liberals allow nothing with the structure of absolutism to enter the liberal grid, so tightly spaced are the lines of the grid. Intolerance for absolutisms within the grid means that liberals treat less than respectfully the conservative groups whose very existence is supposed to be ensured by the existence of the grid. Calcified or extreme liberalism in practice will not merely insist on the freedom of religion envisioned in the United States Constitution, but demand that only secular humanism is defensible.

In practice, what this means is that liberal thought edging toward its extreme tends to find any extensive religious belief somewhat distasteful, perhaps a bit lower class, or at least eccentric. Conservatives are not wrong to sense that liberals not only want to take away their SUVs, but wish they wouldn't carry on so much about how the good Lord put them where they are (if that place is, e.g., in the White House), makes their victories, and generally engineers their success. The good Lord apparently is never responsible for their less glorious moments. Calcified liberalism ends up telling people many things they must do or say: be politically correct, let people have any kind of sex they want, let people kill their unborn children. For liberals, by contrast, it's conservatives who are the great controllers, fulminating with "Thou shalt nots."

In theory, extreme liberals should be brought back out of the extreme territory faster than conservatives, and with a guiltier conscience. A grid is a grid; it's made of two kinds of elements, the overstructure and the undefined spaces between the honeycombs. Liberalism has built into it an acknowledgement of an element alien to it, even if individual liberals, being after all only human, would be just as happy to deny the existence of the other worldview.

If reminded that they are merely the grid that's supposed to allow such things as conservatives who accept Jesus Christ as their Personal Savior, liberals would probably accept that this is so. Conservatives, by contrast, have no natural impetus to be called back to order by someone pointing out that they have succeeded in converting everyone to their point of view, or that they are in the position to do so should they wish. This seems like a blessing from their God, or the way things were supposed to be. Getting along is more of a virtue for liberals than it is for conservatives.

Academia

In an extreme-liberal grid, everyone will think the same way, because they will never be far from one of the wickets of the grid. This is the current situation in much of American academia, which has become just as one-note as the conservative–fascist world it imagines lurking outside.

One form that liberal theories pushed to their extreme takes is the academic love of theories that emphasize "subversion" and celebrate the marginalized. This instinctive love of outsiders and those who challenge authority informs what courses are taught, and what is taught in those courses. "Winners" and those in power are, students are taught, suspect; only outsiders are worthy of interest and respect. In this counterintuitive assertion of intellectual if not real power, liberal thought has tied itself into a self-referential knot. In order to prove something that's clearly untrue, namely that its version of things reflects the world, it piles on the words explaining, explaining, explaining, excoriating the opposition, proving to the choir once more that it's right to come to church. American academia talks to itself within a liberal bubble, and so has largely cut itself off from the reality of American life, which includes another worldview.

At the same time, interestingly enough, academia has recently become interested in the same products of consumer society as everyone else, with Princess Diana and Barbie dolls near the top of the interest list. The posture is one of moral superiority. I'm reading this trash novel to analyze it. In fact, it's being read because it's a guilty pleasure. Academia is interested in movie stars for the same reason everybody else is. Movie stars are pretty.

The language of the liberal bubble around American humanities disciplines for many decades took the form of deconstructionism. Most conservatives couldn't bring themselves to read the work of Jacques Derrida, its founding father—and probably would not have made much of it if they had, and so never understood its intellectual interest. Instead, "deconstruction" as used by conservatives didn't refer to a specific theoretical school or movement, but typically became a synonym for anything liberals do. According to conservatives, this is: deconstruct rather than construct; pick at the people actually doing something; leave a mess instead of offering a viable alternative.

The reaction of one military commentator to an article of mine suggesting that *On War*, the masterpiece of the Prussian theorist Carl von Clausewitz, didn't function very well as a foundational document for courses in strategy, was that I was engaging in just such snide "deconstructionist" debunking.[4] What, he demanded, did I propose to put up in its place? I had to laugh out loud at the suggestion that what I'd done bore the slightest similarity to the works of Derrida. But that isn't the way this responder was using the word—and his way is something we see repeated again and again. In his mind, I had to be one of those deconstructionists he'd heard about who destroyed what others had spent so long constructing.

You always need a foundational document: If you don't like ours, give me yours. This at least is how conservatives think. My point was precisely that we didn't need a foundational document for strategy courses and in any case Clausewitz wasn't a good candidate. This was apparently unthinkable as a serious solution.

For conservatives, debunking something without proposing a substantive alternative is the height of folly: We always have to have an absolute set of actions to aim at. For liberals, pulling down the statues is an end in itself. This produces the situation where there is no overarching absolute structure. The insistence of the French thinker Jean-François Lyotard that "there is no master narrative" was a quintessentially liberal insistence, one guaranteed to make liberals sit up and cheer and conservatives froth at the mouth.[5] (When statues were actually pulled down in, e.g., Iraq, it was largely American conservatives who cheered. I consider later the paradox that people who are conservative in the American context express this by demanding that a liberal structure be imposed by force on the outside.)

For conservatives, lack of a "master narrative" is tantamount to a world without a rudder. The louder the conservatives yelled, however, the better the deconstructionists liked it. This gave liberals more things to deconstruct; if they were making the conservatives scream, they had achieved their goal.

Still, even though most conservatives had never read a word of Derrida, they weren't wrong that deconstructionism was intrinsically more enthusiastic about pulling down statues rather than erecting them. Deconstructionist thought exhibits the quintessential liberal preference for words rather than actions. Its words are its actions. Conservatives weren't wrong either that there's something annoying about it. It assumes that it alone gets to keep its back to the wall. To everyone else it has a response. It rolls its eyes while the opponent talks, then sets about analyzing what has been said. It always gets the last word.

Such thought has a long pedigree in Western thought, starting perhaps with Socrates' insistence that he was only a gadfly, a tiny insect that could do no more than annoy the larger bovine creatures, and that he knew that he knew nothing. Deconstructionist thought at its most interesting, as precisely in the writings of Derrida, makes similar claims to transparency. In the hands of Derrida's epigones, by contrast, intent on their own form of liberal empire building, if only within academia, it solidifies into dogma.

For deconstructionism understood as a precise method of proceeding rather than merely as liberal debunking, the world had to be expressed in polarities. This was an inheritance from the French structuralists who were the forefathers of the deconstructionists. In each pair, insisted the structuralists and the deconstructionists after them, there is going to be one that ends up with the short straw. The deconstruction machine was set up on the basis of Derrida's central intuition, namely that the long straw could be seen as a subgroup of the short, rather than the reverse. As a result the stronger element ends up being, at least in a logical sense, dependent on the weaker.

Black isn't a negative form of white, Derrida might have said, but rather white is a subgroup of "black," where "black" is understood as a technical term not identical to our usual use of black. Such terms were usually expressed by Derrida's translators into English with the French word to indicate this technical nature. Thus, if my example had been Derrida's, this technical sense of "black" would have been expressed by leaving the word, even in English , as "noir," to indicate a kind of "black" that included and subsumed both black and white. The meek really do inherit the Earth, according to Derridean thought—or if not the meek (French intellectuals and their American disciples were anything but meek), at least those who perceive of themselves as downtrodden. Or rather, they assert that they already own the Earth. Our apparently marginalized group is in fact intellectually primary, they insist.

In the related terms of the more political thinker who has since replaced Derrida as the thinker *du jour* of American academics, Foucault, any First-World power presupposes the Third-World ones it purports to look down on. This is not the economic claim that colonial powers intrinsically suck their colonies dry, though this claim is in fact a liberal position, but rather the ontological claim that there is no such thing as neutral taxonomy. Giving names to things is always about establishing dominance. You can't be a First-World power except as a result of the act of differentiating yourself, excluding, and repressing the Third World. The Third World is thus necessary to the First's nature, and its understanding of itself. For Foucault, the only reason you consider something in words is to subdue it. Putting labels on things is always an act of taming them. It clears things up, makes you the powerful one and skewers the thing you've named.

Thus from an American liberal academic perspective, one informed by Derrida and Foucault, there's no such thing as merely doing X and Y. We're always by nature repressing something else. In doing X and Y we're implicitly excluding A and B.

When applied to conservative thought, this translates into a liberal (academic) certainty that conservatives always define their comfortable Inside precisely through the exclusion of the Outside. From this comes the widespread academic conviction that conservative thought is intrinsically fascist. It starts wars and vilifies opponents only to unify its people the more absolutely within.

But this betrays a fundamental incomprehension of the conservative worldview. In all likelihood conservatives aren't consciously suppressing

A and B at all; conservatives may indeed be unaware of the existence of A and B. They may not include A and B, but this is not likely to be as the result of a conscious choice. Nor do liberals typically consider the fact that, while conservatives may in fact not be doing A and B, but by the same token they are equally not doing C, D and so on. This isn't remarked, because for whatever reason, the liberals aren't interested in C and D.

Anyone whose currency is action will tell you that we can only do what we do; most of the time we aren't refusing to do the alternatives, just not doing them. We only have so much time and energy. It is only liberals, with an axe to grind and their heads full of, e.g., A and B (but not C and D), who would claim that in doing X and Y, conservatives were suppressing A and B. It's another example of the fact that people of thought, here academics, fundamentally don't understand people of action.

A favorite text of midshipmen at the Naval Academy is part of Theodore Roosevelt's speech on the subject of "Citizenship in a Republic" in 1910 in Paris, whose central point is the passage about the "Man in the Arena." Indeed, the relevant excerpt was until recently printed as part of *Reef Points*, the book of facts that midshipmen must memorize.[6] It is the quintessential statement of belief of the conservative, and represents everything that American academics make fun of. It's the credo of the man of action, the person taken as a target by liberal American academics; it expresses, well before the fact, the frustration of conservatives at liberal "deconstructionism."

> It is not the critic who counts, not the man who points out how the strong man stumbled, or where the doer of deeds could have done better. The credit belongs to the man who is actually in the arena; whose face is marred by the dust and sweat and blood; who strives valiantly; who errs and comes short again and again; who knows the great enthusiasms, the great devotions and spends himself in a worthy cause; who at the best, knows in the end the triumph of high achievement, and who, at worst, if he fails, at least fails while daring greatly; so that his place shall never be with those cold and timid souls who know neither victory or defeat.

Liberals who make themselves reactive in this way, always using as their raw material the actions of conservatives, have reached close to the logical extremes of liberalism.

Conservatives see themselves as doing, and liberals as criticizing; they see themselves as constructing and liberals as, literally, deconstructing. No wonder they snort when they catch the liberals at it again.

Outside Absolutisms

Another form that liberal excess takes is the apparently paradoxical worship of absolutist societies, so long as they are outside the purview of the liberal grid and present no threat. This means of necessity, what we call traditional societies, preindustrial ones. It is almost invariably liberal tourists who want to go to "untouched" places, or who fight "globalization." Paul Krugman analyzes the pictures in the antiglobalization propaganda put out by protesters of the World Trade Organization meeting in Seattle; their nightmare vision is that Cairo will look like Los Angeles (if only it were so lucky!) and hence not be interesting to tourists.[7] The desire of tourists, which is to say Westerners, for an interesting vacation is driving international politics.

American liberals are almost exaggeratedly respectful of Third-World regimes. In *War Is a Force That Gives Us Meaning*, Chris Hedges pokes bitter fun at the Americans who visited Nicaragua under the Sandinistas and swallowed all the propaganda of that regime.[8] The locals called them the "sandalistas" after their footwear, emblematic of their "hippie" politics. Equally ridiculous, in the eyes of the locals, are the Americans who go to India in search of "enlightenment" and affect a poverty they are not in fact afflicted by. They want to do it like the locals, even if all the locals want is to become like the Westerners.

In the 1980s and 1990s, the American arts scene, which was populated largely by liberals—conservatives act, they don't consider how things look—adopted a similarly adulatory attitude toward cultural artifacts from traditional societies. Westerners were quick to assume that if something came from a simpler, "unspoiled" culture outside our own, it was immediately of greater value than yet another Western industrial or factory-produced product.

Yet what liberals failed to acknowledge was that the precondition of liberal interest in visiting such absolutist cultures is that these allow themselves to be visited, and that they don't pose a threat. And this frequently is only the case after conservatives are finished neutralizing the threat they pose, usually by force. Civilians need the military to make things safe for them to be civilians, as the military likes to point out. This leads to the military's feeling that the civilian world is always chronically in debt to them.

Furthermore, such absolutist cultures outside, as is clear from the World Trade Organization protesters Krugman notes, are expected not to take on any of the qualities of the grid-culture to which they function as apparent alternatives—apparent because seeing them as alternatives presupposes the unquestioned existence of the grid structure.

Paradoxes on the Pacific

Yet respectful interest in conservative cultures "outside" the liberal grid on the part of liberals is always an expression of the grid, not of interest in an alternative to the grid. An example of this was provided by the 1990 Los Angeles Festival, directed by avant-garde then-wunderkind Peter Sellars, and devoted in its entirety ostensibly to the arts of the Pacific Rim countries—which meant, indicatively, to the "traditional" or "indigenous" cultures of those countries.[9] The Sydney Opera wasn't invited. We Western liberals apparently don't want more liberal relativism, which is after all simply more of ourselves: we want absolutist nodes. Yet these must have been rendered so impotent that they do not threaten to take over our comfortable hegemony. We want to enjoy the lion caged, not deal with it uncaged. (I have considered this all in greater detail in my book *Caging the Lion: Cross-Cultural Fictions*.)

Liberal love of the "unspoiled" is, in Schiller's terms, a sentimental rather than a naïve attitude. The naïve is unself-conscious, as we like indigenous cultures to be. To the extent that they are self-conscious, and are merely merchandizing themselves, we're less interested. The Los Angeles festival was a celebration of the sentimental. This means, an expression of the liberal point of view: Though ostensibly a celebration of an alternative to the liberal grid, it was in fact a reiteration of it.

The terms "traditional" and "indigenous" were used interchangeably at the opening ceremonies of the festival, presumably to underscore the difference between what we audience members were about to see and our own nontraditional and non-indigenous society. These opening ceremonies, set at the spectacular site of Angel's Gate in San Pedro, high on a bluff with a view of the sky-blue expanse of the Pacific, placed side by side Maoris with what they referred to as their "younger cousins" from the islands of Wallis and Futuna, wearing beautifully painted bark cloth. These in turn rubbed shoulders with Australian aborigines decorated largely with body art, with Korean shamans in immaculate white robes and high black hats, and with Ikooc dancers from Mexico in scarlet headbands and loincloths. Native Americans brought welcome and blessings. Indeed, each group brought welcome, prayers, and in most cases, dances.

Audience interest in these dances came from the belief that what the dancers wore to perform sprang "naturally" from their cultures as they now are. Yet as soon as the dances were over, many of the most interestingly "native"-looking of the performers pulled on jeans and jogging shoes that had been left aside for the ceremony. One of the preconditions of respectful attention to the Other is that the Other stay Other, and not look too much like us.

Either they should have been dancing in their T-shirts and quartz watches—in which case we would have thought their native culture polluted, and have been radically less interested in watching them—or we should accept this state of (un)dress as a costume in the same sense as our own Western tutus and tights. In this case, however, the result would have been no more "traditional" and "indigenous" than a performance of the French ballet *Giselle* in New York or Paris.

One morning during the festival the aboriginal dancers taught a class outside on the campus of California State University, Los Angeles, where the Dance Critics Association was holding its annual conference. As a television crew dangled state-of-the-art microphones over the dancers heads and circled them with cameras, the critics tried out trilling like birds and throwing imaginary spears while the eerie sound of the didgeridoo breathed in the background. Since the dancers were all citizens of a Western, anglophone country, Australia, they acted in ways and spoke a language comfortingly comprehensible to the media representatives, as well as to the critic-dancers hanging on their words and gestures. One of the Australians wore a T-shirt that said "Florida" in flamingo pink. We would have been less eager to pay respectful attention if the guests had rejected chairs or been afraid of the microphones, and we would have been unable to understand them at all if they, or someone with them, had not spoken our language. On one hand, they were emissaries from another world. On the other hand, they were just dancers, like dancers everywhere. How mysterious yet how reassuring.

The festival was a show for the haves where the have-nots were meant to stay in their places, remain colorful, photogenic, and naked. At the same time, the tabloid-sized program was touting the whole enterprise as a step forward in comprehension of the world, assuring us that "finding out about our ancient and completely contemporary neighbors on the Pacific turns out to be . . . extremely interesting, occasionally shocking, moving, mysterious, and profound, and again and again a huge amount of fun."

Though intermittently moving and mysterious, therefore, the Other is at bottom essentially "fun." It is composed of entire worlds, whose interest for us, however, is merely that they add yet another taste to the variety of our liberal grid. Our tasting them is always tasting them in succession, which is to say an expression most fundamentally of the smorgasbord, rather than of each individual dish. This is a reiteration of the grid.

The airplanes circling out over the ocean and descending toward the Los Angeles airport that day at the opening ceremonies made clear that in spite of our delicious feeling as audience members of having left behind the bustle of our apparently alienating industrial society by retreating to this gorgeous spot on the Pacific, none of these ceremonies would have been audible without the bank of microphones that were continually going on the blink and bringing everything to a halt—we could see them but we couldn't hear them. And none of this could have happened at all without the airplanes that had brought the participants to Los Angeles to begin with.

The paradox was that this very festival in honor of the indigenous world was impossible without the technological achievements of the society to which the groups invited to participate were supposed to present an alternative. The informative program assured us that the festival was "sparked by . . . an impulse to return to our spiritual essence through image, song, and dance." If we Westerners have lost our "spiritual essence," as the program clearly assumed, how ironic that we could only get it back through the very things that—according to most versions of the story of an Eden lost to us by our having moved away from our agrarian roots—are the sign of our loss.

This is the paradox of the confrontation between the war protesters to whom a screaming middle-aged woman is holding up a sign: "My Son is Fighting to Protect You." What to make of this? Clearly the woman with the sign thinks this means: stop protesting. But it can as easily mean just that: he's fighting to make it possible for them to protest.

The hottest items in the sales area at the Los Angeles Festival were at the booth marked "Tahiti"—set next to other booths bearing the signs of places primarily interesting to Westerners as getaway islands. They were T-shirts with a silk-screened print by Gauguin, a European artist whose paintings memorialized places like Tahiti as an Eden already lost, his signs of longing now turned into "indigenous" export. This was sentimental being offered as naïve—our own point of view reflected back at us and sold as the world outside our borders.

Things Fall Apart

The very hallmark of a traditional society is its absolutism, as a reading of the novels of Chinua Achebe about the Igbo in what is now Nigeria make clear. The world of Achebe's most famous novel, *Things Fall Apart*, is that of Igbo society before the arrival of the Europeans. For the first half of the book, we can't date what we're reading about. It might be 1600; it might be 1800. It is only the arrival of Europeans bearing the portrait of their "Queen-Empress" that allows us to date the life of the book's apparent hero, Okonkwo, to the later years of the nineteenth century.

Such a society was, in the sense we would generally use this concept, timeless. Every year there were the same ceremonies for the crops; always the same mechanism for dispensing justice; the endless propitiation of the gods, and under this, the endless cycle of birth and death. Too, there were always wars with neighboring people, the opportunity they offered warriors like Okonkwo to earn personal glory in the form of human skulls from which to drink their wine. The pre-British society of the Igbo portrayed in *Things Fall Apart* was a traditional society.

Achebe makes clear that this predictability came at a price. First, gender roles were rigidly defined. Men always did what men do. When someone born male wanted to do something else, such as Okonkwo's father, he was simply marginalized. Or Okonkwo's son Nwoye, who took more to the animal-filled creation stories of the women than to the bloodthirsty war stories that men were supposed to be interested in. But the son had the good fortune to come of age after the arrival of the Europeans, so more options were open to him than merely the ignominious death which was the only possibility for Okonkwo's father.

There were other disadvantages to life in this traditional society besides rigid gender categories. Muscles and prowess in war were the highest goods, so that those with less immediately useful qualities than sheer brawn were overlooked, and men kept women and children in line by force. Another societal peculiarity was that twins were killed at birth. People could wonder why this had to be, but wondering could not change the fact that it was so. Nor could people ask why they had to follow the word of Agbala, priestess to the god. She ordained, for example, that a young man raised as Okonkwo's foster son should be killed with machetes, despite the warm feelings that had grown up between him and his foster father and between him and his foster brother. Why were there outcasts in this society, called Ozu? People may have questioned, but could not question very publicly, nor could they set about changing the situation. The point was merely to respect these things, giving them public fealty.

To say, in best conservative fashion, that the value of these things was simply that they had always been so, and that the public act of respecting them was its own end, seemed insufficient to the younger generation in Achebe's novel when suddenly there were alternatives. This was so even if the alternatives—here, English Christianity—didn't make any more sense than what they were alternatives to. At least there was suddenly a real point in asking, "What should *I* do?" And this is always the death knell of the conservative viewpoint.

A second viable absolutism on the scene converts the nature of the first, like a chemical reaction that changes the thing to which the second compound was added, altering a conservative worldview into a liberal one. Okonkwo's son Nwoye, who was so ill at ease with his father's martial stories and did not understand why his foster brother had to die, joins the Christians. It is not for the incomprehensible theology of the crucified God that he does so, Achebe tells us, but rather because Christianity seemed to answer questions Nwoye had and had not even been able to articulate.

Nwoye had a vague but insistent sense that it was wrong to kill twins, a sense without a name or a label in the absolute structure he had been born into. Too, he had a vague unarticulated sense that it was wrong to force him to be like his father. His father's shortcomings were clear to him: His father had been successful as a warrior because he was so inept at verbal articulation or at showing love, resorting to violence to overcome his tongue-tied nature, in best Billy Budd style.

The conservative world prior to the arrival of the English could not articulate its alternative, the liberal. It's always the liberal, therefore, that articulates the conservative, never the reverse. From the perspective of a conservative world, e.g., Europe before the Renaissance—or whatever point the hegemony of the Church was broken—the people who explain the world are not conservative, they merely are. Orwell's tatty totalitarianism in *1984* is a world trying to force an absolutist structure on a people who remembered a world in which there were alternatives, albeit only blurrily. Hence is the necessity for the State's smarmy lies and "double-speak." In a world really without alternatives such as the Igbo society before the arrival of the Europeans, double-speak would not be necessary. An assertion of the one possible way would merely seem the way things are.

The Naval Academy presents yet another odd situation. Its members not only remember a liberal world, they came from it and return to it on liberty. Hence is the necessity for differentiating the conservative world from the liberal at every turn. Outside is moral relativism; only within is unity and order.

In *Things Fall Apart*, the liberal structure wins over the traditional, absolutist one. Paradoxically, an extreme Western liberal will see this as negative. Countless Western professors have taught this book as an excoriating critique of colonialism. Yet it is clear that, nostalgic for the old society though he might be, Achebe cannot see this mutation in completely negative terms. As a product of this liberal society, how could he?

Now that we see that the village men in masks who channeled religion and dispensed justice are only people in masks and not spirits, we see alternatives to the received wisdom that is at the basis of all conservative, here traditional, societies. Having eaten of the fruit of knowledge, we won't put it back on the tree—unless we embrace an absolutist structure simply because we are weary of having to choose among many alternatives, or visit it sentimentally, as at the Los Angeles Festival.

Having a label for things is progress. In a world with only a single way of doing things, we do not have articulations for alternatives. Nwoye, in the old structure, was merely a bad Okonkwo, as Okonkwo's father had been merely a failure.

This is the situation that Foucault is interested in, the time when we sense that something is rotten in the state of Denmark but do not know what. Foucault's favorite examples are things like insanity and homosexuality, which, in a taxonomic sense, didn't even exist until the language of sanity and heterosexuality nailed them down with terms that condemned them to second-class status.[10] Foucault would rather have these things un-nailed down, but the fact is that for someone seeking to define himself, giving a name to something that otherwise would be without one is liberation.

This is a good example of one aspect of Foucault that his epigones have typically overlooked. Eager for weapons with which to attack the solid and comfortable, his epigones hear only that naming subjugates. They do not seem to have considered the fact that for Foucault, not having a name at all is the better situation, something, e.g., that a Nwoye could only sense as repression: the lack of a viable alternative, the conservative world rather than the liberal.

When the insane weren't insane but tolerated as village idiots, things, Foucault implies, were better. When homosexuals weren't homosexual but simply not heterosexual, things, apparently, were better. In neither case would somehow who lacked a label (what to call insanity before it was called insanity? What to call homosexuality before it was homosexuality?) have been able to attack the only game in town, sanity or heterosexuality.

For naming the weaker element didn't succeed, as Foucault's epigones seem to imagine, directly on the world where all swam in an undifferentiated taxonomic soup. It succeeded on a world where the weaker element was held not to exist at all, only the stronger. In this situation, clearly it was progress to name the weaker element. Lacking a name for an alternative in the state before doesn't mean that the dominant term failed to exercise hegemony. The village was governed by the sane, not by the idiots.

Foucault would rather be the individual without a name, even if he knew himself not to be correctly described by the only name then available: whatever sane people thought they were before insanity was invented; whatever men who had sex with women thought they were before homosexuality was invented. But for the young man growing up in a small Midwestern town who realizes slowly he doesn't want to have sex with the cheerleaders, at least not the female ones, having a name for what he is is presumably progress. For Nwoye, being able to say, I am X, where X is an alternative to the absolute structure Y he grew up with, is a triumph. It says, there is X and Y, and I am X, an alternative to Y.

If it's true that our American culture wars are the result of conservatives making a power grab, then the most urgent message we have to send is to American conservatives. The message is this: Being convinced that you are doing the right thing only makes you different from liberals, who in fact are not your most absolute enemies. The world is full of groups of people, all of whom are just as convinced they are doing the right thing as you are. Conviction, faith, and belief are not rare things; they are very common indeed. Thus your most absolute enemies are the other conservative absolutisms, of which the world is full. Liberals will at least try to talk with you; other people equally firm in their own beliefs will not talk. They, like all conservatives, will act instead.

6
YIN AND YANG

The philosopher Charles Peirce wrote about Firstness, Secondness, and his resolution of those, Thirdness. Firstness, in a simplified articulation, is the subjective float, the way everything goes perfectly, so long as it remains inside our heads. Secondness is the fact that in reality we bloody our noses on the world. We constantly have to deal with things we haven't planned for. For Peirce, Thirdness is what we're aiming at, their fusion. It's not very clear what Peirce means by this.

The conservative worldview is, metaphorically speaking, locked in Firstness. It isn't subjective as opposed to objective, but it is unsullied by things that contradict it. This doesn't mean that it is unable to acknowledge the existence of Secondness, here understood only as an alternative to what it asserts. But it does mean that Secondness remains outside of its purview. Conservative thought is not "on one hand, on the other hand" thought; it is merely "this is the way things are" thought. Liberal thought strews Secondness throughout its purview.

The American system limiting the reach of any one absolutism in favor of the structure that allows them all could only have been set up by people who were very conscious of the potential for a war of all against all and who had decided that the greatest good was staying alive. Hobbes famously justified absolute kingship for the same reason. Hobbes's solution is more congenial to conservatives than democracy is, because it at least gives us a something, or in this case a someone, the monarch, external to ourselves whom we are supposed to follow. It becomes possible for us to say that we are, primarily, following the sovereign, and only secondarily staying alive. If we make staying alive quite clearly the central issue, as Madisonian notions of checks and balance do, this will leave a great void for conservatives. We are free to do what we want, but what is that? Such a fusion of Firstness and Secondness lacks the most fundamental quality conservatism demands of its ethics: absolute rules for action.

Conservatism will only accept the fusion if we make clear that the fusion is not the same as conservatism, and that there is a purpose in accepting it. In the same way, liberals will not accept a grid that exists for the sole purpose of allowing the absolutisms within it, as long as the grass the system allows to spring up between the metal cross-hatching is presented as fulfilling their own needs.

Democracy therefore will only be acceptable to both liberals and conservatives if it is both presented and accepted as a compromise, something that by definition fails to satisfy either side fully. It is precisely the sense of compromise—the acceptance that things will not fully satisfy either side—that is lacking in the early twenty-first century. This is the reason why our culture wars have become so violent. The conservatives are caught in the absolutist structure of Firstness, while the liberals insist on the binary structure of Secondness. Neither is willing to acknowledge that Thirdness, here represented by democracy, may well be something else entirely, an artificial construction not intrinsic to either of the other worldviews. And yet that is exactly what it is.

To conservatives who see the metal grid as an alien constraint on the grass taking over completely, life will seem to lack purpose. Their options are to challenge that structure, try to overthrow it, or find purpose in other things. One of the things conservatives typically find purpose in is war, as American society seems to be doing in the early years of the twenty-first century. Andrew Bacevich's *The New American Militarism* provides the most chilling contemporary view of a society, like that of George Orwell's *1984*, self-defining through permanent war.[1]

Chris Hedges' point, in *War Is a Force That Gives Us Meaning*, is that great armed struggles give solidity to the group in a way that normal life does not—not merely groups of soldiers on the battlefield, fighting for their buddies, but of civilians who "pull together" back at home. Other societal conditions fulfill the same purpose: East

Germans spoke for a time after the Wall fell of their sense of solidarity before it had done so. Now, it seems, they suffer *die Qual der Wahl*, the pain of too many choices, and must answer for themselves questions that previously had answers offered through circumstances.

The essence of democracy is limiting actions to small, very controlled things like voting. Not killing the opponent. Not taking office by force. Not using the State as a way to enrich yourself and your cronies. This will always be the case in a democracy, and so the danger always exists that conservatives who feel stifled and defensive will break their bonds in order to do these things. Because liberals are the defenders of the grid, by the same token, they have no motivation to encourage the growth of absolutisms that the grid is designed to protect. Indeed, in a world like the American one with a single form of conservatism so dominant, the problem for liberals seems to be opposing this conservatism. No one recommends introducing others in the hope they would compete with this for the available resources and so all end up more stunted. What if one of them takes off and grows bigger than the others? Yet democracy works best when there is a spectrum of small to medium-sized absolutisms, none of which can hope to supplant the others.

Social Contract Theory

Liberals and conservatives aren't natural allies. Nothing will compel them to join forces, and nothing has—any more than people actually agreed to the imaginary social contract so beloved of Enlightenment theorists. Social contract theory was based on the understandable but erroneous view that determining the origin of society would help us understand it. But there's no logical connection between the way things were once, or how they came to be, and how they are now, or how they should be. Showing that the origin of the family fortune was something disresputable doesn't necessarily mean the current fortune-holders aren't completely so.

In any case, as John Rawls has pointed out, the problem with such a social contract theory, like that of Rousseau, was that there was no social contract. Its best to admit this clearly. For this reason, Rawls proposed a hypothetical form of the social contact that outlined what the basis of a "fair" society would be if we were to accept it. Yet precisely this formulation makes clear the problem with Rawls's version of the social contract. If we no longer claim we did accept this social contract, but only could if we wanted to, we have removed any impetus for people to do so—namely the claim that the question is no longer open. We have to agree to accept it; nothing in his reasoning forces us to do so. And this means, the purpose of visualizing in terms of a social contract at all is lost, namely putting it in the past where we can't do anything about it.

Rawls defines justice as what he calls fairness. He defines fairness by imagining a prebirth world where each person gets to give out goods to various individuals' situations, but others get to choose first which situation they would be born in. This may be an academic sense of "fairness" if we stipulate that others get to choose first after we've cut the pieces of cake. Under these circumstances, we'd clearly be well advised to cut equal pieces, assuming that people would always choose the biggest pieces for themselves.

But why (so actual people might reason) should we cut equal pieces given that others in reality don't get to choose first? When I build a bigger house than my neighbor, I don't give that person the choice first of which house to live in. I just live in the bigger one. After all, I built it. All these rules, in any case, are expressed in the quintessential liberal terms of actors rather than Absolute Actions. What if instead I follow such rules of Absolute Actions that by nature do not take account of others? Rawls seemed incapable of conceiving of the conservative worldview as a way of seeing the world at all.

Saying that people never, in fact, actually agreed to a social contract is an obvious way of getting at the even more telling theoretical problem with classical social contract theories. Writing from the perspective of the achieved society, we can explain what advantages it has. But if we conceive of a "before" state that is truly different from the "after," so that we need a social contract to bridge the two states, we cannot, from the perspective of the "before," explain why people would have been able to jump to the "after."

This is a logical difficulty, the result of separating out two states, here the "before" and the "after." It is comparable to the problems usually called Zeno's paradoxes. In one paradox, the arrow speeding toward its target never hits the target. For consider, the arrow first covers half of the distance to the target. Then it covers half of the remaining half, or quarter. Then it covers half of the remaining distance, and half of that, growing asymptotically closer to the target but, because it always has to cover half of the remaining distance, never reaching it. In another paradox, Achilles never overtakes the tortoise he is pursuing in a race: He must cover first half of the distance between them, and then half of that, and so on, growing ever closer but never breaking ahead.

In *Being and Nothingness*, Sartre proposed that Zeno's paradoxes were the result of having a notion of time as divisible into discrete units, rather than conceiving of it as a structural quality of being. From my perspective, the paradoxes are the result of separating off one concept from the other. Only an external, unrelated concept can mediate between the two of them. If we need a social contract to get us where we are, we will never, paradoxically, get where we are, any more than Achilles will ever overtake the tortoise or the arrow reach its target. Conversely, if we are where we are, we don't need a social contract. For the same reason, if we have to assert that the individual is one with society, he or she can't really be so. And if we separate out "is" from "should," there's no way they can really be joined together again.

Social contract theories are liberal attempts to ensure that the absolutist, conservative theories that make up the contents of their grid structures remain within bounds. They are liberal attempts to make liberal theories primary over conservative ones. It isn't liberals they have to appeal to, since they all talk the language of the liberal grid. Predictably enough, classical social contract theories express the liberal grid in terms designed to appeal to conservatives, by placing it in the past: The liberal grid becomes tradition. It's unclear to me why Rawls thought he could dispense with this powerful lure for conservatives and still hope to convince them to sign on for his version of the contract.

Placing the social contract in time is the most likely way of getting conservatives to agree to be swayed by it. Anything, absolutely anything, can serve as the basis of conservative respect and become tradition, even things that in their own contexts were intrinsically liberal. Or even things that were the result of chance, such as who is born a king. If frozen at this particular point, the pattern of that moment can be pored over, interpreted, or memorized whole (as, for non-Muslims, the Holy Qur'an seems to have been frozen). This is the reason why the real United States Constitution is likely to get the allegiance of conservatives, despite its essentially liberal task of setting up an overstructure that allows absolutisms but does not allow any one to take over. This produces the strange state of conservatives on the United States Supreme Court claiming only to be the servants of a preexisting Holy Writ, though in this case the Writ is the nonconservative Constitution.

From inside the perspective of a conservatism, the world lacks boundaries. A strong conservatism, or one unaware of its relative weakness, would therefore have no impetus to accept the permanent restrictions of life in a liberal structure such as social contract theories are trying to guarantee. From the perspective of the conservative, the liberal structure is always the enemy unless it can be used as a temporary shield to fend off competing conservatisms while one conservatism gathers strength.

No combination of liberals and conservatives is intrinsically stable. The American situation may come closer to stability than others, because its liberal overstructure is rooted in the historical fact of the Constitution, something that appeals to conservatives. But conservatives planning a breakout from their self-limitation within the system will not be slowed down by this.

As a result, the question of why most conservatives should or would ever agree to live under democracy can only be answered not by looking at the conservative worldview itself, but at ancillary issues noted earlier like whether they think they can succeed in a hostile takeover, and whether they offer something everyone can achieve or whether they are only accessible by an elect. Similarly, the question of why liberals would ever agree to tolerate nonliberal conservatisms within their grid cannot be answered by the worldview itself. Instead, both sides must agree to the combination. But this requires both sides acknowledging their own nature. The (possibly uneasy) truce between conservatives and liberals is based on each one, for reasons external to its own worldview, having accepted the fact of the other. The end point is nothing more nor less than this acceptance, which cannot be justified by the worldview of either side.

Seen from without, a conservative subgroup is absolutist, repressive. So is the liberal grid structure when seen from the perspective of an absolutism not subsumed by the grid. Democracy cannot be justified from without, or before it is achieved. It can only be justified when it has been achieved and taken for granted. The justifications liberals offer for democracy ring hollow in a contentious world: We can't force conservatives to tie their own hands. We can only hope they will do so.

Democracy

Democracy is most efficiently defined not, as it usually is defined, as a system where the people rule, or where the will of the people decides. The most fundamental definition of democracy is as a combination of liberal and conservative. This means the liberals take care of the traffic lights and the conservatives go where they go, taking care to stop at the traffic light.

Attempts to justify democracy almost invariably evoke some version of "the people" or "the people's will." But if we question the notion of "the people's will," it falls apart like any other concept that suddenly seems strange to us.[2] If we demand further justification for this concept, by definition we will be unable to find it, because we have broken up "the people" into parts that can never be joined together again. We have the same problems of jointure at the other end, where "the people" is expressed in the single elected individuals. If we question that this is so, it seems clear it isn't so at all.

The Achilles heel of democracy is the jointure between individual and collective. This is so for the same reason that "is" cannot imply "should" once the two entities are separated. The individual "I" must somehow be joined into the collective that expresses its will, and this collective re-funneled into the individual elected. Both of these processes lack justification, if we are determined not to accept them. In a sense, the arrow never gets to its target, unless it does. Either we simply accept it, or we don't.

Let's take the mechanism by which, apparently through magic, many individual expressions of will are transformed into something completely different, the "will of the people"—a process akin to alchemy's attempt to change stone or iron into gold. (Apparently alchemists didn't think about what gold would be worth if we could do this.) Any divergence between what I personally want to happen and what the collective "will" is determined to be is unjustified in theory; I either accept the transformation as legitimate or I don't.

One of the more glaring problems of democracy is that of protecting the rights of minorities. If, as they inevitably are, they are outvoted; should their concerns disappear or be held for naught? But equally puzzling is the fact that I might vote for someone who in fact wins, and (let's say) seems initially to mirror my own beliefs. What do we do if it turns out that this person is different than I thought, or takes a new turn? Or if I take a new turn? Have I voted for this person, who is now different? If I'm now different, shouldn't I get to vote again?

Another theoretical difficulty is found in the fact that I may vote based on one issue, and then have to live with the person enacting other policies I disagree with. Or the person begins focusing on issues I approve of but rapidly turns to others. Should I not be able to revote every month? Every day? At every meal? Of course, we could decide on a reasonable interval based on practical problems (all those elections, for one), but the point is that the theoretical issues do not go away. Shouldn't I get to vote on every issue?

It's not that there aren't pragmatic answers to this: what else are you going to do? It's that they lack theoretical justification.

If what we're aiming at is perfect consonance even with my own beliefs—leaving aside the problem of divergence between people—is a four-year presidency, as in the United States, better than a seven-year mandate, as in France, on the theory that the temporal leash is shorter, and the politician has less time to diverge from the views for which I may have elected him or her? But if this is so, a two-year mandate would be better still, at least theoretically (in fact, they'd spend all their time campaigning), and a one day mandate the best of all, until finally we got to a geometrical point.

When we vote, what are we voting for? A person? A set of principles? Promised actions? What of the fact that a person may be (or rather, certainly is) making what we call "campaign promises"—that won't be fulfilled? What if he or she does something we didn't vote for? Or changes his or her mind? What of the fact that many people affected by a country's actions are unrepresented in the choice of its leaders—such as, in the 2004 U.S. election, the European countries? In an increasingly global world, why should the farther-flung reaches of the American Empire, that will pay the price for a wrong choice back in the metropole, not have the right to vote as well? Why, for that matter, should the Iraqis who will be most affected by American policy not vote as well? Is this not denying them representation?

Voting only makes sense insofar as it's an alternative to other things, like killing people. If we look at it out of context, its rationale unravels. Trying to justify voting in democracy aside from the things it's an alternative to is like trying to define liberalism or conservatism out of a context of conflict with the other. Our words ultimately slow, our hands drop to our sides. Trying to justify democracy that has been questioned is impossible. We either accept democracy (e.g., because the alternative isn't pleasant) or we don't; nothing can talk us into accepting it. But this may be the reason we do.

The definition of democracy cannot be the particular means by which the marriage of liberal and conservative is accomplished; it is the marriage itself. The alternative to this is the acrimonious bellicosity of the current age. Having accomplished the union means that all the theoretical objections possible given the fact that we postulate separate individuals at one pole and their association at the other are in fact avoided. In a functioning democracy, the arrow gets to the target, even though logically it shouldn't. But all this means is that we accept the structure. In a similar way, when we arrive alive at our destination, we have failed to be involved in the logical infinity of accidents that could have taken us off course.

Democracies Defending Themselves

Those who have accepted democracy tend to believe that it is a transparent medium, a structure allowing all other structures. This is comparable to the way each of the two worldviews, liberal and conservative, seems transparent to itself. For this reason liberals are sometimes puzzled when the democracy takes steps to protect itself in the form of entities like the CIA or even the military. For some liberals, indeed, there is an inherent contradiction in the notion of a democracy defending itself against domestic enemies and remaining a democracy. Nor do liberals typically feel very enthusiastic even about the notion of a democracy defending itself against foreign enemies.

Liberals have to accept that what they do is something specific that's not equivalent to the whole unwieldy combination structure. Liberals do have a specific function in the whole; they aren't the same as the whole. They take care of the traffic lights. Traffic lights, even though in a sense they are impartial and merely facilitate the flow of traffic, do stop the people they stop, when they stop them. They're a specific thing. And that means, they need to be maintained. But if what liberals do is a particular action, that means it can be threatened. The traffic light can be harmed or dismantled. Of course it is possible to oppose the overstructure, and cause it to take steps to protect itself. There's no way to distinguish on a theoretical level between absolutisms that threaten the overstructure and those that don't. If they do, they do. Force is always an option for conservatives.

What for one context functions as liberalism, a defense of the overstructure, can in another context function like a conservatism. "We want to free you!" is the perennial American assertion to non-American countries and peoples. Those outside the United States see only the force necessary to imposing the structure. The United States Army looks no less menacing as it faces an enemy than, e.g., the Wehrmacht did. An army is an army, and no army questions the politics that sends it into the field.

Militaries all look the same from the inside, too. It certainly feels no different, in its essentials, to be in the United States Navy than it did to be in the German Navy during World War II, or in the Soviet Navy. Nor, undoubtedly, did the fabric of life in the army change when the Soviet Navy became once again the Russian Navy after the fall of communism. All soldiers salute and say the local equivalent of "Yes, sir."

The United States can force others to swallow its democracy at gunpoint. For those being forced, this feels the same as being forced to accept anything else; what they sense is the force, not the thing being forced on them. If they do accept it, swallow it whole, they may see things differently—just as the liberals and conservatives who have agreed to accept each other take each other for granted, but can change their points of view and find this accommodation of the opposing viewpoint unacceptable. Those within the United States point out correctly that if the other people would simply accept the structure of American democracy, it would function for them as it functions within the United States. It would be the traffic light that people would simply accept and the cars would be regulated by it.

But the circularity of this reasoning is clear: In order for democracy to function as a fusion of disparate worldviews, the fusion must be accepted. What is at issue is precisely the difficulty, sometimes impossibility, of forcing acceptance. The whole history of U.S. foreign policy is based on failing to understand—as we have failed to correctly understand the nature of the relationship between liberals and conservatives on the domestic front—that something seen from within is different than that thing seen from without.

The Quiet American

Americans frequently confuse the uneasy truce between opposites of functioning democracy with a substantive "moderate" or "middle" way. Believing that we function in such a middle ground means we've failed to understand the fundamental asymmetry of the two positions.

We also look for it outside, failing to understand that no absolutist worldview can accept incorporation into a relativist one. The Ayatollah

Khoumeini would certainly have rejected being relegated to the position of inhabitant of one more house of worship in church row in an American small town.

The well-meaning young Ivy Leaguer in Saigon in *The Quiet American*, Graham Greene's book about early U.S. involvement in Vietnam—written in 1954, and seeming to predict eerily the events of the following two decades—can show sixteen ways from tomorrow why he, and the United States, are sure to find the "middle way" in Vietnam. His certainty leads to many deaths, among them his own; this is the only way his theories can be called into question. One of Greene's points is that absolutist worldviews aren't disprovable by theory, only by facts lying outside the theory. In this sense, they're anti-intellectual, even though they may take a lot of gray matter to lay out.

In 2004, Americans saw very bright people laying out a breathtaking vision of an abruptly democratic Middle East. For a time, this rhetoric was justified as American idealism, as if idealism were a good thing. But Greene's quiet American was in this sense idealistic, too. "Idealism" is only another word for describing from within something that would be nice. It's not raining on the parade to talk about the real probability (or lack of probability) of this working, as conservatives sometimes feel it is—the "cynicism" that's so criticized at the Naval Academy. It's the only way liberals can respond to conservatives, by asking if what's said is in fact true, or suggesting outright it's false.

Of course, if people would simply accept the democratic structure, it would in a sense disappear into the fabric of their lives. But that is true of all systems. Those within a system that have accepted the traffic light are in a different place than those outside one. For those outside one, accepting this as a given that would allow them to move on to other things is something more easily postulated than achieved.

Conservatives who insist on others simply swallowing the American system aren't completely misguided in thinking this possible. It's true that many human alterations occur, in this fashion of moving from nonacceptance to acceptance, in quantum jumps. First they're there, then they're not. Foucault thought that epochal development in human thought occurred in this fashion as well, the way society goes from seeing sexuality as defined by the action, then by the sort of person.

Such a switch is so fundamental that we can't further say what it is that has caused the switch itself. But just because we can't see the thing preventing people from making this switch (if we make the switch fundamental enough, there's by definition nothing preventing them from making it) doesn't mean they can be compelled to make it when we want them to. We can't merely berate someone who, were he or she "merely" to accept X or Y, would be in a different place. It's as impossible as if we were to demand religious belief from others merely because it is available to ourselves. We've made the leap of faith. They must do it too, here and now, on pain of whatever. American claims for the universalism of democracy amount to saying, "If you could see this from the inside, you wouldn't resist." But this is true of any structure. Accepted is accepted.

Peaceful Coexistence

I have tried to explain the differences between liberals and conservatives. As a way of going beyond these differences, I suggest that each side needs to acknowledge the strengths of the others, as well as focusing on its weaknesses. This may sound a bit like a sort of 1968-style "love-in," or a twenty-first century movie: "Oh, behave!" But this isn't a trivial injunction at all, or a silly one. If we don't simply decide to get along, we have the very real ability to blow apart the uneasy truce of American democracy. The first step toward making sure we don't do this is acknowledging the danger of doing so. The second is meditating on what we would lose if we did.

The end of the world as caused by liberals is an end in ice, a freezing of all motion. Gradually all the cars are slowed to a crawl as a result of the too frequent, too rapidly changing lights. The metal grid designed to allow the grass to grow expands into the areas formerly assigned to grass. The end of the world as caused by conservatives is a world in fire. One particular absolutism makes a grab for power in a great immolation of Principles, and starts the World Culture War, defined by relentless pursuit over the most meaningless and trivial issues that we've so far managed to avoid. If conservatives can't see that one miniscule little victory more over a few inches of no-man's-land won't be worth the fight, we have to make it clear to them why that is so. If liberals can't see that someone's believing in God doesn't mean a person is a fool, we'll have to explain why this is so. (I've attempted to do this in *Science and the Self: The Scale of Knowledge.*)

Liberals and conservatives need each other for American democracy to function, as they need each other for self-definition. At the same time they should accept that each is a different sort of creature. The author John Gray suggested that "men are from Mars, women are from Venus."[3] The point of saying this was not to suggest that either could do without the other. Instead, it was quite the opposite: to eliminate all the fruitless attempts of each side to make the other be like it. If we start off acknowledging our differences, we will ultimately be able to get along because we'll look beyond them.

One of the main thrusts of this book has been to say clearly that conservatives especially need to take care, because of what I've called, after Huntington, their "bloody edges." They must understand that constantly seeking to expand their domain, while intrinsic to their being, is not a good idea. At the same time I have been concerned to convince liberals that conservatism is a real thing, with its own way of doing things. It's not merely schismatic (wrong) liberalism, in the sense that Dante thought Islam to be schismatic Christianity. It's like another religion.

Another major concern has been to convince liberals that conservative thought really does do some things better. If you're a conservative, you state what *is,* and you take steps to achieve it, and you don't worry too much about the fallout. You know you have only one direction to go in: forward. I can understand why many people, most of them lovely people within their own worlds, are conservatives. I can see, too, why most men are conservative. It's closer to how men are men. I think that a lot of liberals fail to see the lure of such a worldview or to understand that conservatives are not, simply, bad or deformed versions of liberals. At the same time I have to convince conservatives that liberals aren't just wimps. Deciding what to do based on the particular nature of the situation is just as valid a way of proceeding as knowing beforehand, even if it has to be done more carefully, and perhaps more quietly.

Liberals do some things better; conservatives do other things better. The pen isn't mightier than the sword; the two are complementary. In terms of the Naval Academy, this means: action doesn't trump, or the reverse. You have to be good at both. Ace your push-ups, but write a good essay too.

Personal Note

I'm a liberal. This is so because I realize that I'm only one alternative among many, not the whole show. I've never been comfortable being a "team player," as we say at Annapolis. After all, I grew up as a fish out of water in a small-town high school where the only game in town was football and the worship of the football team, and where you were supposed to show "school spirit" at "pep rallies" in the gym. It was a world where wearing the wrong kind of shoes or shirt meant you were mercilessly teased. It was a world where the high point of the political decade was a wildly cheered appearance by the extreme right-wing presidential candidate Barry Goldwater: "AuH_2O," as my father's bumper sticker had it. It was a world where "colored" people knew their place, living in a shadow version of the white Main Street (West Main Street) that continued on over the bridge—though Salisbury had voluntarily integrated its stores early enough to avoid the fate of Cambridge, thirty miles down the road, which was largely burned in protests organized by the activist H. Rapp Brown.

I figured out early on this was not a world I could be a part of, though it was undoubtedly warm and comforting to those who accepted its values. I saw no place for people who thought differently, or who were different. Who knows why, as an adult, I didn't become a "born-again conservative" finally demanding the certainty and warmth I'd been denied as a child? Or is this why I've been at the Naval Academy so long?

In the 1960s you could still get up a good head of righteous steam singing "We Shall Overcome" in a racially mixed group. Back then it seemed thrilling. I went to a college that by anyone's standards is liberal, Quaker-founded Haverford College, where respect for others was ingrained, and each person was allowed to so as he or she liked so long as it didn't disrupt the collective. All these are predictably liberal things.

I had a gay brother so I don't see why people get so upset over who puts what where, sexually speaking. (No, the Bible doesn't condemn homosexuality: people who read and interpret the Bible to their own ends do that.) That fact alone makes me a liberal on at least several of the main flash points of the culture wars. I'd say that people probably have a default of one set of sex objects or another. But I also think that we don't even consider the nondefault as an option because that's easier for us, and the way we think things have to be. That's why the nature/nurture debate can never be resolved as an either/or.

I know the virtues of democracy because of having lived in the middle of Eastern Europe, and having spent time, albeit as a visitor of shorter or longer duration, in dictatorships all over the world. For this reason as well, I know that the world is full of people who aren't likely to take kindly to hearing that things they've been doing for centuries are wrong. I know that other people do things differently than we do, and that it's perfectly possible to profess another religion than those with many adherents in the United States. Maybe that's because I have friends who are Hindus and Muslims, and note that they're fully as moral as I am, probably more so.

I think current American anti-French jokes show only American ignorance. Maybe that's because I speak a handful of languages, including French, and have rarely received anything but politeness at the hands of the French. (Of course, there are idiots in every country.) I've lived and taught in Germany, so I know that individuals are individuals, even if my country fought their country for very good reasons.

People are always surprising themselves, I find. We're extraordinarily complex entities. One-size-fits-all principles thus seem to me unacceptably blunt instruments for deciding action. I tend to ask: why don't you wait and see what develops? I'll almost always sacrifice the principle to the individual, rather than the reverse.

This doesn't mean that individuals are always right to emphasize their individuality: I believe that everyone has to adopt standard ways of doing many things, otherwise we wouldn't have anything in common, nor be able to communicate. Nor are individuals always perfect the way they are at any given time: People have to work to achieve prowess at higher and higher levels. We're not doing people a favor by accepting less than the maximum they're capable of, or by deforming the world so the less capable people get their time at the helm in the name of some misguided notion of "fairness." But what they're aiming at is a definition of themselves, which has yet to be determined—not the achievement of a single common outside goal that everyone else is aiming at, too.

I'm not a Muslim, so the Qur'an (I've only read an "interpretation," in English) for me lacks the sense of completeness it has for believers. But by the same token that patchwork that Christians call the Bible lacks for me the finality it has for believers. (Any sentence starting with "The Bible says" seems questionable to me right away. The only people who think "relativism" is the same as moral abomination are the absolutists.) There are too many books in the Bible that almost made it into the canon (such as the Book of Thomas, or the Book of Tobit) and we know too precisely what people determined the doctrine that's now so fought over (e.g., St. Athanasius) for the Bible to seem a perfect somehow trans-human creation. But that's because my worldview is calibrated to notice individuals. I see the people who created the Bible; a conservative acknowledges those people, but holds them unimportant. They fade into the construction of the Truth, like the nameless Egyptians who constructed the pyramids. It's a difference of what you focus on.

The tenets of all religions, if you read them in the cold light of day—which means, if you don't have any reason to believe them—seem screwy. Ever wonder about this "Holy Ghost" thing? What about the Mormon belief that Native Americans are one of the Lost Tribes of Israel? The Muslim belief that Mohammed rose into the air and was transported to Jerusalem? That Jesus walked on water? All those orthodox Jewish food prohibitions? The Hindu belief that Lord Krishna seduced a hundred milkmaids in one night?

I'm a liberal too because, whenever someone claims a distinction as absolute, I immediately want to show them the gray area between the two alternatives. It exists just as clearly as the black and the white areas do. The notion of an intrinsically gray area is anathema to conservatives. Thus I don't think abortion is murder, because we'll never be able to decide the nature of the intrinsically gray area of not-yet-humans. The people defending the "rights of the unborn" are those who in fact won the lottery and got to be born: they feel threatened by the mind game of their own nonexistence. If I had been aborted, they think, I wouldn't be here. So I have to defend the "right to life" of fetuses.

But lots of pregnancy starts don't produce people, for lots of reasons. Abortion is only one. Every person who has been born was surrounded in what Wittgenstein would have called "logical space" by a cloud of non-people, might-have-beens who never even got conceived, much less brought to term. This isn't how conservatives think: all the people who are have to have been planned, from the beginning, with souls. Some of them don't make it to birth, but that doesn't mean we're allowed to impede them ourselves. Conservatives don't deny that the woman carrying the baby has a point of view, only that it's a determinative factor.

It's shortsighted to think of a war as something that kills only your own soldiers. It also kills the other side's, and they're people, too, with beliefs, feelings, and mothers who (with any luck) loved them, too. There are many effects of war beyond the battlefield. War disrupts the whole fabric of civilized life: reading books, sipping tea, talking with the neighbors. It's not being soft to point this out; it's being realistic. But, yes, it involves looking beyond the immediate circle of individual control where conservatives feel at home. Which is why conservatives would rather walk over hot coals than do it. Hot coals they can tough out.

It's not chance that urban, which is to say usually urbane, educated people with university degrees who have traveled are more likely to be liberal than conservative. They know that the world is a complex place. They get to the point of thinking that human happiness might after all be what we're aiming at, not some preplanned theory-world, yet another conservative absolutism. To conservatives, this means they've lost the ability to be idealistic. Yes, and a good thing too, liberals would say. Ultimately life is about whether you get to be with your family and hug your children, not whether you celebrated some great battlefield "victory." The conservatives who know all this are so usually precisely because the world is so complex. You have to have some certainty, they say.

We might think that older people would be more likely to be liberal than conservative, because over time we learn that control is an illusion. But somehow it doesn't work that way. As people age they shut out unpleasant truths, maybe because acknowledging them involves just too much pain. Frequently they become horrible ranting old people, insistent that God's will must be done, or America's, or Allah's. But believing that you have a short line to God doesn't make you right, just one of the crowd. Remember the psycho played by Kathy Bates in the movie *Misery* (based on a Stephen King book), who first saves then kidnaps a popular novelist and forces him to write a novel to her liking before trying to kill him. "God has delivered you unto me for a reason," she tells him, all smiles, as he realizes that he will probably die.

Questions like whether developing humans are people and whether homosexuality is a "choice" are flash points nowadays precisely because we lack the means to resolve the problems. If we could do so, we would have. They're the products of underlying structures. Questions like that are never solved; they're just run into the ground so people walk away with a hangover, wondering what that was all about.

Of course, the two worldviews are different. They're complementary. That means, we'll disagree. But if we don't at the same time acknowledge that the disagreement is what binds us together, we've lost the miracle wrought on the American continent in the late eighteenth century, a miracle that, in an increasingly threatening world, seems increasingly worth preserving.

Notes

Introduction

1. Andrew J. Bacevich, *The New American Militarism: How Americans Are Seduced by War* (New York: Oxford University Press, 2005).
2. Some of these are considered by Jared Diamond in his *Collapse: How Societies Choose to Fail or Succeed*, (New York: Viking, 2004); those of a largely military nature are considered by Barbara Tuchman in *The March of Folly: From Troy to Vietnam*. (New York: Ballantine, 1985).
3. Boris Dewiel, *Democracy: A History of Ideas* (Seattle: University of Washington Press, 2001), 143.
4. http://www.aynrand.org/site/PageServer?pagename=education_campus_libertarians.
5. Charles Krauthammer, "No-Respect Politics," (*Washington Post*, July 26, 2002), A33.
6. Paul Krugman, *The Great Unraveling: Losing Our Way in the New Century* (New York: Norton, 2003), Introduction, 3 ff.
7. Writers such as Michael P. Lynch note that liberals aren't as good at being scrappy as conservatives are, and Lynch asks, in an article for the *Chronicle of Higher Education*, "Where Is Liberal Passion?" April 22, 2005, pp B7–9.
8. This is the sense in which my view here is pessimistic, and in which I do not share the views of Lynch that "democratic politics . . . is aimed at getting others to see things your way." *Chronicle of Higher Education*, "Where is Liberal Passion?" April 22, 2005, p B9.

9. George H. Nash, *The Conservative Intellectual Movement in America Since 1945* (Wilmington, DE, Intercollegiate Studies Institute, 1996), xiv.
10. Louis Hartz, *The Liberal Tradition in America* (New York: Harcourt, 1991), 4.
11. Horkheimer and Adorno, *Dialektik der Aufklärung.* Also, "Culture Industry Reconsidered," in *The Adorno Reader,* edited by Brian O'Connor (Oxford: Blackwell 2000), 230–38.
12. *An Essay in Post-Romantic Literary Theory; Modernism and Its Discontents: Philosophical Problems of Twentieth-Century Literary Theory; Art and Argument.*
13. In *Disappointment or the Light of Common Day*, Lanham, MD: University Press of America, 2006.
14. I make these points and other related ones in *Caging the Lion*, especially the chapter "Reflections on Rwanda," (New York: Peter Lang, 1991).
15. Clifford Geertz, *Works and Lives: The Anthropologist as Author* (Stanford, CA: Stanford University Press, 1990), 1.
16. Renato Rosaldo, *Culture and Truth: The Remaking of Social Analysis* (Boston: Beacon, 1993), 20–21.
17. Laura Bohannan, "Prince Hamlet in Africa," *Norton Reader: An Anthology of Expository Prose,* 3rd Edition, edited by Arthur M. Eastman et al., (New York: W.W. Norton, 1973). 498-507.
18. Northrop Frye, *Anatomy of Criticism: Four Essays* (Princeton: Princeton University Press, 2000).
19. Achebe, Chinua, "An Image of Africa," *Massachusetts Review* (1977), 782–94.
20. Shklovsky, "Art as Technique," in Lee T. Lemon and Marion J. Reis, *Russian Formalist Criticism: Four Essays* (Lincoln, NE: University of Nebraska Press, 1965).
21. In *An Essay in Post-Romantic Literary Theory.*

Chapter One

1. http://encarta.msn.com/college_articleConservativeColleges/ Top_10_Politically_Conservative_Colleges.html
2. Andrew Bacevich, *The New American Militarism.*
3. Bruce Fleming, "Not Affirmative, Sir," (*Washington Post*, February 16, 2003), B02.
4. Dan Baltz, "Disparate Coalitions Now Make Up Two Parties, Study Finds," (*Washington Post*, May 16, 2005), A15.
5. Joseph Steffan, *Honor Bound: A Gay Naval Midshipman Fights to Serve His Country* (New York: Villard, 1992).
6. I've considered this in my book *Sexual Ethics: Liberal vs. Conservative.*
7. Isaiah Berlin, "Two Concepts of Liberty," In *Liberty,* (Oxford: Oxford University Press, 2002), 166-217.
8. Percy Bysshe Shelley, "Defense of Poetry" and Shklovsky.

9. I have considered this in my book *Disappointment*.
10. George Lakoff, *Moral Politics: How Liberals and Conservatives Think* (Chicago: University of Chicago Press, 1996), 366.

Chapter Two

1. I read this syndicated columnist in the *Annapolis Capital*, May 16, 2005, A8.
2. *Democracy*, 111.
3. T. E. Hulme, "Romanticism and Classicism," in *Speculations: Essays on Humanism and the Philosophy of Art*. Edited by Herbert Read (London: K. Paul, Trench, Traubner, and Co., 1924), 116.
4. Ibid, 117.
5. George Lakoff, *Moral Politics*, 236 ff.
6. *Art and Argument*.
7. John Searle, "The Logical Status of Fictional Discourse," *New Literary History* (1975): 319–32.
8. Robert Kaplan, *The Ends of the Earth: A Journey at the Dawn of the Twenty-first Century*, (New York: Random House, 1996).
9. Geza Vermes, *Jesus the Jew: A Historian's Reading of the Gospels* (Philadelphia: Fortress, 1981).
10. Victoria de Grazia, *Irresistible Empire: America's Advance through Twentieth-Century Europe* (Cambridge, MA: Harvard University Press, 2005).
11. *Protestant Ethic*, Chap. 4, ff.

Chapter Three

1. http://www.cnn.com/2003/US/10/16/rumsfeld.boykin.ap/.
2. Bernard Lewis, "The Roots of Muslim Rage," *The Atlantic Monthly* 66, no. 3 (1990): 47–60.
3. Alfred Jules Ayer, *Language, Truth and Logic* (New York: Dover, 1946).
4. I have considered the historical discussion of the purpose of sex in *Sexual Ethics*.
5. Summarized in John Corvino, ed., *Same Sex: Debating the Ethics, Science, and Culture of Homosexuality* (Lanham, MD: Rowman and Littlefield, 1997).
6. *Jesus the Jew*, 68.

Chapter Four

1. I've considered miracles elsewhere, in *Disappointment or The Light of Common Day*, and *Science and the Self*.
2. Huntington, *Clash of Civilizations*, 254 ff.

3. *On War.* One of Clausewitz's most famous concepts is that of the "fog of war." I have considered this and other topics in Clausewitz in "Can Reading Clausewitz Save Us from Future Mistakes?"
4. Alexa Hackbarth, "Vanity, Thy Name Is Metrosexual," (*Washington Post*, November 17, 2003), C10.
5. John Berger, *Ways of Seeing* (New York: Penguin, 1995), 45, 47.
6. The literature is vast. Most concise is Craig A. Williams, *Roman Homosexuality: Ideologies of Masculinity in Classical Antiquity* (Oxford: Oxford University Press, 1999).
7. Michel Foucault, *The History of Sexuality: An Introduction* (New York: Vintage, 1990).
8. I have considered this in greater detail in *Sexual Ethics.*
9. Eve Kosovsky Sedgwick, *Epistemology of the Closet* (Berkeley: University of California Press, 1992), 35.

Chapter Five

1. Amitai Etzioni, *The New Golden Rule: Community and Morality in a Democratic Society* (New York: Basic Books, 1996).
2. Paul Duggan, "Montgomery Mother's Stand on Sex-Ed Begins at Home," (*Washington Post*, May 19, 2005), A01.
3. http://archives.cnn.com/2002/WORLD/europe/09/20/germany.election/.
4. Response to my article on Clausewitz, cited above, by Chris Brassford. *Parameters: U.S. Army War College Quarterly* 34, No. 2 (2004), 123–25.
5. Jean-François Lyotard, *The Postmodern Condition: A Report on Knowledge* (Minneapolis: University of Minnesota Press, 1984).
6. Speech at the Sorbonne, April 23, 1910.
7. Krugman, 370.
8. *War Is a Force*, 36.
9. I considered this in *Caging the Lion: Cross-Cultural Fictions.*
10. Michel Foucault, *Madness and Civilization; A History of Sexuality.*

Chapter Six

1. Andrew Bacevich, *The New American Militarism.*
2. *A Theory of Justice.* A briefer restatement of the main ideas is found in *Justice as Fairness*, which echoes the title of an earlier paper incorporated into *A Theory of Justice.*
3. I have considered the phenomenon of suddenly regarding a hitherto unexceptionable concept with "amazement," at which point it seems to cry out for justification, in *Art and Argument.*
4. John Gray, *Men Are from Mars, Women Are from Venus: The Classic Guide to Understanding the Opposite Sex* (New York: Perennial Currents, 2004).

Bibliography

Achebe, Chinua. *Things Fall Apart*. New York: Anchor, 1994.

———. "An Image of Africa." *Massachusetts Review* 18 (1977): 782–94.

Adorno, Theodor. *The Adorno Reader*. Edited by Brian O'Connor. Oxford: Blackwell, 2000.

Atwood, Margaret. *The Handmaid's Tale: A Novel*. New York: Anchor, 1998.

Ayer, Alfred Jules. *Language, Truth and Logic*. New York: Dover, 1946.

Bacevich, Andrew J. *The New American Militarism: How Americans Are Seduced by War*. New York: Oxford University Press, 2005.

Berger, John. *Ways of Seeing*. New York: Penguin, 1995.

Bohannon, Laura. "Prince Hamlet in Africa." In *The Norton Reader: An Anthology of Expository Prose*, 3rd Edition. Edited by Arthur M. Eastman et. al. New York: Norton, 1973: 498–507.

Brassford, Chris. "To the Editor" (response to Fleming, "Can Reading Clausewitz Save Us From Future Mistakes?"), *Parameters: U.S. Army War College Quarterly* 34, no. 2, (2004): 123–25.

Clausewitz, Carl von. *On War*. Edited and trans. by Michael Howard and Peter Paret. Princeton, NJ: Princeton University Press, 1976.

Corvino, John, ed. *Same Sex: Debating the Ethics, Science, and Culture of Homosexuality*. Lanham, MD: Rowman and Littlefield, 1997.

Dewiel, Boris. *Democracy: A History of Ideas*. Seattle: University of Washington Press, 2001.

Diamond, Jared. *Collapse: How Societies Choose to Fail or Succeed*. New York: Viking, 2004.

Etzioni, Amitai. *The New Golden Rule: Community and Morality in a Democratic Society*. New York: Basic Books, 1996.

Fleming, Bruce E. *Annapolis Auntumn: Life, Death and Literature at the U.S. Naval Academy*. New York: New Press, 2005.

———. *Art and Argument: What Words Can't Do and What They Can*. Lanham, MD: University Press of America, 2003.

———. *Caging the Lion: Cross-Cultural Fictions*. New York: Peter Lang, 1992.

———. "Can Reading Clausewitz Save Us from Future Mistakes?" *Parameters: U.S. Army War College Journal* 34, no. 1 (2004): 62–76.

———. *Disappointment or The Light of Common Day*. Lanham, MD: University Press of America, 2006.

———. *An Essay in Post-Romantic Literary Theory*. Lewiston, NY: Mellen, 1991.

———. *Modernism and its Discontents: Philosophical Problems of Twentieth-Century Literary Theory*. New York: Peter Lang, 1994.

———. "Not Affirmative, Sir: A Well-Meaning Admissions Board's Absurd Reality." *Washington Post*, February 16, 2003: 2(B).

———. *Science and the Self*. Lanham, MD: University Press of America, 2004.

———. *Sexual Ethics: Liberal vs. Conservative*. Lanham, MD: University Press of America, 2004.

Foucault, Michel. *The History of Sexuality: An Introduction*. New York: Vintage, 1990.

———. *Madness and Civilization: A History of Insanity in the Age of Reason*. New York: Vintage, 1988.

Frank, Thomas. *What's the Matter with Kansas? How Conservatives Won the Heart of America*. New York: Metropolitan Books, 2004.

Frye, Northrop. *Anatomy of Criticism: Four Essays*. Princeton: Princeton University Press, 2000.

Fussell, Paul. *Class: A Guide through the American Status System*. New York: Touchstone, 1992.

Geertz, Clifford. *Works and Lives: The Anthropologist as Author*. Stanford, CA: Stanford University Press, 1990.

Gray, John. *Men Are from Mars, Women Are from Venus: The Classic Guide to Understanding the Opposite Sex*. New York: Perennial Currents, 2004.

Grazia, Victoria de. *Irresistible Empire: America's Advance through Twentieth-Century Europe*. Cambridge, MA: Harvard University Press, 2005.

Greene, Graham. *The Quiet American*. New York: Penguin, 1996.

Hackbarth, Alexa. "Vanity, Thy Name Is Metrosexual." *Washington Post*, November 17, 2003, 10(C).

Haddon, Mark. *The Curious Incident of the Dog in the Night-Time*. New York: Vintage, 2004.

Hartz, Louis. *The Liberal Tradition in America*. New York: Harcourt, 1991.

Hedges, Chris. *War Is a Force That Gives Us Meaning*. New York: Public Affairs, 2002.

Hulme, T. E. "Romanticism and Classicism." In *Speculations: Essays on Humanisum and the Philosophy of Art*. Edited by Herbert Read. London: K. Paul, Trench, Traubner, and Co., 1924: 111–140.

Huntington, Samuel P. *The Clash of Civilizations and the Remaking of World Order.* New York: Simon and Schuster, 1996.

Krauthammer, Charles. "No-Respect Politics." *Washington Post,* July 26, 2002, 33(A).

Krugman, Paul. *The Great Unraveling: Losing Our Way in the New Century.* New York: Norton, 2003.

Lakoff, George. *Don't Think of an Elephant: Know Your Values and Frame the Debate—The Essential Guide for Progressives.* New York: Chelsea Green, 2004.

———. *Moral Politics: How Liberals and Conservatives Think.* Chicago: University of Chicago Press, 1996.

Lakoff, George and Mark Johnson. *Metaphors We Live By.* Chicago: University of Chicago Press, 1980.

Lemon, Lee T. and Marion J. Reis, eds. and trans. *Russian Formalist Criticism: Four Essays.* Lincoln, NE: University of Nebraska Press, 1965.

Lewis, Bernard. "The Roots of Muslim Rage." *The Atlantic Monthly* 66, no. 3 (1990): 47–60.

Lynch, Michael P. "Where is Liberal Passion?" *Chronicle of Higher Education Review* (cover story), April 22, 2005, B7–B9.

Lyotard, Jean-François. *The Postmodern Condition: A Report on Knowledge.* Minneapolis: University of Minnesota Press, 1984.

Madison, James. *Federalist Paper 51.* In *Federalist Papers,* by Alexander Hamilton, James Madison, and John Jay. Edited by Charles Rossiter. New York: Signet, 2003.

Nash, George H. *The Conservative Intellectual Movement in America Since 1945.* Wilmington, DE: Intercollegiate Studies Institute, 1996.

Rawls, John. *Justice as Fairness.* Cambridge, MA: Harvard University Press, 2001.

———. *A Theory of Justice.* Rev. ed. Cambridge, MA: Harvard University Press, 1999.

Riesman, David. With Nathan Glazar and Reuel Denney. *The Lonely Crowd: Revised Edition.* New Haven: Yale University Press, 2001.

Roosevelt, Theodore. "Citizenship in a Republic: The Man in the Arena." Speech at the Sorbonne 23 April, 1910. http://www.theodore-roosevelt.com/trsorbonnespeech.html

Rosaldo, Renato. *Culture and Truth: The Remarking of Social Analysis.* Boston: Beacon Press, 1993.

Sartre, Jean-Paul. *Being and Nothingness.* New York: Washington Square Press, 1993.

Searle, John. "The Logical Status of Fictional Discourse." *New Literary History* (1975): 319–32.

Sedgwick, Eve Kosovsky. *Epistemology of the Closet.* Berkeley: University of California Press, 1992.

Shklovsky, Victor. "Art as Technique." In *Russian Formalist Criticism: Four Essays,* edited by Lee T. Lemon and Marion J. Reis. Lincoln NE: University of Nebraska Press, 1965: 3–24.

Steffan, Joseph. *Honor Bound: A Gay Naval Midshipman Fights to Serve His Country.* New York: Avon 1993.

Tuchman, Barbara. *The March of Folly: From Troy to Vietnam*. New York, Ballantine, 1985.

Vermes, Geza. *Jesus the Jew: A Historian's Reading of the Gospels*. Philadelphia: Fortress, 1981.

Weber, Max. *The Protestant Ethic and the Spirit of Capitalism*. New York: Scribner's, 1958.

Williams, Craig A. *Roman Homosexuality: Ideologies of Masculinity in Classical Antiquity*. Oxford: Oxford University Press, 1999.

Index

For Product Safety Concerns and Information please contact our EU
representative GPSR@taylorandfrancis.com
Taylor & Francis Verlag GmbH, Kaufingerstraße 24, 80331 München, Germany